GW01003806

BRITISH BROADCASTING CORPORATION

**THANKS TO**

*Chris Lent* – for editing the book, producing the series and dreaming up the whole idea.

*Carole Montague* – for invaluable help in getting the show on the road and keeping it there!

*The TV Production team* – including Deborah Perkin, John Wooler, Horacio Queiro and Peter Chapman.

*Everyone at BBC Publications* – but especially Roger 'the Riff' Fletcher, Annette Peppis, Tony Spaul, Josine Meijer, Jennie Allen, Huw Davies and Rob Calcaterra.

And, lastly, thanks to Peter Riding and Maggie Bebbington for giving us support through the difficult bits!

This book accompanies the BBC Television series
*Rockschool*, first broadcast on BBC 2 from 1 November 1983
and repeated on BBC 1 in June 1984

Series introduced by Deirdre Cartwright (guitar), Geoff Nicholls (drums), Henry Thomas (bass), and produced by Chris Lent

Published to accompany a series of programmes
prepared in consultation with the
BBC Continuing Education Advisory Council

This book is set in 9 on 10 point Univers Light Monophoto
Printed in England by Jolly & Barber Ltd, Rugby, Warwickshire
Cover printed in England by Belmont Press Ltd, Northampton
and bound by Hartnolls Ltd, London

© The Authors 1984
First Published 1984
Published by the British Broadcasting Corporation
35 Marylebone High Street, London W1M 4AA
ISBN 0 563 21059 1

This book grew out of the BBC TV *Rockschool* series and looks at the technology, techniques and musical vocabulary you need to play guitar, bass and drums in a band. The *Rockschool* presenters, Deirdre Cartwright, Geoff Nicholls and Henry Thomas, have each written chapters on their respective instruments; and there are contributions on the hardware from Gary Cooper and Rick Palmer of *Music UK* magazine. Also cropping up from time to time are comments from some of the leading players featured in the TV series.

Because the book covers so much ground, there are one or two points you should bear in mind when using it:

★ Be prepared to look at sections relating to all three instruments, and to all four styles, even if you're only immediately interested in playing one of them. If, for example, you only want to play HM bass, you will miss out on a lot if you turn straight to that chapter without looking at the sections relating to HM guitar and drums and blues bass, guitar and drums. Music does not fall into separate self-contained compartments and neither does this book.

★ It's important to read the sections on basic technique first. Once you're happy with these you can move on to the styles, where you'll find more advanced techniques discussed. Again, you will have to refer to different styles, and in some cases, different instruments.

★ Don't be put off by the musical theory and examples. Pages 6 and 7 give a rudimentary guide to the forms of notation used in the book and should be used for reference while reading. Three different methods are used for writing out chords and melody: box diagrams, tablature and standard notation. The three are often shown together for easy comparison.

★ In the guitar and bass sections, we talk about the 'left (neck) hand' and 'right (plectrum or plucking) hand'. This is intended to help left-handed players who are often neglected in tutors. For the drums, however, directions are only written for right-handed players. Left-handers will have to reverse these directions. This may be annoying, but remember that drummers, more than other musicians, should be ambidextrous.

★ If you are just starting out in a band, we hope that *Rockschool* will help you to understand how the three instruments central to rock work together to produce different sounds and styles. Pass the book around among the different members of the band and discuss the points raised by it. If you've been playing for years, then maybe this book will help you to plug those gaps in your musical knowledge that all musicians have, no matter how experienced they are. We certainly learned a lot in writing it!

CHRIS LENT

# Contents

In this book we'll be covering the styles of blues, rock, funk and reggae. You don't have to read music to play any of these styles. But knowing some of the rudiments will help you to stay sounding fresh and inventive. Standard musical notation is as much about rhythm, time, accent and volume as it is about the pitch of the notes you play. So the dots will give you the beat as well as the sound!

We also use guitar tablature and box diagrams to help with chord shapes and lead lines. Drum parts are shown in standard drum notation.

Keep referring to these pages while using the book, especially when you come to the later chapters.

### Staves and Bars

Music is written on and in-between groups of five horizontal lines called STAVES. A stave is divided by vertical BAR LINES into separate BARS or MEASURES. There are different kinds of bar lines and they have different meanings:

A double bar shows the end of a composition or portion of it.

A section of the music to be played twice is indicated as follows:

repeat the music in between.

Sometimes a repeated passage has a different closing when played the second time. In this instance first and second endings are used:

This means repeat the previous measure.

Each bar or measure represents a fixed space in time. The total time value in each bar is shown at the beginning of the music by a TIME SIGNATURE consisting of an upper and lower number. The upper indicates the number of beats you count within each bar; the lower number explains the time value of each count:

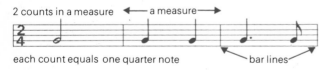

2 counts in a measure ← a measure →

each count equals one quarter note — bar lines

So this example represents a count of ONE-TWO, ONE-TWO in the TIME of four even beats.

Common time signatures:
2 3 4 3 6 9 12
4 4 4 8 8 8 8

### Notes

Notes represent the RHYTHM and PITCH of the music. Each different type occupies a set space in time. Its position on the stave indicates its pitch. Let's look at time values first. These are used in drum notation too.

Eighth notes and notes of shorter duration in time can be joined together in groups by cross bars called BEAMS

1 beam    2 beams    3 beams

### Note values
### Count

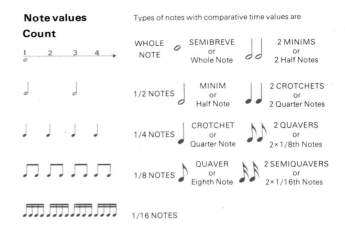

Types of notes with comparative time values are

| | WHOLE NOTE | SEMIBREVE or Whole Note | | 2 MINIMS or 2 Half Notes |
| 1/2 NOTES | | MINIM or Half Note | | 2 CROTCHETS or 2 Quarter Notes |
| 1/4 NOTES | | CROTCHET or Quarter Note | | 2 QUAVERS or 2×1/8th Notes |
| 1/8 NOTES | | QUAVER or Eighth Note | | 2 SEMIQUAVERS or 2×1/16th Notes |
| 1/16 NOTES | | | | |

The short notes are usually grouped together in twos or fours. The 1/16 note or semiquaver, for example, is fitted into the time of two quavers or one crotchet:

To get the sound of this rhythm into your head say 1-e-an-a, 2-e-an-a, 3-e-an-a, 4-e-an-a.

A dot behind a note = add half the value of the previous note.

$o.= o + d$    and lasts for six 1/4 notes (crotchet beats).

$d.= d + d$    and lasts for three 1/4 notes (crotchet beats).

$\flat.= \flat + \flat$    and lasts for three 1/8 notes (quaver beats).

$\flat.= \flat + \flat$    and lasts for three 1/16 notes (semiquaver beats).

A tie ⌢ (above/below) two notes means the first note is continued until the full duration of the second.

lasts for 1 2 3 4    1 2 3 4
                        off

lasts for 1 2 3 & 4
                off

lasts for 1 2 3 4    1 2 3 4

### Triplets

1/8 note triplets have three evenly spaced notes over one 1/4 note beat.

COUNT  1        2        3        4
SAY    1 2 3    2 2 3    3 2 3    4 2 3

A 𝅘𝅥𝅘𝅥𝅘𝅥 1/4 note triplet has three evenly spaced beats over one 1/2 note beat. For example:

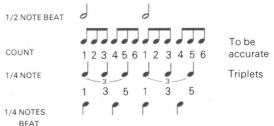

1/2 NOTE BEAT

COUNT          1 2 3 4 5 6 1 2 3 4 5 6    To be accurate

1/4 NOTE       1 3 5 1 3 5               Triplets

1/4 NOTES BEAT

6

## Rests

An absence of sound is called a REST. This can last for part of a bar, for a whole bar, or for several bars. There are different symbols to describe the length of the rest.

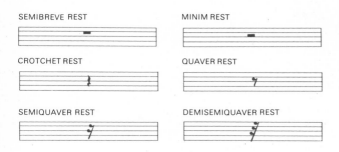

## Accents & Crescendos

If one beat is stressed more heavily than the others, it is said to be ACCENTED and has this symbol  >  above or below the note:

This should not be confused with crescendos or diminuendos which indicate an increase or decrease in volume, thus:

———— Indicates a gradual increase in volume (loudness) called CRESCENDO.

———— Shows a gradual decrease in volume called DECRESCENDO or DIMINUENDO.

## Pitch

A CLEF sign appearing at the beginning of each stave fixes the pitch of each line in the stave. There are two clef signs:

Treble Clef (G Clef) fixes G on the 2nd line

Bass Clef (F Clef) fixes F on the 4th line

The position of all the "natural" notes on the bass clef stave and the treble clef stave are as follows:

When notes go above or below the stave, they are written on leger lines.

There are various symbols which indicate alterations in pitch to the natural note. These are called SHARPS and FLATS, and are placed before the notes to raise or lower their pitch:

♯  raises the note one half-step (*semitone*)

♭  lowers the note one half-step (*semitone*)

♮  cancels the sharp or flat; restores note to original pitch

✗  raises the note two half-steps (*whole tone*)

♭♭  lowers the note two half-steps (*whole tone*)

Examples of flats & sharps

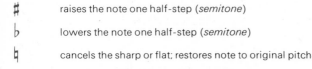

## Tablature

This was designed for guitarists who could not read standard musical notation. It is particularly useful because it can show you *how* to play as well as *what* to play.

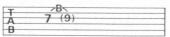

Each line represents a string. The top line is the high E (1st string) and the numbers indicate which fret to play on.

This example tells you to bend the G (3rd string) up from the fret until it sounds like the note fingered at the 9th fret.

B  indicates a bend

H  indicates a hammer-on

P  indicates a pull-off.

These techniques are described in detail later on.

## Box diagrams

This is a standard method of describing chord shapes.

A D major chord is illustrated.

The horizontal lines are the strings, the vertical lines are the frets, a darker line means the nut. The frets are numbered at the top.

×  means don't play this string

○  means play the open string

1  indicates where you should fret the note and the number inside tells you which finger to use.

## Drum notation

Traditionally, drum parts have been written on the BASS CLEF. But since drums do not have specific pitches, this is a bit misleading.

Today drum rhythms are often written on a FLEXIBLE STAVE indicating no specific pitches and with as many lines as there are drums and cymbals. This seems to be a much more sensible system and is used throughout this book.

Drums are indicated by standard musical symbols

Cymbals are marked with an 'x'

Accents are shown thus  >

'Grace' notes look like this

HI-HAT/RIDE

SNARE

BASS DRUM

This is a standard rock'n'roll drum pattern.

# CHAPTER 1

## Guitars, Amps and More!

## Gary Cooper

★ Despite challenges in recent years from low-cost, electronic keyboards, the guitar probably remains the most favoured instrument in popular music. Its rise to this position has been a slow one, particularly if you define the instrument as including the whole plucked string family (lutes, lyres, harps, etc). The earliest examples, working from this broad definition, stretch as far back as the Hittites, the Babylonians and Assyrians, through the Ancient Greeks and the Romans, and via them into the mainstream of early European culture.

If we accept a more rigid definition of the guitar, however, then we can safely say that instruments with metal frets and six strings tuned to modern standards (E A D G B E) were in existence by the late 18th century. To find the guitar as we know it in popular Western music, we have to look to European emigrés to the USA, who developed the so-called 'Spanish' guitar into its almost universally recognised offspring during the course of the 19th century.

For practical purposes, today's guitars are divided into three basic categories: acoustic, electric and bass (although the bass is clearly a hybrid, being designed to feel like a guitar but function as a bass). Within these categories there are many variations, but they provide a starting point. It is the purpose of this chapter to look at the instruments most widely used in rock — the solid-bodied electric guitar and bass ★

## The electric guitar

Discovering the origins of the electric guitar isn't easy. Throughout the 'jazz age' numerous players experimented with various devices to enable their guitars to be heard above the brass and woodwind instruments which dominated the period. It was during this time that a phenomenal rate of progress was made towards the evolution of the modern guitar.

Leading the field, probably, was Gibson. Orville Gibson had died in 1918, leaving behind him a company whose guitars, mandolins and other stringed instruments were rated as being among the finest produced. The legendary Lloyd Loar joined the Gibson company in 1920 and his arrival saw a development in the instrument which led directly to the electric Gibsons of today.

To begin with, the truss rod was introduced. This was a steel re-inforcement of the neck, enabling slimmer, easier-to-play models to be produced so that guitarists could experiment with solo playing styles which had previously been virtually impossible.

Loar also developed the 'cello' guitar, an instrument with a solid top, which dispensed with the traditional soundhole on acoustics in favour of 'f-holes'. These provided a more cutting tone, enabling acoustic guitars to be distinguishable amid the other instruments of jazz bands of the period. He is also credited with the invention of the adjustable height bridge so that guitarists could select the height of their strings for a preferred 'action' (string height above the fingerboard). This major development, once again, encouraged a new style of playing which was to reach its peak with the electric guitar.

Meanwhile, individual performers were desperately trying to amplify their acoustic guitars with microphones to try to make themselves heard. No one really knows who made the first breakthrough in the development of the guitar pickup, but certainly the first commercially offered electric instrument on the market was the Rickenbacker 'Frying Pan', an electric 'steel' guitar launched in 1931. Some people maintain the Rickenbacker was not really a guitar, but, either way, it was then that the concept of using a magnetic pickup was established.

*A later version of the basic 'cello' design, the Gibson Super 400 (right)*

The De Armond-Rowe company also developed an electric guitar in 1931, the Dobro company manufactured a very few of their 'resonator' guitars with pickups in 1932, and by 1935, Gibson had their ES150 electric semi-acoustic on the market. Nevertheless, Rickenbacker, by general consent, take the prize for getting their electric guitar on the market first. As with most scientific developments, Nature seems to have set many people on the same track at the same time.

For the most part, though, these early electric guitars were little more than the previous generation's acoustics with primitive pickups. The development of the *real* electric guitar was to be left to a radio repairman, who had watched the struggles of early electric guitarists to overcome the problems of feedback when they tried to amplify their hollow-bodied guitars. That repairman was Leo Fender and it was he who introduced the world's first solid-bodied electric guitar (the Broadcaster, later re-named the Telecaster) in 1948. Fender, working with ex-Rickenbacker employee 'Doc' Kauffman, soon realised that only a solid instrument would properly counteract feedback problems encountered by traditional instruments fitted with pickups. The rock'n'roll guitar had arrived.

As if all this weren't enough, Leo Fender then went on to launch his Stratocaster in 1954. If any guitar epitomises rock'n'roll, it is the 'Strat'. Somehow its shape refuses to date, regardless of who is making it fashionable at the time, be it Hank Marvin, Jimi Hendrix, Mark Knopfler, or Stuart Adamson. Probably more Fender Stratocasters have been made than any other single guitar. It has been modified, altered, copied, improved and degraded, but it remains *the* electric solid-bodied guitar of all time — not bad for a 1954 model!

Other makers had also anticipated the rise of the electric guitar. Epiphone had a semi-acoustic electric jazz guitar on the market during the late 1940s, as did Gretsch, and a solid-bodied guitar was built by Paul Bigsby and Merle Travis in 1947. But it was Gibson who responded with a vengeance to the Broadcaster/Telecaster when, following extensive development, they launched the Les Paul model in 1952.

*The Fender Stratocaster, used by guitarists for 30 years, is still a favourite among today's most innovative stylists, like Stuart Adamson (left) of Big Country, and The Edge (above) of U2*

the most comfortable possible fit to the body.

Furthermore, the Strat featured three single coil pickups — most guitars only had one or two. The pickups could be used individually, but it wasn't long before players discovered that if you were careful and set the pickup selector switch between two settings, you could use two pickups at once. This is the famous 'in between' or 'out of phase' position so often spoken about. The pickups were controlled by a single rotary volume knob along with two tone controls, one each for the neck and the middle pickups.

The guitar featured an ingenious tremolo arm too, a system which remains more or less unchanged to this day, and which is still regarded by many as the only production system worth using. Unlike earlier tremolos, the Strat was reasonably good at returning the strings to their normal tuning after use and it was coupled with a bridge which was far in advance of others in terms of its adjustability.

On its own, through the clean-sounding amplification of the period, the Strat had a remarkably pure tone. The maple neck was easy to play, the thin frets made it especially suited for speedy handling and the ultra-thin body and futuristic looks made it a natural choice for the rock'n'roll players of the late 1950s. It was a hugely successful instrument and, despite numerous detail changes, remains more or less the same guitar to this day.

Perhaps the major advocate of the Strat in the USA during that early rock'n'roll era was Buddy Holly. In Britain Hank Marvin is said to have been the first player to have brought one into the country and he almost single-handedly ensured its place in British rock history. But the biggest success for the Strat was when Jimi Hendrix took his essentially clean-sounding guitar, played it through his Marshall valve amps and tortured and twisted the output from those three single coil pickups, forming a unique and revolutionary sound.

### The Gibson Les Paul
Whereas the Fender Stratocaster is essentially the same guitar today that it was when originally launched, the Gibson Les Paul (undoubtedly the other contender for the 'world's most popular electric guitar' award) has seen many different variations since its first appearance in 1952.

The Les Paul guitar went on to become the only serious rival to Leo Fender's Stratocaster as the world's best known guitar. If Fender had Jimi Hendrix and Eric Clapton, Gibson could respond with an equal number of 'name' users, including Jimmy Page and Jeff Beck.

Even today the vast majority of guitars are still based on concepts which originated with the Les Paul and the Fender Stratocaster, and those two instruments in their own

*Jeff Beck playing a Les Paul. Note the twin coil Humbucker pickups*

right command probably the majority of professional guitarists' loyalties.

### • The Fender Stratocaster
Right from the start the Strat was the trend-setter among electric guitars. Like the earlier Telecaster it had a solid body, fashioned from either alder or ash, but that body was carved and shaped to provide

track recording techniques. Indeed, it is frequently said that he invented the first eight-track recorder.

As early as the 1930s, Paul had been making solid-bodied guitars, had become a noted guitar player in jazz and country circles and, with his wife, Mary Ford, had made numerous hit records. Eventually, having played many guitars of his own design, he teamed up with Gibson and 'his' guitar was soon made available to an eager world.

There were (and still are) many differences between the Les Paul and the Strat; the twin P90 pickups, the thicker body (made of mahogany, topped with a carved piece of maple), a shorter scale (the Les Paul had 22 frets on a $24\frac{3}{4}''$ scale length, the Strat offered a $25\frac{1}{2}''$ scale and 21 frets), the absence of a tremolo unit, the fact that the neck was glued onto the body on the Gibson, whereas the Fender's was bolted in place. In fact, there are so many differences in both playing qualities and sound that many players own both, using whichever one bests suits the number they are performing.

Various other Les Paul models followed that auspicious 1952 launch, including the flat-topped guitars which appeared in 1954, the Les Paul Special and Les Paul Junior. But the guitar that was to become just about *the* Les Paul to own (and which, as a vintage instrument, is probably the second most generally sought after of all vintage guitars) was the 'Fretless Wonder' or 'Black Beauty' — the 1954 Les Paul Custom.

---

> 'There's a lot of things you can get from a Strat, because when you turn it down it doesn't get duller and duller like a Les Paul does. You can set the pickup switch between *the* pickups to get a funky sound (newer models have five-way selector switches), you can use the front pickup to get a really jazzy sound. But the really classic Stratocaster sound, I suppose, is that hard biting tone.'
>
> *GARY MOORE*

Like the Strat, the Les Paul first appeared with single coil pickups (known as P90s). It was a thick-bodied instrument, not ultra-slim like the Fender and perhaps owed more to traditional guitar manufacturing ideas than did the Strat.

Younger players (and those becoming interested in guitars for the first time) have been heard to ask 'Who's Les Paul?'. As it was really *his* vision which lay behind the development of this instrument then perhaps a short diversion is justified.

Born in 1916, Les Paul is probably one of the very few modern musicians who justifies the use of that much overworked word 'genius'. His achievement with the Les Paul guitar is matched by less well known, but equally important successes — like being the first player to use multi-

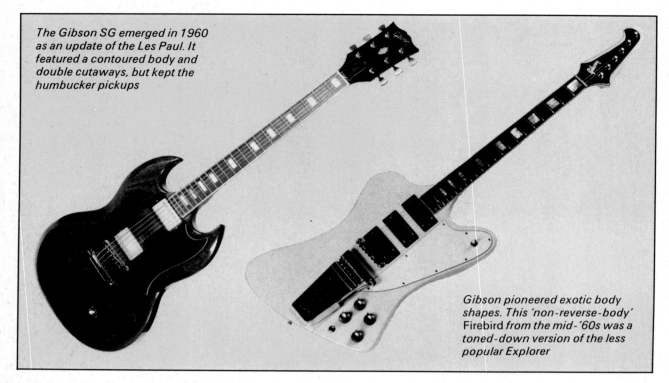

*The Gibson SG emerged in 1960 as an update of the Les Paul. It featured a contoured body and double cutaways, but kept the humbucker pickups*

*Gibson pioneered exotic body shapes. This 'non-reverse-body' Firebird from the mid-'60s was a toned-down version of the less popular Explorer*

This model had some highly desirable 'extras', such as an ebony fingerboard, all-mahogany body, supremely low, flat frets, and it was wonderful to play. As a collector's guitar the Custom is probably second only to the 1958 Les Paul Standard, with sunburst colouring on its flame maple top and two 'humbucking' twin coil pickups. There were even twin cutaway Les Pauls (which were developed into the almost as popular SG models), but if you mention a 'Les Paul' to most players, the single cutaway model is what they will immediately think of.

It was the development of the twin coil pickup which really high-lighted the differences between the Strat and the Les Paul. This innovation gave rise to the development of all the other guitars produced by the Gibson company which have left their marks on rock; the Flying-V, the Firebird, the ES335 and the SG. All these models have Hum-bucker pickups of various kinds, and all have a distinctive 'Gibson sound'.

The development of the hum-bucking pickup came about through the problems encountered by early users of single coil designs. Despite their harmonic clarity and purity of tone, these tended to suffer badly when they picked up electrically induced hums and buzzes, caused by electrical interference.

Gibson had undertaken considerable research into the problem, research which was mostly carried out by Ted McCarthy and Seth Lover during the mid-1950s. They finally came up with the twin coil 'humbucker'. A twin coil pickup of this type uses a simple principle to eliminate electrical interference problems — that of two coils placed next to each other, wound in contrary directions and wired parallel with opposite magnetic poles, so that each coil will effectively cancel the hum of the other.

It wasn't, however, the hum-cancelling effect of the new Gibson pickup (which began to appear on Les Pauls and other models during the late 1950s) which really impressed guitarists so much as the thicker, warmer, somehow *creamier* sound that the Les Paul fitted with these pickups could create.

Possibly the first person to discover what could be done with a Les Paul was Eric Clapton. On the early John Mayall *Bluesbreakers* album in 1966, Clapton is pictured with a Les Paul plugged into his Marshall combo, and with that combination he learned that the high output of the Gibson, its tremendous sustain and ability to overdrive a valve amp to distortion, could give him a guitar sound which few players since have equalled — though possibly hundreds of thousands have tried!

### The 1960s

The early 1960s saw the building of many fine guitars, some of which are still sought after today (and which can fetch considerable prices as collectors' items). Gretsch supplied much of the country and early 'beat boom' markets (and their guitars were used by players from George Harrison, through Keith Richard, to Chet Atkins). Rickenbacker scored with John Lennon, Pete Townshend and later Jim McGuinn of The Byrds. Guild (although always a smaller manufacturer) had their users too, and even Harmony (still, at that stage, producers of American-made, lower-priced guitars) were played by well known guitarists including Steve Marriott of The Small Faces.

Ace Heavy Metal axeman Michael Schenker, seen here with another exotically designed Gibson guitar: the distinctive black-and-white 'harlequin' Flying V which has become his trademark

Throughout the 1960s guitar and amplification sales boomed. Companies rose to fantastic heights of production in trying to cope with the demand (and in nearly every case they managed to damage their reputations as producers of quality instruments!). There was simply no way that makers like Gibson, Fender, Gretsch and Rickenbacker could cope with the demand without sacrificing some elements of quality control. Their prices, too, seemed to go on rising and rising. But all this changed with the arrival of the Japanese on the scene.

As they had previously done with cameras, motorcycles and other mass market consumer goods, the Japanese attacked the West with an army of 'copy' guitars, instruments of frequently execrable quality, which looked like famous American models in shape, but did not sound or feel anything like as good!

Those early copy guitars could have spelt long-term disaster for the Japanese manufacturers. But they were cheap and appealed to beginners who, even if they couldn't afford a *real* Les Paul, liked to be seen on stage with a guitar which at least looked like one, regardless of what it sounded like! Soon some of these copy guitars were getting so good that the quality of models from makers like Ibanez and Aria began to approach that of the originals on which they were based. Even their pickups (probably the major area of weakness on early Japanese copy guitars) began to improve significantly.

Today, several Japanese manufacturers — Yamaha, Aria, Ibanez and Westone — all offer guitars which will take a player from the very beginning of their career (at a price which American manufacturers cannot approach) to the point where that guitarist becomes professional and even thereafter.

## The current scene

The guitar market contains more guitars now than ever before, featuring a bewildering array of choices which baffles the professional player as much as it does the beginner. In essence, however, not much has changed (impossible though that may seem) since the Fender Stratocaster and the Gibson Les Paul, were launched back in the early 1950s.

Most guitars are still designed around these two models. Either

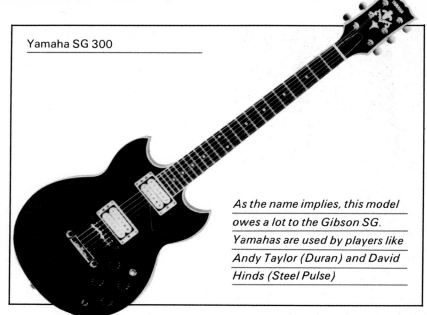

Yamaha SG 300

*As the name implies, this model owes a lot to the Gibson SG. Yamahas are used by players like Andy Taylor (Duran) and David Hinds (Steel Pulse)*

they have bolt-on necks, single coil pickups, single sided headstocks and Fender-like necks (following the Strat's example), or they feature twin coil pickups, glued neck/body joints, fatter frets, thicker wood bodies and a generally beefier sound (*à la* Gibson Les Paul). In fact, if you scratch the surface of any guitar on the market today, most of them (whether they purport to be of an 'own design' or not) follow either one or the other of these fundamental types. Other instruments may be closer to Gibson Firebirds, Explorers, semi-acoustic 335s, or Fender Telecasters, but there is very little around today that is genuinely new, apart from technological improvements in pickups, bridges, strings and other accessory areas.

An absolute beginner on the electric guitar today may well find that the price of current Japanese-manufactured guitars is high. There is no doubt that the Japanese guitars (with so few exceptions as to be almost a rule) are well made and sound excellent, but they have moved up in price to a point where a newcomer to the instrument might well need to look for something cheaper. Here the choice is largely from instruments made in Korea, although a few come from Taiwan and even Italy. In general, Italian guitars are very underrated by most players whereas the opposite is true of those from Korea. Despite having mastered the art of finishing, many Korean instruments leave a lot to be desired from the point of view of manufacturing quality. They may superficially look to be of excellent

value, but the quality can be so inconsistent that it is often necessary to sample quite a number of individual guitars before finding a good one. When they *are* good, however, they can represent excellent value.

Perhaps the most unexpected development in the guitar business in recent years has been the steady growth of numerous individual 'craftsman makers'. The UK especially seems to have produced a crop of genuine 'artist builders'. Although the trend may have started with individual developments in bass guitars (*see* the next section on the bass guitar p. 17), makers such as the Manson Brothers, Overwater, John Diggins, Chris Eccleshall, Roger Griffin, Gordon Smith and many others have begun to challenge the established names in the production of quality guitars.

These makers are capable of producing superlative instruments, hand-manufactured from exotic woods, at a cost frequently below that of mass-produced models. An increasing number of professional (and even semi-professional) musicians are turning to these craftsmen and, although their combined output is tiny compared with that of leading Japanese or American manufacturers, the influence wielded by this new breed of guitar makers is becoming increasingly powerful.

The result of all this competition is that there is a greater choice of price, quality, design and appearance than there has ever been before. Whatever your particular leanings, there is a guitar out there for you — all you have to do is find it and that

*Suzi Quatro using a Fender Precision on the set of* Top of the Pops *during the early '70s*

ment to the string bass players of the time. After he had given guitarists power without feedback (he'd helped them on their way with a few excellent amps too), bass players found that their instruments were almost totally inaudible.

Thus it was that in 1951 Leo Fender introduced his first electric bass. Although it was picked up by many players who admired its portability and sound (not to mention the ease with which this fretted instrument could be played), bass players were to be very much the poor relations to guitarists for many years to come (and not without some justification if one listens to the early recorded work of rock'n'roll bassists!).

### The Precision

The instrument itself, however, was a huge success for the Fender company. Called the Precision it sold massively well. Very early Precisions bore a strong resemblance to Fender's first solid-bodied guitar, the Broadcaster/Telecaster, having a rather square body formed from ash, a maple neck (maple was used on all Fender instruments of the time), with the strings tuned to E A D G, an octave lower than they are on a conventional guitar to correspond to the tuning of a double bass. The Precision bass had just a simple, single coil pickup, 20 frets and a set of four massive open-backed Kluson machine heads.

In 1954 the first series of Precisions was replaced by an updated model, which has since become (virtually

that bit hotter, the woods rarer and end up with what is very much your own guitar.

### The bass guitar

Much of what has already been said about the current state of the electric guitar market applies to the bass too. However, there are some significant differences, not least of which is an even greater influence from individual makers on the design of the instrument.

Historically speaking it is far easier to be definite about the origins of the bass than it is about the solid-bodied electric guitar. To find the bass's first incarnation we have to look no further than Leo Fender, the same individual who started the whole solid guitar trend with his 1948 Broadcaster.

In some senses Fender almost owed the development of the instru-

may be easier said than done unless you analyse carefully what you want and how much you can afford to spend.

What has happened to the electric guitar is perhaps best summed up by the typically oblique French saying which, translated roughly, says 'the more it changes, the more it stays the same'. Almost regardless of which guitar you buy today, its ancestry will be plain, and perhaps the basic choice to be made is still between a Fender or Gibson-like instrument. The difference today is that you can now, as a beginner buying at a beginner's price, get a worthwhile and satisfying instrument, or, at the other end of the scale, go to a craftsman and have your instrument's neck just that shade narrower, the pickups just

The Precision

*Note the finger rest on this 1953 Precision. In those days, you were expected to play with your thumb!*

*Fender have re-issued their vintage models with the* Standard *series*

*The Yardbirds (below) with Paul Samwell-Smith (left) using an* Epiphone *Rivoli*

*Jack Bruce in action with a* Gibson *EB-3. Note the pickup selector switch*

without alteration) the best-selling bass guitar of all time. But in 1957 one major change was made — Fender added a split pickup. This pickup was unusual in that it had one half working on the top two strings and the other handling the bottom pair, the idea being to give a better frequency coverage. Each half of the new pickup had four pole pieces and the new sound made a considerable difference to the Precision's uses.

In 1960, Fender decided that it was time for a new bass altogether and brought out the Jazz model. Superficially similar to the Precision,

the Jazz bass has an offset body and a neck which is considerably narrower at the nut, making it faster to handle. The Jazz also featured two pickups and offered a much better tonal range than the Precision.

Needless to say, the changes to the first style of Precisions didn't meet with universal approval (bassists being as contrary as guitarists!), so in 1968 Fender introduced the Telecaster bass, which sought to replicate many of the qualities of the original 1951 Precision model. It is the Precision, however, which still remains the yardstick by which other basses are judged.

### Gibson basses
Gibson, having seen Leo Fender's new instrument make considerable waves, decided that they would follow suit and in 1953 launched the EB-1, an ungainly looking shorter-scale instrument which was to provide the model for the Hofner Violin bass later adopted and immortalised by Paul McCartney. The Gibson instrument was hardly a massive success, however, and its value as a collector's item today is more the result of its extreme rarity than its quality as a bass.

But having one flop on their hands didn't deter Gibson. They carried on making basses and managed to score some success with a semi-acoustic instrument, the EB-2, which they launched in 1958. Essentially this model was a large version of their popular ES-335 guitar and, alongside the contemporary (and Gibson-manufactured) Epiphone Rivoli bass — which was a virtually identical instrument once its pickup had been changed to the EB-2's type — it sold well and was the mainstay of many 1960s beat groups.

Gibson basses were never rivals to the success of the Precision, but the later single pickup short-scale EB-0 and EB-3 models (based on the solid-bodied twin cutaway SG series of guitars) did, for a brief period, sell remarkably well. This was largely owing to the world-wide popularity of Jack Bruce, who virtually single-handedly invented lead bass playing when he was with Eric Clapton and Ginger Baker in Cream.

The short-scale Gibsons launched in 1960 produced a fuzzier, fatter sound than the Precision, and Bruce's use of the EB-3 became a legend. McCartney (with his Hofner and, later, a Rickenbacker) had shown that bassists could be melodic, but Bruce showed that they could play an audible counterpoint to lead lines which enabled the three-piece Cream to produce a titanic sound, and were capable of providing a musical (as opposed to purely rhythmic) platform for Clapton's extended blues-based solos.

Gibson's period of glory in the bass field was, however, short-lived. The instruments declined in popularity very quickly and EB-0s and EB-3s command low prices on today's secondhand market. Since 1960 they have launched bass model after model and of course, probably only the massive and idiosyncratic Thunderbird bass has secured any serious following. Although it is hopelessly unbalanced to hold (the headstock is far too large), it has a unique sound and those who love it appear to do so with a real passion. Gibson briefly re-introduced the Thunderbird in 1976 as a 'bi-centennial' version but it failed to make any great impression, and neither did models like the Grabber, Ripper, or Melody Maker.

## Other competitors
But the contest to produce the best bass wasn't just left to the two giants of the electric guitar world.

*Chris Squire of Yes, one of rock's most melodically inventive bassists, here using a Rickenbacker 'blond'*

Probably the second biggest seller after the Precision has been the Rickenbacker bass which somehow still manages to look modernistic, despite its 1950s pedigree. The Rickenbacker is an unusual instrument by any standards and, like all of this maker's models, is unique in most aspects of its design.

The 4000 (affectionately known as the 'Ricky') was followed by the 4001 which featured twin pickups and a stereo output (though few

Rickenbacker users have ever bothered to use their instruments in stereo it seems). The Rickenbacker basses had extremely slim and easy-to-play necks compared with previous bass guitars produced by other manufacturers and they also had a sound which was very different from that of a Fender. Over the years Chris Squire of Yes and Paul McCartney have probably done more for the Ricky bass than any other users — Squire, in particular, on account of his melodic playing which made full use of the 4001's enormous clarity of sound to carry his distinctly musical style.

Other Rickenbacker users include Lemmy from Motorhead (who uses one fitted with a pickup salvaged from a Gibson Thunderbird to suit his unique chordal approach to playing), Geddy Lee of Rush, Paul Simenon and Bruce Foxton.

Strangely, the next significant development in the bass guitar was not to come from any of the major manufacturers but from the specialist designers and builders, notably the San Francisco-based Alembic company. Alembic's reputation grew from their association with the Grateful Dead and individual players like Jack Cassady from Jefferson Airplane. They made the first major strides in developing the use of battery-powered pre-amplifiers which enabled bassists to effect enormous tonal changes in their sound. This was something which had been lacking on all the previous 'passive' instruments, whose only tone facility (as with guitars) had been to work by cutting frequencies out of the output signal. Actives actually *added* frequencies and boosted them considerably.

The reputation of Alembic spread rapidly across the world and top players flocked to buy their instruments. One of the first international superstar bassists to use one was John Entwistle, who has a collection of Alembics, some shaped like Gibson Explorers with amazing decorations on them. The legendary Stanley Clarke is an avid Alembic user too. If Entwistle influenced pure rock bass players like no other, Clarke did the

Rickys galore! A classic Rickenbacker 4001 'Black Beauty' in the hands of Deep Purple's Roger Glover

same for jazz/rock players, having a speed and agility which is probably unmatched. Clarke was the person who, in many ways, inherited the post-Cream mantle of Jack Bruce, taking the bass so far that it became a pure lead instrument. The active Alembic was the perfect bass for this role.

The Japanese have managed to bring active-powered instruments of good quality within the reach of semi-pro bassists, notably models from Westone and Aria.

The greatest advance of all in bass guitars has recently begun to make astonishing progress — an all-synthetic bass with no headstock. The Steinberger bass, one of the most unusual-looking instruments ever made, has produced a revolution in the short time that it has been in existence. This bass was developed by an American engineer, Ned Steinberger, who had been asked by a small US-based manufacturer to look at the whole concept of the bass guitar, not from the point of view of a player or someone who had previously made instruments, but rather as a design exercise.

Steinberger came up with some novel ideas. To begin with he decided that the presence of a headstock was of little value to a bass. He went further and maintained that in many cases it even caused unpleasant 'overtones' to the notes. His answer was to place the tuning mechanism on the bottom end of the guitar, developing a unique system to achieve this.

*Motorhead's Lemmy playing chords on a Rickenbacker which he's had specially modified*

*Paul Simenon uses a Rickenbacker to get the fuzzy tone associated with The Clash*

The Steinberger is made of carbon graphite and fibreglass with a fingerboard of phenolic resin — there's no wood in the bass at all. Basses (and a few guitars) have already featured 'straight-through' necks (necks which ran the full length of the instrument with wood joined to either side of them to form the body), but Steinberger took the idea even further. His bass is one complete moulding and thus the sustain it produces is unimpeded by any joints between different materials. Furthermore, the strength of the materials used means that the neck cannot warp or twist. The tiny body comes with a rotating backplate so that the instrument can be played in any position, owing to a perfect centre of gravity. Despite its unconventional appearance, the Steinberger is gaining in popularity with a host of top players, from Sting and Bill Wyman, to John Taylor and Robbie Shakespeare.

## Oddball basses

Not *all* basses have had just four strings. Back in 1962 Fender attempted to start a new trend by announcing their Bass VI, a six-string bass with a tremolo system. Not unlike the Jaguar guitar in looks, the Bass VI was tuned exactly one octave below a normal guitar and had three single coil pickups. There were various problems with the instrument and it was reputedly difficult to amplify in such a way that the top two strings didn't drown the bottom four, but it

was used for a while by Jack Bruce, and Phil Lynott is known to have used one. Overall, however, it was a failure for Fender and they dropped the experiment in the early 1970s. They later tried again with a five-string bass but that, too, failed to capture many players' imaginations.

Rather more successful unconventional basses have been produced by custom builders. Alembic, for example, have produced a fair number of eight-string instruments which have been quite popular (John

Paul Jones used one with Led Zeppelin from time to time). Geezer Butler from Black Sabbath has a John Diggins eight-string bass and Jimi Hendrix used a Hagstrom model on 'Spanish Castle Magic' on his *Axis Bold As Love* album. Although it has never achieved the popularity of the fretless bass, the eight-string instrument is effective for reinforcing riffs and has had some success over the years.

## The fretless bass

One of the most significant departures from the standard four-string bass guitar has been the fretless type. Initially this was almost exclusively used by jazz players, especially those working in jazz/rock where a double bass would have

*Sting of The Police playing a fretless Ibanez bass*

been inaudible, and the peculiarly fluid and woody sound of a fretless electric bass produced a tone more suited to jazz than a conventional bass. It was brought to prominence by Jaco Pastorius when he was with Weather Report and has since become a strong favourite among players of many types of music. Pastorius literally removed the frets from the neck of his Fender, but others haven't had to go that far since manufacturers have been quick to offer fretless versions of their normal models. Most basses on the market today can be bought in fretless versions and the instrument as a distinct type can be heard playing everything from pop to jazz, famous users including Sting, Mick Karn and Stanley Clarke.

Initially the fretless bass can be an extremely difficult instrument to play (especially for a bassist who has long been used to having frets on his or her instrument!), but perseverance usually works wonders. The ability to slide from one note to another and the unusual harmonic content of the notes plus the distinctive tonality has won the instrument many supporters.

## Pickups

Any guitar pickup operates fundamentally in the same way. When a guitar or bass string vibrates, it moves a magnetic field through the coil windings around the magnetic pole piece, creating an identical frequency in the coil as that at which the string is vibrating. This generates an alternating current which is fed back down the guitar lead and into the pre-amplification circuit of the amplifier.

There are really just two basic pickup types which you will find on most electric guitars — the single coil design (common to nearly all Fender guitars) and the humbucker, or twin coil, developed and used mostly by Gibson. There are variations on these two basic types and the number of windings on the coil, the size, shape and quality of magnets used can all have a tremendous effect on the way in which the pickups work (and thus how they sound). The principles, however, remain the same.

Before making any changes to your pickups, however, it is essential to have at least *some* idea of what you are doing. If you don't, seek

*The Who's John Entwistle with an Alembic bass, one of the first makes to use active circuitry successfully. Note the tremolo arm too*

professional guidance. A knowledge of the basic types available will undoubtedly help, so here is a brief description of how pickups work.

### Single coil pickups

The single coil pickup, at its most basic, can be either a 'bar magnet' type (using one single bar stretching across the width of the unit) or it can have individual pole pieces (magnets) as is found on the Fender Stratocaster. Around this magnet (or magnets) is wrapped a continuous coil of ultra-fine gauge copper wire, which, together with the magnet itself, provides the mechanism for the frequency transfer from the string to the amplifier via the changing size and shape of magnetic fields as outlined above.

Effectively, it is the size of the change within the magnetic field which determines the volume of the output from the pickup. The strength of the magnet used is probably the major determining factor in how high the output is from the pickup

and, hence, how loud the guitar sounds. Overdo it, however, and you can cause magnetic anomalies which result in a 'double' note effect caused by the over-strong magnetic pull on the strings. This is a common fault on guitars where the action (the height of the strings above the fretboard) has been set low but the pickups remain set high. As soon as the strings are played the pickups' magnets pull the strings down excessively and create this unwelcome effect which can often (if you don't realise what is happening) make you think that the guitar is constructionally at fault.

### Twin coil pickups

Twin coil pickups, as we have seen, were invented by Seth Lover in 1955. All pickups fall prey to interference of one sort or another but the humbucker is less prone than a single coil type. It doesn't however, *sound* the same, which is one of the major reasons why players use both Fender *and* Gibson-type guitars — the pickups on each are quite different, the single coil sounding thinner and cleaner, the humbucker warmer and smoother. Each has its distinct advantages over the other.

Humbuckers use two coils of wire and two sets of pole pieces. They are wired in such a way that the current flows sequentially from one to the other but out of phase. Unwanted signals, therefore, are cancelled out. The pole pieces, however, have opposing magnetic polarities which is what allows the pickup to amplify the string vibration and not cancel it out along with any interference.

One dodge, supposedly capable of allowing a guitar fitted with a humbucker to sound like it has a single coil as well, is to fit the pickup

> **❞The sound I used to use was the sound which most bass players used — clean and bassy . . . but if you play that at a thousand watts in an auditorium, it sounds like a B17G bomber flying overhead! On the trebly side of things, the bass sounds too thin. But if you combine the two with active circuitry, you get something with a lot of cutting power and a lot of depth, and you can use that to play lead lines on bass, or whatever you want. ❞** *JOHN ENTWISTLE*

with a 'coil tap' which is supposed to work by cancelling just one of the twin coils, so that what you are left with is a fully functioning single coil pickup. This works fairly well but it is no more than an approximation of the real thing.

Other tricks can be used, such as altering the magnetic 'phase' relationship of either the twin coils of a humbucker or of two single coil pickups. This gives a thin and funky 'out of phase' sound.

There are so many ways of wiring guitar pickups that an almost infinite number of sounds can be obtained. The problem is that the more switches and options you have, the more complicated a guitar can be to use. It is, nevertheless, a subject well worth studying if you want to improve your guitar's sound.

### Active circuitry
Active circuitry in a guitar or bass simply means the provision of a small pre-amplifier fitted inside the body of the guitar, which amplifies the signal from the pickup. The current required to achieve this is usually supplied from either one or two batteries also 'on board', although some systems have been designed which draw their power from an 'outboard' transformer, thus powering the guitar from stepped-down mains voltage.

As well as boosting the signal level from the pickup (making it easier to overdrive your amplifier and resisting outside electrical interference from stage lighting, PA faults etc), active power enables a guitar to be fitted with sophisticated tone circuits if desired.

Active circuits have appealed more to bass players than guitarists by

and large, and quite a number of current models feature this facility, instruments from Westone, Aria, Ibanez, Fender, Gibson and many of the custom builders being good examples. Those who wish to convert existing 'passive' guitars can even buy small ready-made circuits which can be fitted inside their instruments to convert them.

### Strings
Originally guitar strings were manufactured from animal gut (despite being frequently called 'cat gut', feline lovers needn't worry — sheep intestines were invariably used!). Today strings are either made from nylon or metal. For the most part, nylon strings are only used on Spanish or 'classical' guitars and therefore don't really concern us.

Metal strings are available in many different types and thickness. The type you should choose is very much a matter of what suits your style, your guitar and the sound you want.

Briefly, strings are sold in gauges — the thinnest strings starting at around 0·008", the thickest types going up as far as 0·060" — quite a range! For practical purposes it makes sense to divide strings into three basic types, those for electric guitar, acoustic guitar and bass.

### Electric guitar strings
Originally, electric guitar strings were very much the same as the metal strings used on acoustics, but different playing styles have brought about a considerable reduction in average string thicknesses. This development began in the mid-1960s when British blues guitarists, wanting to be able to bend their strings

to express blues playing styles (epitomised by the early work of Eric Clapton, Jeff Beck and Peter Green), began fitting banjo strings in place of conventional heavyweight types.

Earlier strings had often been 'flatwound' too, being made of a central core of steel with metal tape wound round them. This provided a smooth feel and reduced the annoying squeaking which players experienced when sliding from note to note, something which particularly bothered jazz players as they were playing at low volumes where such problems were easily noticed. Flatwound strings, however, failed to give the bright attacking tone that rock guitar players wanted and so they turned to 'roundwound' types. These had the central steel cores wound with round wire and are far and away the most popular today. Flatwound strings are still available but they can be harder to find and are mainly used by jazz players.

In addition to wanting thinner gauge roundwound strings, the 1960s blues players (whose use of string bending techniques, light gauge strings, amplifier distortion etc have formed the basis of nearly all current rock guitar trends and styles) also wanted unwound third strings. In much solo playing the third string (the G) is used extensively for bending. As a result, a flatwound third tended to suffer from considerable wear on the winding since abrasion against the fret caused windings to strip prematurely. String makers responded by making sets with plain thirds; again, strings of this type are almost universal today, although a few players still like wound thirds.

In the quest for speed and ease of bending, lighter gauge strings became popular among lead guitarists during the late 1960s and 1970s. On the face of it, these strings might seem to have everything in their favour but there are disadvantages. Obviously, the thinner the string, the less volume it produces when it's plucked. It also suffers more from tuning problems and tends to sustain the note for less time than a thicker string. The craze for ultra-light strings led manufacturers to produce sets so light (starting with, say, a 0·008" top E string, going down to a bottom E of around 0·036–8") that many users found their tunings slipping and their output power to be too low — especially when playing chords.

'The strings I use are a little heavier than most people's, and I like the action highish. I don't go for playing six million notes up the neck, so I don't want the action right down. It's more for the sound. I think the gauge of strings you use should be the heaviest you can manage to do what you want to, because the heavier the string, the better the sound you get from it. It gives a louder, truer note. And it stays in tune better.'

WILKO JOHNSON

During the past two or three years some sense has begun to prevail and a slow move back to thicker gauge strings, often set slightly higher against the frets, has begun. A good compromise on most electric guitars is a set starting at 0·010″ and ending up at around 0·050″. Strings of this gauge are easier to keep in tune, deliver more power on chords and solos and yet are still fairly easy to hold down and bend. Because electric guitar strings need to have a magnetic property, the metals used for their windings now tend to be of different materials to those used on acoustics. Stainless steel, nickel, silver plate and various alloys each have their advantages and adherents.

## Bass guitar strings

Thicker (and, regrettably, considerably more costly) than conventional guitar strings, bass strings have been subject to some considerable research in recent years too. Originally, bass strings tended to be flat-wound but modern styles have turned them over to roundwound for the most part. At various times black nylon strings have been tried (to give a more double bass-like sound), but these have never proved very popular.

One of the most influential figures in the bass-string world has been The Who's John Entwistle. An early user of roundwound types, he worked closely with one of the world's leading string makers (the British company, Rotosound) to develop their bass roundwound sets, which are available in many different gauges and string lengths (as, of course, are most guitar and bass strings these days). The development work undertaken by Rotosound and Entwistle revolutionised the bass guitar string and the distinctive growling sound which Entwistle obtained from his various basses inspired just about every other string maker in the world to follow suit.

In addition to conventional flatwound strings (still used by a few jazz-style bassists and some fretless players), other makers developed a half-and-half type of string where the steel or nickel windings were ground down after manufacture to provide a smoother playing surface, reduce fret wear and give a generally smooth sound. Other makers have replied with a newly developed finish where the bass strings have no metal ground away from them but still offer a softer feel. Grinding metal away from the string, it is claimed, damages the string's fundamental tonality.

> 'When I started off with Whitesnake, I used to use flatwound strings, because the middlyness really poked through. But they're really hard to play, so I gave them a rest and took up groundwound strings. They don't have so much twang on top as roundwound, but they still have a middly sound.'
>
> NEIL MURRAY

Superwound bass strings are a recent development which have created a major change in players' attitudes. With these strings the windings terminate before passing across the bridge so that, in effect, only the central core of the string rests on the saddle.

Early Superwound strings had to be fitted carefully and adjusted for length manually, but there is now a wide range offered to suit the many different string lengths needed on different basses. The idea behind the Superwound string is that it will pass a far purer and stronger note through the body, it will sustain better and sound harmonically purer. The Superwound string has proved a tremendous success — makers like WAL, Steinberger and many others fit them as standard and they are becoming increasingly popular.

## Buying strings

Once you have settled on what gauge of strings suits your needs

> 'I don't really like to change the strings daily. I like to leave them on and let them settle in. And of course a bass string is a pretty fat string and if you start stretching it and pulling it, and changing it every day, you're never going to sound in tune. So I like to keep them on as long as I possibly can . . . plus, it's cheaper!'
>
> BERNARD EDWARDS

there remains a bewildering array of types and brands available on the market today. There is not, however, an equal number of manufacturers! So profitable are guitar strings that quite a few well-known brands are little more than marketing names, companies buying strings from various sources and having them packaged in fancy materials, supported with considerable advertising, claiming various merits over other, cheaper, types. It isn't, therefore, necessarily true at all that the more you pay for a guitar string the better

quality you are getting. Two brands may look quite different in their packaging, may cost quite different prices, but can well come from the same production line.

The best advice, therefore, is to shop around and try as many different string types as you can before deciding what you like best. Try different *gauges* of string too. Don't be too surprised if a cheaper string seems to last as well and sound as good as a premium brand — beneath all the ballyhoo and marketing they could well be the same strings!

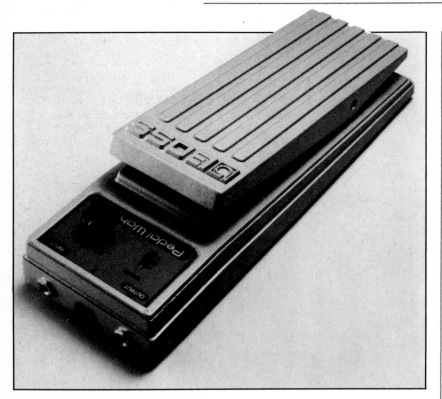

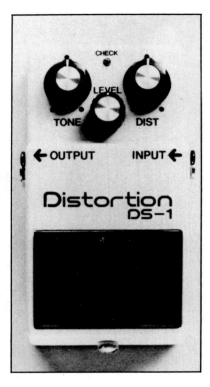

## Effects units

Effects units come in an astonishing array of types and sizes, although actually there aren't as many basic effect sounds as one might think.

The first effects to appear on the market were those offered with early amplifiers from manufacturers like Fender and Vox — notably a spring delay system (called reverb) and the long since largely abandoned 'tremolo' or 'vibrato' circuits. Reverb is still probably the most popular of all effects, perhaps because what it does is provide a short delay which simulates a natural effect. Tremolo systems produced that wavering note effect beloved of 1960s guitarists. Tremolo refers to the effect which varies the *volume* of a signal, whereas vibrato alters its *pitch*, although the two have grown so confused these days that most people say tremolo when they mean vibrato, and vice versa!

There was a long gap between the effects mentioned above and the appearance of the first of the pedal types, now so common. The breakthrough came when a designer by the name of Gary Hurst developed an earlier idea into what became known as the 'fuzz box'. This artificially dirtied the guitar's signal and deliberately sought to undo the work of amp designers by making amplifiers sound distorted as opposed to clean.

*The Boss Wah is only the latest in a long line of different pedal designs that go back to the late '60s*

Hurst's first name-user was probably Jeff Beck, who used the 'Tone Bender' with his single pickup Fender Esquire (essentially a one pickup Telecaster) while with the Yardbirds. The Spencer Davis Group also used the effect to grab themselves a hit single or two and Keith Richard immortalised the essence of the fuzz box's sound on the Stones' 'Satisfaction' single. Basically, the fuzz box worked by generating a square wave frequency which could be variably blended with the normal output of the guitar. In some senses it seeks to simulate the effect of an overdriven valve amp but, since a valve amp doesn't produce square waves of that type, it is only ever a poor simulation and is best regarded as a quite different effect.

As an effects unit, distortion pedals of one type or another have remained easily the biggest selling pedals. Today there are dozens of different kinds on the market, ranging from expensive mains-powered types to 'dirt cheap' battery-powered ones. The sounds vary so much that there can be no rules as to which is the best to buy. Some of the generally better types, however, don't just rely on square wave generation but actually boost the guitar's output signal

*Distortion will 'fatten up' the sound of a single coil guitar, but should be used sparingly on twin coils*

to help overdrive the first valve in the pre-amplifier. These are most often called 'overdrivers' by their manufacturers and are quite different devices from standard fuzz boxes. Following the early success of the fuzz box, effects next went into a bad period when most of them were offered with 'Siren' or other gimmick sounds. It wasn't until the Wah Wah pedal was developed (again in the UK), that the whole effects business started looking up again. Wah pedals work by the user pushing a foot pedal up and down, usually in time to the beat of the song. This works a rotary potentiometer which creates a shift in tone. The sound is exemplified by the work of Jimi Hendrix (who raised its use to that of an art form) on tracks like 'Voodo Chile'. Eric Clapton, too, used the Wah pedal to great effect on Cream's 'Tales of Brave Ulysses'.

Since those days in the 1960s, many other effects have come and gone. Phasers were probably the next type to capture guitarists' imaginations — these sought to duplicate the tape phasing effects obtained in the recording studio, used on such all-time favourite tracks as the Small Faces' 'Itchycoo Park' and some Beatles recordings. Jimi

*Phase will give your guitar a sweeping, spacey sound useful for chords and percussive rhythm styles*

Hendrix (probably the finest user of effects units there has ever been) was an early advocate not only of the phaser but also of its half-brother, the flanger. Flanging, although somewhat similar to phasing in sound, isn't *quite* the same effect. It too originated in the studio, where it was achieved by the physical manipulation of the speed of one of two tape machines replaying identical signals. The engineer placed his hand on the 'flange' of one of the tape spools, hence varying the speed of one track against the other. Flanging pedals, as opposed to phasers, tend to be more versatile these days and probably out-sell the latter quite considerably.

Another popular effect is chorus. This almost single handedly sold one particular amplifier (the Roland Jazz Chorus Series) since its built-in chorus effect was definitive and unobtainable, initially, from any pedals on the market. Today chorus pedals can be bought from many sources (including Roland, with their Boss range) which are as good as or better than, that of the amp itself. Chorus is probably today's most popular effect. What it does is delay one signal against another (obtained by splitting the original

output from the guitar). The delay (variable in pitch and length) makes an instrument sound like several simultaneously. It is widely used to 'thicken up' chords and can help a six-string guitar sound a little like a twelve-string. It is also one of the very few effects used widely by bass players and is a favourite with many guitarists, including Andy Summers from Police.

Taking delay still further, ADT (originally standing for 'Automatic Double Tracking') was also originally a studio effect. The provision of the right amount of delay can make one guitar sound like two playing in unison. Pitch shifting is also possible with some effects and others seek to give an extra note one octave above or below the guitar's to increase the impression of twin guitars at work.

One final effect which deserves a separate mention, is the echo unit. This emerged in the early 1960s with the British Watkins Copicat and the American Echoplex. Both used tape systems to provide delay times which could be varied from lengths which were almost short enough to be called reverb, to those which were distinct vintage rock'n'-roll echo effects. Despite having been largely superseded by purely electronic 'analogue' and, lately, 'digital' delay machines, tape echoes (using loops of tape to delay signals) provided a high quality of repeat

*Used in funk, Chorus gives a 'double-tracked' effect, which can also make a cheap guitar sound good!*

and are still popular with many players. In fact a more modern kind (the Roland Space Echo) is the mainstay of many PA systems' echo facilities, and the role of the WEM Copicat is still far from over since it has proved to be cheap and reliable, and can produce a variety of tape delay effects which can only be expensively duplicated on the better digital machines. Delay can also be obtained from pure electronics, either in small pedal forms or from larger units. Some use what electronics engineers charmingly call 'bucket brigade devices' where, roughly speaking, a signal is stored, overflows and 'pours' into the next device, thus creating a delay. The idea is similar in concept to a 'bucket brigade' of fire fighters!

Digital delays convert an instrument's signal into 'bits' (as with computer signals) which allows for an almost unlimited number of things to be done to process and modify it. Digital delays have been around for a while in recording studios but only in the last year or so have they become cheap enough to be considered for stage use. They are very much the delay systems of the future.

The problem with effects units, especially the cheaper types, is that they are often used as a poor substitute for playing ability and, more importantly perhaps, they can induce all manner of extraneous noises caused by the picking up of interference. Effects units need to be used with understanding and subtlety to get the best out of them, otherwise they can be far more trouble than they are worth.

## Amplification

Before going on to look at the individual types of amplification available today, it would be a very good idea if we started off with some sort of understanding of the terms used to describe the loudness of various units, if only because this is an area which very few players really understand properly and which causes enormous confusion.

Commonly, amplifier power is talked about in terms of watts — 'such and such an amp has an output rating of 100 watts', for example. Regrettably, although this is so common as to be almost universal, it is also meaningless! You cannot relate the actual perceived loudness of any two pieces of amplification equipment by talking in terms of their output in watts alone.

The only true measure of the sound we hear from an amplifier is what engineers refer to as the resulting 'sound pressure level'. This measurement is in decibels (dBs for short) and depends *not* on the output power of the amplifier alone, but on various other crucial factors like the efficiency of the speaker in converting electrical energy into

sound, the type of enclosure in which that speaker is mounted and many other considerations.

It *might* be true to say that two amplifiers each delivering 100 watts into two identical speakers mounted in the same enclosures might sound as loud as each other, but it isn't even that simple in practice as it depends on them having identical characteristics in other respects as well as having equal input signals.

Using the term 'watts' is, therefore, at best a rule of thumb — and even then only if it is quoted against a standardised reference, such as the term RMS. This, in effect, means the *average* sustained maximum output power of the amp. Terms like 'Music Power' or 'Peak' are to be avoided as they only confuse the situation. RMS is a fair average measurement whereby you can compare like with like — but only if you understand that there are other, equally important factors. The only really satisfactory solution (unless you have the inclination to make a study of the complex principles involved) is to use your ears and your common sense!

For practical purposes amplifiers can be divided into two distinct types (which apply equally to guitars and basses) — heads (or amp 'tops') where the amplifier is cased on its own, and 'combos' where the

amp is in the same enclosure as the speakers.

Most amplifiers today are combos — they combine portability and convenience for storage and transport with sufficient power and reliability to do the job asked of them. Heads and separate speaker enclosures ('cabs') are still used, however, where output power is high (especially with valve amps) or where, in bass use, the danger of low frequency vibrational damage to sensitive components in the amp means that it is safer to separate the speaker cab from the amp.

## The background

The combo was the first type of amp available to electric guitarists and has served them faithfully down the years. All early combos worked by using valve amplification principles (the only technology available at that time) and largely developed

*By the mid-1970s, vast stacks of bins, horns and speakers were common at rock gigs. Monitor systems alone were probably more powerful than the PAs used by bands ten years before*

from the amplification used in radio receivers during the 1940s.

What was needed for the electric guitar, though, was something much more powerful than the average radio, so American engineers (among whom Leo Fender — yet again! — was one of the pioneers) began to look at what could be done to obtain the necessary output power.

Using the valves available at the time, Fender (working with Donald Randall) had a guitar amp on the market as early as 1949, and by 1954 they had some eight models on offer, including the Bassman — the first bass guitar amplifier. Already this model could deliver a very impressive 50 watts, as could the Twin, which featured two 12″ speakers in combo form.

In the States, Fender amps remained easily the biggest sellers for many years (they probably still are, in fact, although relative newcomers Peavey must be a close second) whereas in the UK Vox and Selmer were their opposite numbers — Vox being very much the more professional of the two makes.

Right up until the 1960s 50-watt combos were about the loudest amps that you could get. They were more than adequate for most purposes, but the dawn of Mersey Beat Mania in 1962 created a desperate need for something louder to enable bands like The Beatles to be audible above the screams of their audiences! At a Beatles' or Rolling Stones' concert in 1963 you were lucky to be able to hear one note in every half dozen played, so inadequate were the amps available.

The drive for more power was undertaken (mainly in the UK) and various companies offered louder amps to cater for the new demand. Vox tried to move up to 100 watts with their AC 100 model (which rode on top of a single enclosure containing four 12″ speakers and two high pressure horns) and Selmer also offered 100-watt versions of their Treble'N'Bass amps as well as combos like the Thunderbird and Zodiac. Unfortunately, none of these were quite right for the demand.

Once the Beat Boom bands got to the States the situation became even more ludicrous. The Beatles played the massive Shea Stadium using Vox AC 30 (combos rated at a 30-watt output into two 12″ Celestion speakers) for guitar, with Paul McCartney relying on a hopelessly inadequate Vox AC 50, 50-watt amp driving two 15″ speakers.

*An early shot of The Rolling Stones. Note the Vox amps, and the absence of any PA paraphernalia besides microphones. This set up would have been inadequate for large venues.*

Necessity, being the mother of invention, *should* have delivered something louder for those early beat groups but nothing of any real significance happened until the *sound* changed as well as the volume.

No one really knows who first turned his amplifier up so loud that it fed back and distorted. Probably a thousand players had done it by accident, but they always hastily turned down again and spent the next few minutes banging at their ears to get their hearing back. Some crazed Englishman, however, some time around 1964, decided *not* to turn his amp down — he *liked* the sound. Legend has it that we *can* identify the player in question — step forward, Jeff Beck. Others say that it was Pete Townshend, but Beck seems to be the more likely candidate.

Beck was (is) unique. His blues-based playing with the Yardbirds (he replaced Eric Clapton, who had gone off to play some *real* blues with John Mayall) was savage and barely controlled. Beck wasn't prepared to stick to conventions and although Clapton had been remarkably *good* with the Yardbirds (witness

his work on the album *Five Live Yardbirds*), his sound had been very conventional. Beck it was, though, who overdrove his Vox amps and, when the feedback set in, began to use it as a deliberate effect to develop a whining sustained sound which had never been heard before. Single handedly (assuming that it *was* Jeff Beck) he had invented a need for distortion and overdrive which still obsesses the vast majority of electric guitarists. Usable distortion is probably still the most sought after (and argued about) quality in any guitar amplifier today.

That desire for distortion baffled many amp designers, who were pupils of the school which taught (as it still does in hi-fi and PA amplification, of course) that a *clean* sound, faithful to the original signal, was what people liked. Despite guitarists snapping up valve amps like the Vox AC30 and deliberately making them overload and distort, amp designers continued their quest for the perfectly clean amp. Not for the first time, equipment manufacturers were completely out of step with what their customers wanted and some musicians feel that only during the past five years have the majority of manufacturers reconciled themselves to this requirement.

Because the *quality* of the distortion sought by guitar players is

almost impossible to measure scientifically, the whole subject still causes considerable contention. What no one has yet done is to make an amplifier which is universally regarded as producing the ideal distorted sound, although, if anyone, Marshall have got the closest to this holy grail.

An ex-professional drummer who had made a considerable name for himself as a drum teacher (teaching such well-known players incidentally, as Mick Waller and Mitch Mitchell), Jim Marshall is undoubtedly the most important figure in the history of guitar amplification. Because of the influence he was having on drummers, guitarists and bassists were also in the habit of dropping into Marshall's shop. They told him how they were stuck for powerful enough amplification (especially the bass players) and so he started to build properly designed bass cabinets for them, fitted with 18" speakers.

Eventually, a regular visitor to his shop, Ken Bran, suggested to Marshall that he started building his own amplifiers, rather than selling other people's. Together, they began work on a bass amp but it turned out to be ideal for guitarist customers like Pete Townshend, Brian Poole and the Tremoloes and others. It was a 45-watt valve amp and it was followed by the most famous speaker cabinet ever — the slope fronted 4 × 12″ Marshall enclosure.

Later, Pete Townshend (always one to look for more power) asked for 100 watts and Jim Marshall and Ken Bran obliged; they also provided him with two of their 4 × 12s which he proceeded to mount, one on top of the other, with the Marshall amplifier crowning the set-up — the stack was born!

From then on there was no looking back. The Who exploded onto the scene with unprecedented vitality and were followed by Jimi Hendrix (who had been introduced to Marshall by Jim's former pupil, Mitch Mitchell), Cream and countless others. At last there was a set-up which combined power and the sound that players had been looking for all those years. Not only was this new set-up from Marshall loud (easily the loudest amplification arrangement yet produced for musicians), but it also distorted so sweetly that it combined those two factors most called for — absolute volume and a distortion which is still recognised as the fundamental voice of rock guitar.

Right through the late 1960s and the 1970s the race was on for more power — Deep Purple, Led Zeppelin, The Who and others piled stack after stack on stage (as much for the

image they presented as for the power they could deliver) and that trend still continues today with bands like Judas Priest and Iron Maiden, who use a backdrop of Marshall stacks to enhance their visual might.

While worries were beginning to be voiced about possible damage to the hearing of players who used these massive stacks, far more sophisticated PA systems were also being developed. This enabled guitarists and bass players to use smaller amps on stage, feed the sound from them through the PA system and then rely on the power of thousands of watts of PA to fill the massive venues which were being played in the USA. To some extent this brought to an end the need to use multiple stacks of amp heads and cabinets. One good stack or a decent combo could take the place of a wall of gear. The combo was beginning to stage a come-back.

### The guitar amp today

Today's amps come in a wide variety of types. For the beginner there is everything from tiny amplifiers which plug into the jack socket of a guitar (boxes no larger than a cigarette packet) to headphones with built-in amplifiers, to small 3- and 4-watt types with minute speakers, up through combos with increasingly larger speakers delivering as much as 200 watts, through to the massive Marshall valve heads and speaker stacks.

The average combo amp used by semi-professional musicians today delivers somewhere around 30–50 watts into a variety of different speaker types. With the developments that have taken place in speaker design over the past few years, it is no longer necessary to have multiple speakers to take 30 or 50 watts and, indeed, some costly professional units can handle more than 200 watts each!

Amplifiers (and this goes for heads as well as combos) work by having two distinct fundamental stages: the pre-amplifier (which takes the minute output from the guitar and raises it to a level suitable for the next stage, whilst also adding tone to the signal, as required) and the power amplifier, which boosts the signal up to a suitable level to drive the loudspeakers.

The number of inputs and tone controls can vary, as can a multitude of other factors such as the amp's sensitivity to the power output of the guitar. Some amps have built-in distortion circuits, some have advanced tone circuits and control systems (either graphic or parametric equalisers), some feature built-in effects, whilst others appear to do nothing much more than provide the bare amplification with the minimum of tonal alteration — the one you use depends on the money you have to spend and what sounds right to your ears. It is vital to note that *all* amplifiers sound different. Loudspeakers have different tonal characteristics, each maker has his own idea of what sounds best and there are no rules as to whose amp you should favour. There is, however, one major factor which differentiates two basic amplifier types — whether they use valves or transistors.

## Transistors *versus* valves

From a purely technical point of view it is probably fair to say that transistor devices are capable of a more faithful reproduction of the input of signal than valves (although there are many who would quibble with even this basic statement).

Up till the 1960s all amps employed valves (as did televisions and radios, of course) but the development of early transistor technology seemed to provide an opportunity for guitar amp makers to capitalise on the invention. Using transistors, amplifiers could be cleaner, lighter, offer better tonal control, be more reliable — the list of potential advantages seemed endless. Early efforts at transistor amps were, however, tremendously unsuccessful. Vox introduced their T60 bass amp (it was a flop), others followed, but they too could not appeal to guitarists who, by now, had begun to abandon the whole quest for *clean* sounds anyway. What was wanted now was a warmer, creamier overdrive, which could only, at that time, be obtained by using valves.

> **"***I use a transistorised combo which is a standard model except I've had heavy duty PA speakers put in it. I find it's better to have a combo — I don't need piles of speakers on stage, I don't need that kind of power. . . . One of the things I liked about trannies when I first tried them out, was the fact that they give a cutting, clean kind of sound, rather than the valve distortion. They have more of an edge, and that's the sound I like.***"***
> *WILKO JOHNSON*

For years a bitter controversy raged. Manufacturers insisted that transistors were inherently superior, guitarists claimed that valves sounded better, whatever their considerable cost disadvantages or other problems.

Because of the way it works, an overdriven transitor tends to produce an emphasis on *odd order harmonics* which sound harsh and discordant to the human ear. An overdriven valve, on the other hand, emphasises *even order harmonics* and these seem to be warmer, smoother and generally more acceptable. Even this is a vast over-simplification, however, as the best modern transistorised amplifiers can produce a sound which is very acceptable to many. Whatever their reasons, many (if not most) rock guitarists seem to prefer valve amps, and valve amps are probably still the world's most popular professional type generally. Valve amps, however, cost more to make than transistor types and so it tends to be true that amateur and semi-pro players use transistor combos until they can afford valve ones. Despite several years during the late 1970s when it was widely claimed that the valve was dead (no other industries used them and thus supplies would eventually dry up), there has been a pronounced swing back to valves. Marshall, Fender, Pro-Amp, Peavey, Burman, Laney, Ampeg, Vox and others are still producing valve amps. The death of the valve looks like having been very prematurely announced!

Good transistorised amps, however, will often get very close to the valve's natural sound and may, of course, be ideal for the player who doesn't *want* to use distortion.

## Buying an amplifier

The most relevant considerations when looking at which amp to buy for the electric guitar are relatively simple. The first thing you have to ask is what you need the unit for. Will you be playing small gigs in clubs, pubs and school or college halls? If so then a combo of around 50 watts output will be sufficient. Will you want a distorted lead guitar sound? If so, do you prefer valve sounds and, if you do, can you afford a valve amp?

If you also want to be able to use the amp at home and still have a distorted sound for practising solos, can that be done? Many amps today have a 'master volume' control which lets you select a low output power but a high pre-amp gain; this will achieve that sound you want (or very nearly so) at relatively low volume levels. Others have built-in distortion circuits (of widely varying quality) — your ears will tell you which suits your guitar best.

For tone controls, look at what is *needed*. There's no point paying extra for an amp with a very expensive tone circuit if you only want a limited range of sounds from it.

If you intend to use a lot of effects, does the amp offer a facility to plug these in *after* the pre-amp (a system which guarantees the minimum of effects units noise)?

If you only want an amp for home use then somewhere around 10 watts would be suitable; for small rehearsals only, then 20–30 watts will suffice. For bigger venues, 50–100 watts will be necessary, especially if you're unable to mike up your amp through the PA system. At this level start to think about separate

amp heads and speaker cabinets as well as combos. It may be that you would get a better spread of sound and a more pleasing effect overall from having the two units separate beyond the 50 watts mark.

Above all, try as many different amps as you can (and always try them as loud as you will ever want to use them, low volume tests can be deceptive). Buy the one which suits your pocket and suits your ears. Carefully reading the reviews in the music press will help guide you, although, in the final analysis, it is only what suits *you* that counts.

## Bass amplification

Most of the considerations above also apply to selecting bass amps. Their history is much the same as that of guitar amps too, although bassists have been even worse served down the years than guitarists.

The bass guitar is a difficult instrument to amplify successfully. As we've already seen, the tendency of the human ear to register higher notes as being louder tends to mean that a bass player will always need the loudest amp in the band's backline. Also he/she probably won't want distortion, so needs an amp that can be run below its maximum output power and still sound clean as well as being loud.

As a rule of thumb, it could be said that a bass player needs double the power of a guitarist. So, if your guitarist has a 50-watt amp, you really need to look for around a *minimum* of 75 watts of power and, probably, 100 watts.

Two other special problems afflict bassists. One is that low notes place far more strain on loudspeakers, the other is that they can set up vibrations which can damage components within the amp section. For this reason higher power amps are usually sold as heads and cabs, although good combos of up to 150 watts can be found. They need to be used with some discretion, though. Ideally, a bass speaker will be fitted into an enclosure specially designed to assist the speaker's ability to reproduce faithfully your bass guitar's lowest notes as cleanly and loudly as possible. These enclosures should be sealed and they tend to be large. For this reason many combos (especially the cheaper types) can represent a severe compromise between cost, ease of transport and ideal design qualities. One school of thought maintains that *all* bass combos are a

compromise, but that's probably over-stating the case. Do test any potential purchase at high levels though, because cheap speakers in badly designed cabinets will rasp and sound very poor.

As with guitar amps, speaker types make a great difference to a bass sound. Guitar players tend to use 10″ or 12″ units, whereas most bass combos and separate cabs use either 12″ or 15″ types. As a general rule a 15″ speaker will probably do a better job, but there is a very good argument for mixing the two sizes. Some players even use 10″ speakers as well and there is a feeling that 10″ units in one cab and 15″ speakers in another could be the ideal set-up.

There has been a trend during the past few years for top professional players to use what amounts to a mini-PA system on stage for their basses. This could comprise a large power amp or two, one feeding one set of speakers, the other feeding another cabinet loaded with speakers of a different size. It's an expensive option but the result can be an amazingly clean and yet full sound. Exponents of this approach, like Stanley Clarke, can spend thousands of pounds on such a rig.

Some manufacturers have even brought this concept down to more affordable levels. Although still not cheap, they can provide various options of sophisticated pre-amp tone controls, outputs to second power amps and different speaker sections for handling different parts of the frequency range, via frequency splitters, known as crossovers. It remains, however, a luxury approach.

Bassists have to be very careful when buying small combos. If they find themselves in competition with better equipped guitarists or keyboard players they might well have to drive their smaller amps and speakers too hard, which will result in a dirty sound or even eventual failure. Better to buy the most powerful amp and speakers you can afford and run them below maximum settings to achieve a safe but loud level of clean sound.

Because bassists tend not to be looking for distortion, overdriven valve amps are generally not sought after, and transistor amps usually satisfy the bass player. Some, however, still prefer what they see as the natural warmth of valve amps (even run undistorted) and so valves have their place here too.

Look for well constructed speaker cabs using properly designed bass speakers and an amplifier section designed to enable you to get the best tonal range from your bass. As always, test it at full volume and listen for weaknesses like rattles, rasps from the speaker and a sense of the whole unit straining.

## Buying a guitar

Faced with such a massive range to choose from, buying a guitar looks like a particularly daunting exercise, unless you start with a very clear idea of what you're after.

Obviously, the first consideration is price. You alone can decide how much you can spend on your new guitar and it is wise to set yourself a ceiling before you go into a shop.

Once you know how much you can afford to spend it's sensible to work out what *type* of guitar you want. As we've already seen, most guitars are really variations on two basic themes — they either have single coil pickups and are Fender-like in most aspects, or they use twin coil pickups and follow Gibson lines, although there are some models available which are a sort of hybrid of the two and others which are genuinely unique, these tend not to be beginners' instruments and are expensive.

To make a sensible decision about which type you want to own there are two simple tests; firstly, ask yourself what sort of sound your own tastes propel you towards. Are you partial to the Hendrix/Blackmore sound? Do you prefer the thinner, cleaner sound of single coil pickups, which turn savage and attacking when they overdrive an amp, or do you go more for the thicker, meatier guitar sound of early Clapton, Beck or current Gibson users like Michael Schenker or Ted Nugent.

Having let your ears guide you thus far, try both styles of instrument. Sample a type of each and see if the sound you get is what you expected and, more importantly still, whether the basic differences in neck shapes, fretting styles, control positioning, action and feel suit your playing style. If you've never played a guitar before, or have never owned an electric guitar, you could simply opt for the type which *feels* right for you — you can always change your mind later on.

Having settled on the *type* of guitar that you like, consider whether a secondhand purchase would be

better for you than a new guitar. Secondhand instruments (and that isn't meant to include prestige 'vintage' American guitars) can obviously be a good buy, but you do need to have some knowledge of what you are doing — especially if buying privately where you may have no come-back against the seller if things go wrong with your purchase later on. Buying from a shop may cost you more, but a retailer has certain legal obligations which he must fulfil with regard to the quality of merchandise he sells. Unless you are certain about what you are buying, a retailer will offer you safeguards over a private sale.

Having decided on whether to buy privately or from a shop, and having some idea of the *type* of guitar you want (a semi-solid, a solid of the single coil or twin coil varieties, fitted with tremolo or without one), you may now be confronted with a guitar which you like the look of and which sounds pretty good to your ears. How do you know whether it's going to be a good buy? Obviously, reading reviews in the music press will have helped familiarise you with some of the major brand names, and you may even have been pointed in the direction of the guitar you are considering by a favourable review which has appeared on that model. But since quality control is not fail-safe, how do you tell if you have a good one in your hands?

There are a few very basic rules to follow, probably the *best* of which is to try and take a knowledgeable friend along with you when you buy. He or she will probably be able to spot problems that a beginner might miss, but if you can't find a suitable adviser, the following guidelines should assist.

Firstly, be very suspicious of ultra-cheap guitars; they can prove to be more trouble than they are worth. Stick to the best you can afford and, to an extent, rely on the better known brand names who have the most to lose from offering a bad quality instrument.

When you first hold the guitar, how does the neck feel to you? Can you get your fingers round it easily enough? Are the frets sharp on top and rough-feeling, and do they protrude from the edges of the fingerboard so that you could snag your hands as they slide up and down the neck? Comfort matters a great deal on a guitar as anything which

makes you feel uneasy with it will hamper your freedom to play.

Start to play the guitar. Are there buzzes when you hold the strings down? (Make sure you try playing along the whole length of the neck.) If the instrument buzzes too much (nearly all guitars buzz a bit), then perhaps the frets aren't of an even height (a common problem on worn guitars or badly made new ones). Maybe the neck is warped? You can check this by sighting the guitar's neck like an arrow, looking from the nut down towards the bridge. No guitar will have a dead straight neck but look for obvious humps or twists. Bear in mind, however, that a correctly set-up guitar *will* show a slight tendency to bow a little away from the strings, so don't take too much notice of this test unless you're sure what to look for.

Next, what about the guitar's action? Are the strings set so high that they are hard to hold down onto the neck? Action can be altered but a badly made guitar will often have its strings set high to disguise inherent faults. A guitar with a sensibly low action which plays in tune right up the neck is a safer bet than one which is set up with a high action, where you are told that it could be set lower. Take the guitar as it is, not as it is promised it will be after setting up. That should have been done *beforehand*!

Tuning problems on guitars have so many causes that only an experienced player can tell precisely what fault is causing which difficulties in this area. The flaws could be anything from a simple case of worn-out strings to wrongly placed frets or a badly designed or placed bridge, to neck warps. Unless you know your guitars, only accept one which is in tune the full length of the neck when you buy it.

The basic test for what is known as 'intonation' (which, basically, means that you will get the guitar sounding in tune regardless of where you are playing on the neck) is to check the harmonics directly above the 12th fret. To do this, lightly touch the string with a finger of your left or neck hand directly over the 12th fret. You should get a ringing note when you pluck the string with a pick. This is the string's 1st harmonic. Now hold the string down and play the same note fretted, ie just *behind* the 12th fret. The two notes should be identical. If they are

not then you have a fault. It's almost certainly something which can be cured by fitting new strings and/or adjusting the effective length of the string by moving the string saddle in question backwards or forwards, depending on whether the fretted note is sharp (high) or flat (low) against the harmonic. If the fretted note is flatter than the harmonic then you need to shorten the string (ie move the saddle towards the nut), if the fretted note is sharper, the saddle needs moving back. Again, this is an easy enough job, but you shouldn't have to do it with a new guitar nor, really, with a secondhand one being offered for sale. Later on (especially if you start changing your string gauges), you may well have to do the job yourself, so it is as well to know how.

Having satisfied yourself that the guitar is comfortable to handle, that the instrument plays in tune up and down the neck, what about the electrics? *Insist* on trying the guitar with an amp (preferably, of course, one you're familiar with). Turn all the controls up full and see if the rotary knobs crackle and spit when they turn. Check the pickup selector is tight and that all the pickups work properly. Listen for excessive hums, which can indicate poor earthing or internal shielding of the components. Fortunately, guitar electrics are so simple (except on actives) that there is little that can go wrong with them, but it's worth a few minutes spent checking them.

If the guitar passes these tests, you like the sound you are getting from it and the price being asked seems fair (you *have* looked around first, haven't you?!) then it's almost certainly a safe bet to buy it.

These days guitar players are better served than ever before by manufacturers — especially when it comes to cheaper guitars. The Japanese makers offer some fine-value guitars and basses and most of the big names have some good buys too. Mind you, there are bargains to be had from other makers, so keep an open mind and, above all, try as many different guitars as you can before deciding which is the right one for you. The mechanical tests for the quality of a guitar are fairly simple — the personal tests for satisfying your needs as a musician will take time and experience.

Whatever guitar, bass or amplifier you decide to buy, don't worry if you seem to have outgrown it with-

in six months or so (especially if it is your first purchase). Settling on the perfect equipment for you will take a long time, and even professional players of many years' standing can suddenly feel the need for a change. But remember, the best instrument, the best effects and the best amplifier will never be any substitute for your skill as a player. Give a top

guitarist a cheap instrument and he or she will *still* sound like the musician he/she is. The converse, unfortunately, isn't true. However, a bad guitar (or just the wrong guitar) can impede your development, so keep on trying new ideas as you develop and change your style and tastes. Above all, try to sound and play like *yourself* — the world isn't

*Mick Jones of The Clash tends to use a variety of Gibson Les Pauls*

looking for the best Angus Young sound-alike nor *another* Mick Jones impersonator. What the world *is* waiting for is someone good, different and, above all, an individual — could that be you?

**"** *I'm very much a purist — I like all my drums to be made of wood. They're of normal sizes, but of fairly heavy construction. The shells are eight-ply, which helps to give a denser sound. I like drums to have some power to them. I can't stand disco-sounding drums and I can't stand studio kits. I can't actually play them when they sound like that. I physically don't want to touch them. It's a matter of being big and warm and monstrous.* **"** *IAN PAICE*

# CHAPTER 2

## Drums and Cymbals

### Rick Palmer

★ It is probably true to say that drummers are rarely the most flamboyant members of rock bands (Keith Moon being a notable exception) — they sit behind a comforting wall of drums and cymbals apparently doing their own thing in splendid isolation from the screaming horde in front of them. However, who can deny the fact that the drummer invariably has an enormous contribution to make to the overall 'feel' of a song or even the characteristic sound of the band as a whole. The inner satisfaction of achieving this, together with being what should be the band's focal point in times of uncertainty goes a long way to compensating for not being fully in the limelight.

So, having decided that you have a great sense of rhythm and that the drums are for you, what should you look for? The following pages will try to help you appreciate what goes into making the major parts of a drum kit (shells, heads, hardware, cymbals and so on) and how the sound of the kit is influenced by the construction of its various components. There is also a short section on some of the more unusual items around, which also points a finger as to where things might be going in the future ★

## Construction

The heart of any drum is the shell. This is an open cylinder made of wood and carefully shaped at the ends to provide an even lip which the head fits over.

The shells of mounted and floor tom-toms are invariably made from several laminations of wood (normally somewhere between six and nine), carefully formed into the correct shape by a heat, steaming and glueing process. By the very nature of the shell-forming process, a join is required in the shell, and it is the objective of drum manufacturers to make this join as rigid as possible and to minimise the effect it has on the tonal qualities of the completed shell. This has meant that most manufacturers have developed their own special processes for making shells, often jealously guarded by patents.

The type of wood used for the shells has a considerable effect on the tone and also, unfortunately, on the price. Maple and birch are often used in the more expensive drums, whilst cheaper sets are made from all sorts of less costly varieties. Generally speaking, the denser woods give a much fuller, warmer sound with better depth. Thus you would expect a good rock drum shell to be fairly heavy. Jazz-orientated shells tend to be a little lighter and, as such, are a little more responsive to the touch of the player, although they normally lack power compared with a rock drum of similar size.

In order to protect the wood from the ravages of moisture and other external factors, the shell is finished with varnish both inside and out. The inside is then smoothed and is normally left as a natural wood finish. The outside of the shell comes in for considerably more attention, of course, often receiving the full 'cosmetic' treatment, and there are now a wide variety of exotic finishes available.

The inner surface of the shell isn't always left with its natural finish, and it is now becoming quite common for some kind of extra treatment to be applied here too. This usually takes the form of a fibre/epoxy coating, which is designed to improve sound depth and projection. Unfortunately it can also be used to hide inferior workmanship, so if the rest of the drum doesn't look particularly well made, beware of internal finishes!

The next important variable in shell manufacture is the size. This is expressed in diameter and depth of shell and as yet is still quoted in inches. For tom-toms, the range of standard sizes is broadly encompassed by the following:

| diameter | | depth | |
|---|---|---|---|
| 14'' | × | 14'' | Floor- |
| 16'' | × | 16'' | standing |
| 18'' | × | 16'' | tom-toms |

| diameter | | depth | |
|---|---|---|---|
| 8'' | × | 5½'' | |
| 10'' | × | 6½'' | |
| 12'' | × | 8'' | Mounted |
| 13'' | × | 9'' | tom-toms |
| 14'' | × | 10'' | |
| 15'' | × | 12'' | |

Bass drums, on the other hand, usually only vary in diameter from 18'' to 24'' with a standard depth of 14''.

As a general rule, jazz drummers tend to stick to the smaller sizes while rock drummers use the middle to top sizes, unless of course they can afford to have the whole lot!

In addition to the sizes quoted above, many manufacturers have started offering drums with 2'' or so added to the standard depth. These are designed to give a more powerful sound and as such are aimed generally at rock drummers.

## Snare drums

Snare drums require special attention for there are quite a few more variables involved. Firstly, it is very common to find snares made with metal shells; secondly, there's quite a variety of depths to choose from given the almost universal snare drum diameter of 14''. And as if that weren't enough to worry about, there's the snare mechanism too!

In choosing which features to go for, you first have to decide what you want from the drum. Metal

*Brass shell snare drum with conventional snare mechanism*

*Brass shell snare drum with parallel action snare mechanism*

*Wood shell snare drum with aluminium stress rings*

drums in general will sound much brighter and snappier than wooden ones, and nowadays the lower priced snare drums are almost exclusively metal. Greater depth of drum gives a deeper pitch and generally more body to the sound. It is not un-common to find 8″ deep snare drums used to get the very solid sound that's so much in vogue nowadays. When playing live, how-ever, and especially if your kit is not miked up through a PA system, a prime consideration will be the snare drum's ability to cut through the sound made by the rest of the band. A metal drum is well suited to this job, with a depth of probably 5″ or 6½″.

The snare mechanism should be easy to engage and disengage (believe it or not some are quite inconvenient) and should provide positive snare engagement, ie no buzzing. Most of the lower and mid-priced snare drums incorporate a movement which lowers one end of the snares, thus reducing the tension in them and allowing them to fall away from the lower head of the drum. Very expensive snare drums often incorporate a feature called 'parallel action' snare engage-ment, which enables both ends of the snares to be moved to and from the drum together while maintaining tension on them. This gives you greater control over the engage-ment and response of the snares,

but the relatively complicated mech-anism required certainly doesn't come cheap! However, the traditional snare tensioning method is by and large perfectly adequate.

*A standard 5-drum set up, showing the range of general hardware – stands, pedals, cymbals, and stool*

## Hardware

Most of the other bits and pieces which make up a drum kit are known collectively as *hardware*. This term covers a multitude of items which can conspire to make your life at rehearsal or, worse still, on stage a nightmare unless you take a certain amount of care over their selection. The main items are listed below, together with a few tips on what to look for when buying them.

## Nut boxes and head dampers

These two items will, of course, come fitted to the drums, but take a good look at them as they will often be a pointer to the manufacturer's overall attention to detail throughout the rest of the kit.

The nut boxes should all be rigidly attached to the shells and check that none of the attachment screws are missing by having a look inside the shell (quite easy to do if clear heads are fitted). Check also that the tensioning screws can turn easily in the nut boxes and that the threads aren't stripped — very important when looking at secondhand kits.

The damping mechanism should be checked for smoothness of operation and freedom from any looseness, which could cause unwanted rattles during playing.

## Bass drum pedals

A lot of engineering goes into bass drum pedals nowadays. You will probably become quite attached to yours over the years and a good initial selection should turn it into an old friend.

All bass drum pedals work on some kind of spring principle, and by and large these can be grouped into *tension spring* and *compression spring* types.

Try out as many as possible and see which one has an action that

you feel happy with. Many pedals have adjustable spring tension, which enables you to set the amount of force that you have to exert to make the beater hit the drum. So if you try a pedal that seems to have a very stiff action, check to see if the spring tension setting is too high.

Apart from the feel of the pedal, the other important point to think about is whether the design has tried to minimise the likelihood of squeaks and rattles developing during the life of the pedal. Many pedals now have nylon in some of the bearings which can help reduce potential squeaks. Wear and tear can nevertheless result in some noise developing, but a little extra care in looking after the pedal will often eliminate this. A small amount of grease regularly applied to its moving parts will go a long way to help increase the life of what is really a small machine in its own right.

## Hi-hat pedals

The basic rule to follow when selecting a hi-hat pedal is really the same as that for selecting a bass drum pedal, ie find one with an action that you like. This is particularly important at the lower end of the price range where the spring tension is not always adjustable. The other considerations are a little different.

For example, the stability of the pedal assembly once it has the cymbals mounted on it is very important. In order to achieve this, the tripod feet should have a reasonable spread and they should also be able to prevent movement of the pedal during playing. Manufacturers are now often making use of large rubber feet to prevent sliding, and this is a good idea as many club managers (and not to say long-suffering parents!) don't take too kindly to having their floors gouged up by the spikes that are normally offered as an alternative.

The pad which supports the lower cymbal should also be sturdy, as should the clutch assembly which holds the upper cymbal. Some manufacturers, unfortunately, make economies here. What is really important is to get a positive location of the top cymbal onto the spindle, and you may well find that it's worth buying a separate clutch assembly in addition to the one supplied with a cheap hi-hat stand.

A worthwhile feature, if it's available, is a memory lock or jubilee clip on the height setting of the stand, as you can then always be sure that the hi-hats will be at the position you want them. This in fact applies to all the stands: it stops them from slipping and helps you to get the same set-up each time you play.

*A hi-hat stand. Note the rubber feet, the memory lock on the height setting, and the cymbal clutch assembly*

*A bass drum pedal (above) with a standard felt beater. Note the side-mounted spring on this model*

## Cymbal stands

The cymbal stand must provide a secure and stable base for your cymbals and enable you to mount them in such a position that you can reach them comfortably.

There is a current tendency to go for ever heavier grades of cymbal stand, which is fine as long as you can afford to pay for all the extra metal involved and you don't personally have to lug all the stuff around. In the more realistic world, however, it's as well to choose a reasonably heavy grade of stand without going overboard. The tripod base should be fairly wide and should preferably have effective non-slip feet, although slippage will not be anything like as severe as it is with the hi-hat stand.

Constructional aspects of the stands worth checking are the smoothness of the bushing between the telescopic sections (the use of nylon in many products has resulted in a great improvement here) and also the ease and security of action of the joint wing nuts. The latter will primarily be dependent on the size of wing nut, and fortunately the manufacturers seem to have adopted a policy of making these pretty chunky. This really helps to get a positive lock on the whole assembly.

One final point, and in fact this applies to all hardware, is the quality of the chrome plating. With a cheapish stand you will not necessarily get a first class job so watch out for slivers of chrome breaking off and sticking into your fingers.

## Snare drum stands

The most common snare drum stand has a base that is similar to a scaled-down cymbal stand. The point of interest is the assembly which actually holds the snare drum in position. This consists of a three-arm arrangement with rubber claws which can be adjusted to grip the drum tightly. The stand will also incorporate a system for tilting the drum to the desired angle. As with cymbal stands, the overall considerations are stability, ease of set up and solidity.

## Stools

Last but not least comes the drummer's stool, or 'throne' as it's sometimes known. The three points to look for here are stability, solidity and comfort. Many stools have tripod legs similar to a cymbal stand, and this gives a good base. Don't go

for too wide a base, though, as this can get in the way of all the other bits and pieces such as bass pedals and hi-hat stands. The solidity of the whole assembly is absolutely vital (remember that it has to support *all* your weight) as there's nothing more embarrassing than an unplanned collapse behind the drum kit! Lastly comes comfort. There are probably very few stools around that are truly unusable in this respect and so really all that is needed here is a quick check that nothing is protruding where it shouldn't!

## Drum Heads

The problem of breaking heads virtually disappeared as a regular occurrence with the advent of the plastic drum head. This, however, has also led to quite an increase in the types of head available, and the variation in sound attainable by using different heads is very marked. The poor drummer is thus faced with yet another decision to make!

A full discussion of all the heads available, together with a description of their relative merits, would almost fill another book, so the next few paragraphs simply give a rough guide as to the more common types and their main characteristics.

## Coated heads

The coated head is the standard head available and is generally found on most of the cheaper kits. The coating is sprayed over the outside of the head's plastic film and this provides some damping of the natural vibration of the plastic, helping to make the sound a little more solid. A plain coated head is a perfectly adequate starting point for a new drummer, and even if you progress to using more exotic heads, coated heads are perfectly good as bottom heads on double-headed drums. In addition, it should be noted that these, and indeed most other types of head, can come in a variety of thicknesses. As might be expected, the thicker heads give a rather more solid sound, but at the expense of a little sensisivity.

## Clear heads

The clear head is the other basic type of head available, and by and large clear heads give a rather more open sound than coated heads. They can also be considered purely from a visual point of view, as they really look good with transparent drum shells.

Another very popular addition to the basic clear head is known as the control spot. These are silver or black discs about 4'' in diameter which are struck onto the centre of the head. The effect of this is to alter the resonant characteristic of the head, generally adding power and at the same time tightening up the

'The oil-filled head for me is a little bit too dull, a little bit too jungle-like in the tom-tom sound, and I don't really go for that plodding, heavy metal drum sound. Also, they're difficult to play in that there's no rebound from them at all. You've really got to work incredibly hard for that sound.'

*CARL PALMER*

sound quite a bit. These heads are currently very popular for general purpose rock work.

### Oil-filled heads

Oil-filled heads consist of two thin layers of plastic head material with the space between them filled with a fairly thin oil. This has the effect of making the sound of the drum much deader, which is often the prime objective of many sound engineers who may be miking up a kit for stage or studio work. The main reason for choosing a dead sound is that it then provides a platform on top of which various sound treatments can be added, thereby enabling a specific drum sound to be established. There is no doubt that oil-filled heads do an excellent job, but they do work out rather more expensive, as might be expected from the complexity of their construction.

## Extras

Many drummers today add roto-toms, electronic drums and/or timbales to their conventional kit. In fact, roto-toms can be used in place of conventional tom-toms, and, as you've no doubt seen, electronic drums *can* replace the whole ac-coustic drum kit but not, as yet, the cymbals!

## Timbales

These latin drums are single-headed and are mounted on a central stand with a cowbell. The shells are usually metal. Played separately from the drum kit, with special lightweight sticks, timbale technique involves rhythms incorporating beats on the cowbell and shells and rims of the drums. Used as part of the kit, timbales can add a latin flavour to your band, and are a feature of reggae drumming.

## Roto-toms

These are basically shell-less tom-toms. The head is tensioned over a metal rim via an ingenious mechanism which can be quickly rotated to raise or lower the pitch. Since there is no shell, the sound is very clean. It is therefore possible to tune roto-toms very easily to definite pitches. They can therefore replace con-ventional tom-toms, but have less tonal colour.

## The future

Recently there have been many quite staggering innovations in the design and construction of drums. As far as drumming itself is con-cerned, the most interesting inno-vation is the electronic drum kit, with the very popular Simmons SDS5 unit currently leading the field. This represents a major break-away from previous notions that electronic drums were a gimmick solely for use in reggae and disco music. The kit is played in the normal way (and indeed is generally supplemented with regular cymbals), but the fact that the beats are all synthesised allows a huge variety of unusual sounds to be generated in addition to most realistic 'natural'

*John Keeble of Spandau Ballet uses a wide selection of electronic and conventional drums combined*

sounds. The very resilient playing surface provided on the 'pads' also allows the possibility of developing a rather different playing technique by virtue of the enhanced stick response.

Other electronically based equip-ment centres around a crop of recently released drum 'computers'. These machines are programmed

> *'I think that any electronic per-cussion is a good idea. Drum machines can sound a little sterile because they don't have enough emotion built into them to speed up and slow down which a drummer automatically does, and sometimes that can help the music a lot. But I think that individual electronic drums can be an excellent addition to a drummer's kit.'*
>
> *CARL PALMER*

rather than played and are really a development of the rhythm box. Real drum sounds are stored digitally in the machine and can then be re-called in almost any timing desired. This can result in the most mind-boggling rhythm patterns, but the *feel* of these machines is nearly always robotic.

Aside from the electronic inno-vations, the main area of future development in drumming lies in the use of alternative materials for various parts of the kit. Mention has already been made of fibreglass and perspex drum shells, and one won-ders how far away a usable moulded plastic shell may be. The cost-reduction possibilities of this would be immense.

## Cymbals

It is all too easy to underestimate the importance that cymbals play in contributing to the overall sound and excitement of your drumming. And whereas the sound of a drum kit can be modified and improved by tuning, damping and using different heads, there's not much you can do to alter a cymbal. Cymbals should therefore be chosen and looked after with care. A few years ago, it was relatively easy to decide what to buy from the limited range avail-able, but now it's starting to get very confusing with a much greater range of sizes, weights and grades. A set of top-grade cymbals can easily be as expensive as a good drum kit.

There are now some very good cymbals at less frightening prices, but beware of the cheaper cymbals which may have a dominating and discordant note. A good cymbal will vibrate to a certain extent in sympathy with the tuned instruments around it, and so blend in with the sound.

When choosing cymbals listen to them close to and from a distance, and always try to hear the whole cymbal set together to see how they blend with one another.

## Construction

There are two main methods of cymbal manufacture, each one pro-ducing a characteristic cymbal sound. The traditional method uses a pro-cess called *spinning* to form the shape of the cymbal itself. With this process, the cymbal starts life as a flat circular 'blank' and this is rotated as it is formed into its final shape, somewhat similar in fact, to a potter making a bowl. A more recently de-veloped process is *stamping*. Again

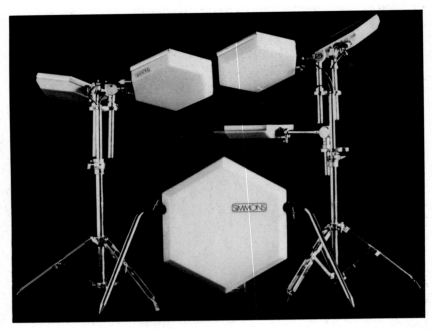

the starting point is a flat circular blank, but the metal is forced into shape purely by the action of a press coming down on the blank. This process is akin to the way in which car bodies are formed from flat sheets of steel.

The two different kinds of manu-facturing process use essentially the same metal, ie bronze, but it is usual to find that the pressed cymbals have a rather higher percentage of tin in them (bronze being an alloy of copper and tin).

After being shaped, the cymbals are then 'hammered'. This process gives the cymbals their characteristic sound and has to be carefully con-trolled by the manufacturers to ensure consistency in their products. It is in fact this process which really stops the cymbals from sounding like the proverbial dustbin lid!

Finishing is rarely an important feature of cymbal construction, as most cymbals have a polished metal finish. However, some cymbals are available in what is called 'brilliant' finish, where a special polishing and lacquering process is used.

The manufacturing process, as well as the hammering, has some-thing of an effect on the sound of the cymbal, and as a general rule you will probably find that 'traditional' cymbals sound a little mellower than their stamped counterparts. However, the golden rule is to listen to the cymbal as objectively as possible without worrying too much about its manufacture, and if it sounds good, take it!

*Is this the shape of drums to come? A Simmons SDS 5 electronic kit*

## Types of cymbal

Cymbals fall into four main types, and the characteristics of each are described below.

### Hi-hats

The hi-hat is probably the part of the kit which is most frequently used, so it's worth investing in something decent. They are always supplied in pairs and are mounted on a stand which allows them to be moved together and apart by means of a foot pedal. They are normally positioned just to the left of the snare drum (for a right-handed drummer) and, together with the snare and bass drum, form the basis of most beats.

A prime consideration of the per-formance of hi-hats is the crispness of the sound, and its ability to cut through that of the other instruments. Cheaper hi-hats are commonly rather thin and have a weak sound, often with an unpleasant ring to it. Any cymbals showing these ten-dencies should really be avoided as this is one area where compromising on sound definitely doesn't pay in the long run. A common feature nowadays is to have a heavier weight bottom cymbal sometimes with holes drilled in it too. This latter feature prevents air being trapped between the two cymbals as they are brought together and so creates

a crisper sound. This can work well but is not essential if you are able to buy a good pair of hi-hats and set them up properly.

Hi-hats come in a range of sizes generally between 13″ and 15″. The smaller sizes are somewhat higher pitched, and in fact the most commonly used size is probably 14″. A good pair of hi-hats is absolutely essential to the establishment of a solid overall sound and patience in saving up the money for them and careful selection really is worth it.

### Ride cymbals
The ride cymbal is often used to fill out the sound of the band during a guitar solo or to add some more depth to the basic beat when required. It can also be used as a crash cymbal. For this reason there are two things to look at when evaluating ride cymbals; the basic 'ride' sound and the crash sound.

For rock music the ride cymbal is normally of fairly heavy weight and

needs to have good definition to the sound each time the cymbal is struck. This has resulted in some ride cymbals being manufactured with a very small or even non-existent cup at the centre. Such types generally give a very good ride sound but unfortunately are not very versatile. This may seem to be

OK for you, but bear in mind that the ability to change the ride completely by playing at or near the bell is often very handy.

*Police skin-beater Stewart Copeland surrounds himself with an impressive array of accessories, ranging from splash cymbals to roto-toms*

Ride cymbals come in a large range of sizes from about 18″ to 24″, and in a selection of weights covering most of the standard range.

Variations of the ride cymbal include 'sizzle' and 'swish' cymbals, which have small holes drilled in them fitted with loose rivets. This means that, when the cymbal is struck, the lighter vibrations are increased, giving a continuous 'sizzling' beneath the ride rhythm.

### Crash cymbals

Crash cymbals are the last in the 'basic' category before you start considering the world of special effect cymbals. They are used for punctuation rather than for continuous rhythm. The crash cymbal will usually be of lighter weight than the ride. If you're lucky enough to have more than one crash cymbal it is important that you arrange their pitches so that their individual characteristics are obvious. As with any instrument, your personal taste will be the main guide, but points to look out for when buying crash cymbals are durability (the very thin cymbals might sound good at first, but will they survive long?) and absence of any unwanted overtones during the decay of the cymbal. The length of decay is also another thing to consider. Do you want to have a very short 'tight' crash or a longer, more gong-like one? Try to answer these basic questions before you go out looking, or better still try to have an idea of the sound you're looking for in your head as this will help to avoid paying out a lot of cash for something that doesn't sound right.

Crash cymbals come in a very large range of sizes and weights, with the pitch generally becoming lower as size and weight increase. The smaller, lighter cymbals tend to have a much shorter decay time and do sound rather brighter. Very small crash cymbals (less than 13″ or so in diameter) are usually known as 'splash' cymbals, except for one very heavy 8″ which is known as a 'bell', because that's what it sounds like.

The 'China crash' cymbal tends to be on the thin side and differs from a regular crash by having upturned edges and a cup rather than a bell at the centre. It can be played on either side to good effect, but the current fashion is to play it upside down. This gives a very sharp and shallow gong-like crash.

## CHAPTER 3

# Basic Guitar Technique

## Deirdre Cartwright

### Playing positions

If you want to sit down to play or practise the guitar the most important thing is that you should be comfortable, so don't sit in a chair with arms as this will restrict *your* arm movements. Cross your legs and rest the guitar on your thigh with the neck slanting upwards so that the head of the guitar is about level with your shoulder. Tilt the guitar body back slightly and then if you lean forward slightly you should be able to see the fingerboard easily.

However, you'll find that most solid body electric guitars are designed to be played standing up and some of the more exotic angular body shapes are extremely awkward to play sitting down. So make sure you buy a good quality strap and check that you can raise the guitar as high or low as you want it. A wide strap will help distribute the weight on your shoulder. As for the height of the guitar, jazz players tend to have them just below their chins and heavy metal players just above their knees! So again it really is a matter of personal preference. A higher

playing position will make fast fingering and plectrum work easier, so keep this in mind while posing in front of the mirror!

### Left-hand positioning and technique

There are many functions of the left (neck) hand. These range from fretting notes to create melodic lines and chords, to damping techniques to prevent unwanted notes sounding or to cut off their duration, to vibrato, string-bending, hammering-on, pulling-off, trilling etc. We'll be covering all these in detail in later chapters, but for the moment let's just concentrate on the basic positioning.

The classic left-hand position is with the thumb placed behind the

centre of the neck and the fingers arched over, resting on the strings. There should be a gap between the side of the neck and the palm of your hand. Try to keep your fingers

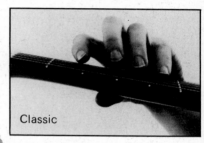

Classic

roughly parallel with the frets — this will help you to use your 4th finger which tends to be weaker than the others. This is a good *general* playing position to adopt, though with some of the blues and rock guitar tech-

Rock

niques it's actually better to rest the guitar neck between the thumb and 1st finger.

To play a note, make sure you place your finger just behind the fret so that you get a clean, clear sound.

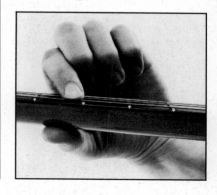

One of the hardest gigging rock guitarists in the world. Joan Jett of The Blackhearts

Finally, you should in general keep to the 'one fret per finger' rule, ie each finger should be responsible for a fret space and play all six strings on that fret. When you change position, your fingers move to cover four new frets.

## Right-hand positioning and technique

The right or plectrum hand controls the timing and volume of the notes selected by the left (neck) hand, using combinations of up and down strokes and damping. In this book we'll be concentrating on plectrum technique, though some guitarists play with their fingers, or a combination of plectrum and fingers.

Plectrums come in a wide range of sizes and thicknesses and can be made from many different materials — the choice is really up to you. Holding a plectrum may seem rather strange at first but you will soon get used to it. The usual method is as follows: curve your first finger, place the plectrum on the first joint and place the tip of the thumb over it.

When striking the strings with the plectrum you should make the minimum of movement with your right arm. Your wrist should be relaxed and the plectrum moved up and down by rotating the wrist and forearm. Do not tense your arm and move it from the elbow as this will severely restrict your ability to build up speed and smoothness.

## Plectrum exercises

You can strike the strings with a plectrum either using a downstroke, ie away from you towards the ground, or using an upstroke, ie towards you.

↓ means a downstroke
↑ means an upstroke

Count a steady 1–2–3–4, tapping your foot to each beat and on an open string play a downstroke to each count. When that feels okay, play an upstroke to each count.

Now, keeping the same tempo, say 'and' between each count. The 'and' coincides with your foot rising up off the ground. This is called the 'offbeat'. Now play alternate up and down strokes like this:

1 and 2 and 3 and 4 and etc.
↓ ↑ ↓ ↑ ↓ ↑ ↓ ↑

Try this, on each of the six strings, building up the speed of the exercise but keeping the strokes smooth.

You can also try striking different strings using alternate strokes, eg

downstroke on the 6th string,
    upstroke on the 4th
downstroke on the 5th string,
    upstroke on the 3rd
downstroke on the 4th string,
    upstroke on the 2nd

downstroke on the 3rd string,
    upstroke on the 1st

Keep the strokes even and play it slowly until you can hit the strings accurately, then try playing the exercise back down the strings —

upstroke on the 1st string,
    downstroke on the 3rd
upstroke on the 2nd string,
    downstroke on the 4th, etc.

An exercise like this really helps you gauge the distance between the strings and will help you build up the essential coordination between your left and right hands. Try to think up some yourself.

> 'Like a lot of rock guitarists, I actually began with a hammering-off style — making my neck hand do the work — because of people like Jeff Beck. But when I joined Colosseum II, I had to play a lot of phrases with the keyboards — unison and harmony lines — and to make all the notes come out cleanly, I had to really work on my picking technique. I had to do chromatic scale exercises, making sure that every movement was up and down with my plectrum hand.'
>
> GARY MOORE

## Tuning methods

The 'pitch' that the note of a guitar string produces depends on three things: its length, its thickness and the string tension. On the guitar all strings have the same scale length, ie the distance between the bridge and the nut, but you can see that they all have different thicknesses or gauges. The thickest (6th) string gives the lowest note and the thinnest (1st) string the highest note. The notes that the open strings are tuned to are as follows:

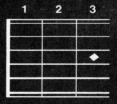

1st string to E
2nd string to B
3rd string to G
4th string to D
5th string to A
6th string to E

Note that although the 1st and 6th strings have the same note and 'sound', the 1st string is much higher in pitch than the 6th string

We looked at string gauges and types in the opening section of this book. Once you have chosen your strings, you have to keep them in tune. A guitarist in a band is faced with two problems, tuning to the other instruments in the band and tuning the guitar to itself.

There are, of course, several different tuning methods. Let's start with those which involve tuning the guitar to a separate reference note.

### Tuning to an instrument

The strings of the guitar are tuned to the notes E, A, D, G, B, E, which correspond to the notes of the piano as shown in the diagram. Remember this diagram or keep it with you so that you can actually find the notes on the piano.

Strike the E key and while the note is still ringing, pluck the E 1st string

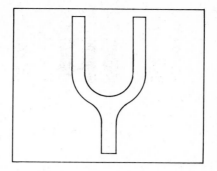

### Tuning fork

This is a metal fork which, when struck, vibrates giving a tone of A at 440 cycles per second. The tuning fork can be placed on the bridge of the guitar or over the pickups so that the tone (A 440) can be amplified. The A string is tuned to this note and then the remaining strings are tuned in relation to the A string.

### Scales and chords:

#### their relationship

There has always been a tremendous amount of confusion amongst guitarists about the relationship between chords and scales. How do chords work together? How do you improvise a solo over a particular chord sequence? And so on.

You can easily get the impression that you either need to study complex systems of theory or do it all by 'ear' and by 'feel' — whatever that means! Well, *all* music is based on relatively few theoretical principles, and if you understand them, you'll understand how your guitar works. This takes much less effort and is much more rewarding in the end than, for example, memorising hundreds of chord shapes without understanding what you're doing.

Throughout this section we'll try to help you understand what you're playing (mental knowledge), hear what you're playing (aural knowledge) and see what you're playing (visual knowledge).

Play any open string and then play the same string at the 12th fret. You'll hear that the sound of the two notes is similar but the second note is higher in pitch. The distance between any two notes is called an *interval*, and this particular interval is called an *octave*. Compare the notes of any string 12 frets apart, eg the 1st and 13th fret, the 2nd and 14th fret, and you'll hear that they are all an octave apart.

In Western music, we divide the octave into 12 *semitones* and on the guitar each semitone corresponds with one fret. A *tone* is two frets.

All these 12 notes have names. Seven of them are named after the first seven letters of the alphabet:

A B C D E F G

The other five notes are said to be *enharmonic*. They have two names, according to their relation to the nearest note with an alphabetical name.

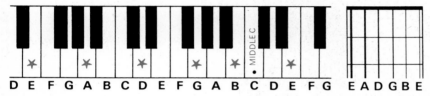

D E F G A B C D E F G A B C D E F G     E A D G B E

and compare sounds. If your guitar string sounds higher or lower in sound than the piano, adjust the tuning peg until the two sounds correspond exactly. Keep striking the piano key as the sound soon dies away. When the E string is in tune, repeat the process for B, G, D, A and E strings.

### Pitch-pipes

When blown, this instrument produces the notes E, A, D, G, B and E. You then use your ear to tune the guitar strings to the pitch of the notes.

### Electronic tuners

These are straight forward. You simply plug into the device and set the selector switch to the desired note. Then, pluck the string and turn the tuning peg until the needle is in the centre, or the correct frequency is reached, repeating this process for all the strings.

Don't worry if it takes you a long time to tune at first, you are having to compare the relative pitch of two notes so this is good ear training. It's also better to slacken the string so that its note is flatter or lower in pitch than the reference note and then bring the note *up* to the correct pitch using the machine heads.

Tuning the guitar to itself is called *relative tuning*. Make sure that at least one of the strings is tuned to a reference note or is roughly at the right pitch. The tuning process is called the '5th fret method' and is based on the fact that guitar strings have a certain relationship to each other as follows:

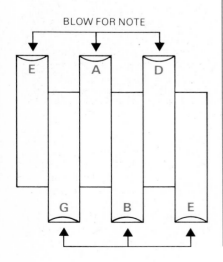

BLOW FOR NOTE

When in tune,
A on the 5th fret of the 6th string is the same as the open 5th string
D on the 5th fret of the 5th string is the same as the open 4th string
G on the 5th fret of the 4th string is the same as the open 3rd string
B on the 4th fret of the 3rd string is the same as the open 2nd string
E on the 5th fret of the 2nd string is the same as the open 1st string

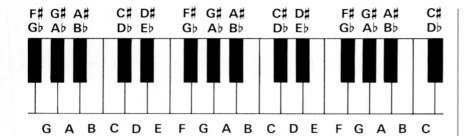

The keyboard gives a strong visual image of this system since the white notes are the alphabetical ones and the black notes are the enharmonic ones. You can see that the note between F and G can be called F sharp, which is written *F#* (usually called this if *ascending* to it) or G flat, written *Gb* (usually called this if *descending* to it).

> *'Being familiar with the keyboard helps a lot. Not that you have to be a piano player or anything, but knowing how to play a C-scale and a few basic major chords really helps to train your ear and helps you to start thinking in terms of tone as opposed to note.'*
>
> LARRY GRAHAM

Of course the guitar has no black and white notes so this is how it looks on the guitar.

As you can see from this diagram and from the section on relative tuning, many notes on the guitar can be played in two or three positions:

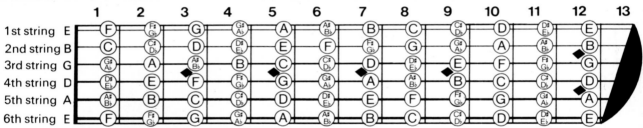

> *'As you get older and as you get more experienced, you can tell if a guitarist is on the 1st string or on the 2nd and 3rd, because each string has a voice of its own. And when you get to stealing licks and copying from people, you can begin to work out when they go from the 4th to the 2nd or whatever, because of the tonal quality of the note played.'*
>
> CHET ATKINS

## Scales

Most scales that we use are simply a way of dividing the octave into a series of steps (scale comes from the Latin 'scala' meaning ladder). The sound of the scale will depend on the *number* of steps you take and the distance or *interval* between each step. So each type of scale has its own particular step pattern.

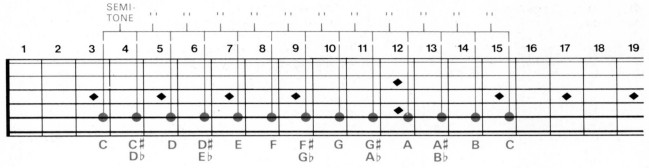

One octave chromatic scale starting on C

## Chromatic scale

If you take every possible step between a note and its octave, ie on the guitar you would play every fret along one string until you reached the octave, you are playing a *chromatic* scale. This scale has 12 steps, each one a semitone apart. Try this scale with the starting or *root* note on C (5th string, 3rd fret).

## Major scale

We're now going to play a different scale with a different step pattern. The *major* scale has seven steps in it but the intervals between the steps

aren't regular as in the chromatic scale. Again we'll make C the root note.

If you play the step pattern TONE (two frets), TONE (two frets), SEMITONE (one fret), TONE (two frets), TONE (two frets), TONE (two frets), SEMITONE (one fret) up one string you'll be playing a one octave major scale. This sounds like singing Do re mi . . . etc.

Notice that the scale of C major has no sharps or flats in it — it corresponds with all the white notes on a keyboard (see piano diagram on p. 52). If you need just these

notes to make up a tune then you'd be playing in the key of C major.

You can start a major scale from any note by keeping to this step pattern — try starting it on G (6th string, 3rd fret).

Notice that the scale of G major includes an F♯. Any sharps or flats in a scale are indicated by a *key signature*. Each major scale has its own particular key signature. If you make up a melody using notes from, for example, the C major scale, then you would be in the *key* of C major, and the 1st note of the scale is called the *key note*.

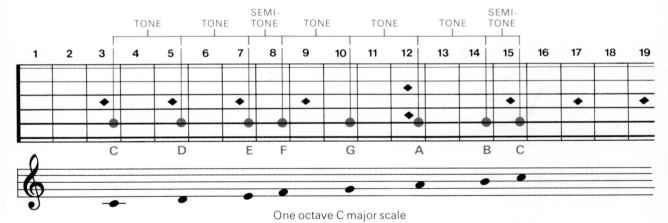

One octave C major scale

One octave G major scale

## Major scale fingerboard patterns

Of course, on the guitar you don't play along the length of one string, because there are easier ways of playing a major scale by moving across different strings. The patterns we have just given were to help you become familiar with the sound and step pattern of the major scale.

These next few major scale patterns are *movable*, ie if you started one on the note of C, that would be the scale of C major. If you moved the root note up one semitone (ie up one fret) to C♯, then, using the same pattern, you could play the scale of C♯ major, and so on.

Remember — it's still the same major scale step pattern even though it looks different

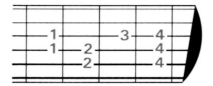

Fingering pattern for one-octave major scale, root note on the 5th string

Fingering pattern for one-octave major scale, root note on the 3rd string

You can join these two shapes together to make up a two-octave major scale. Make the last note of the first example the same as the first note of the second example.

Here's another fingering pattern for a two-octave major scale:

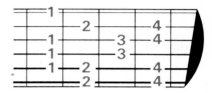

Two-octave major scale, root note on the 6th string

## Major intervals

We've already talked about one of the intervals in the major scale — the octave — but every note forms an interval with the key note or root note. Let's look at the intervals formed by the notes in the major scale, eg in C major:

C–D    Major second
C–E    Major third
C–F    Perfect fourth
C–G    Perfect fifth
C–A    Major sixth
C–B    Major seventh
C–C    Octave

If most of this theory is new to you,

don't worry if you don't take it all in at once. Come back to it and break it down into smaller sections to look at. Remember, these last few pages on scales and intervals hold the key to all chord formation and chord sequences, so it's worth spending some time trying to understand it.

## Minor intervals

Some of you will have heard of *minor* intervals and *minor* scales. If you flatten a major interval by a semitone, ie move down one fret, you will form a minor interval. So, in the key of C these are the minor intervals:

## Minor scale

There are several different minor scales, but one of the most useful is called the *natural* minor. This con-

tains a minor third, minor sixth and minor seventh interval. So, making C the root note, play this pattern:

We'll be talking more about the natural minor scale at the end of this chapter.

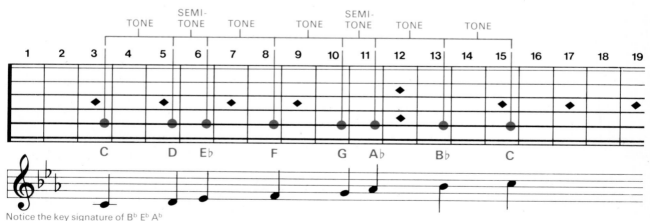

Notice the key signature of B♭ E♭ A♭

One octave C natural minor scale

## How to practise scales

1 Play all scales ascending (up) and descending (down) smoothly and evenly. Start by playing them really slowly so that you don't make any mistakes and then gradually build up your speed.

## Chord construction

A chord consists of a minimum of three different notes played together, although on the guitar you can play *part chords* using only two notes, or *extended chords* with up to six different notes in them.

We're going to look at three different types of chords — major chords, minor chords and seventh chords. The name of the chord is determined by the root note, that is, the one on which it is built, eg whether the chord is C, D, or E etc.

The sound of the chord is deter-

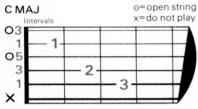

C MAJ
Intervals
o=open string
x=do not play

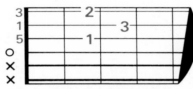

D MAJ

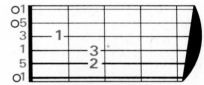

E MAJ

When we form a major triad (the interval between the first and third notes is a *major* third) this is the equivalent of four semitones or four frets apart on the guitar. This interval gives the chord its distinctive major sound.

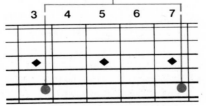

TWO TONES=MAJOR THIRD

SAME INTERVAL USING TWO STRINGS

If we flatten a major interval by a semitone, ie move down one fret, we get a *minor* interval. By flattening the major third one semitone we get a minor third — this is the equivalent of three semitones or three frets apart on the guitar.

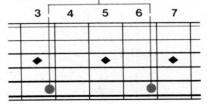

THREE SEMITONES=MINOR THIRD

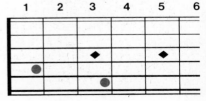

SAME INTERVAL USING TWO STRINGS

2 From the beginning develop your sense of timing and rhythm. Count a slow regular 1–2–3–4 and/or tap your foot. Now play a note to each count or beat, using plectrum down-strokes. When you feel familiar with the notes on the fingerboard, play the scale using alternate up and down plectrum strokes. A good speed and timing exercise is to start by playing one note to each beat, then double up the speed and play two notes to every beat and finally double the speed again and play four notes to every beat. If you were playing in C major, the three versions would look like this (left) in music notation form.

3 Remember the one fret per finger rule. All the patterns illustrated only cover four frets so make sure that this applies to your execution of them.

4 Practising scales will help you become familiar with the notes on the fingerboard, and help build up your technique and coordination. However, don't neglect to build up your melodic sense, your 'ear tech-nique'. Listen to, and sing the scales. Pick out all the intervals I mentioned earlier and gradually learn to recog-nise each of their sounds. Try making up musical phrases by changing around the note order of the scale.

5 How long should you practise? Well, practising regularly for short periods is better than a long session every now and again. It's also not only a case of how *long* you practise but *how* you practise. You'll improve much faster if you observe the previous points and practise things that you know you have difficulty with.

mined by the intervals between the root note and the other notes. This produces a particular harmony, eg whether the chord is major, minor, or seventh etc.

### Open chords
With these chord shapes remember to press the fretted note down firmly so that it 'rings' properly and make sure that your fingers do not inad-

vertently dampen an open string.
### Major chord shapes
Major triads consist of the first, third and fifth note of the major scale (though not necessarily in that order)

#### F MAJ
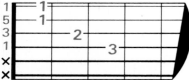
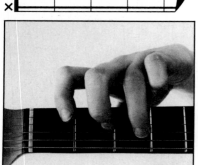

#### G MAJ
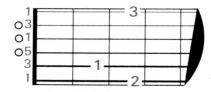
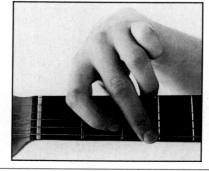

#### A MAJ
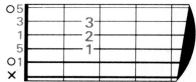

### Minor chord shapes
Minor triads consists of the first, flattened third and fifth notes.

#### E MINOR
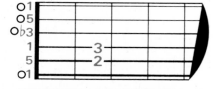

#### D MINOR
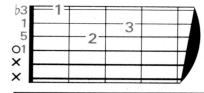
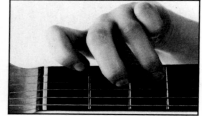

#### A MINOR
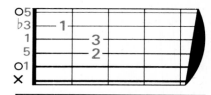
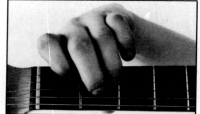

Compare the sound of the major chords to the minor chords — you'll hear that the minor chords sound more 'sad or 'melancholy'. They differ from the major by that one note, the flattened third. You can see this by comparing, for example, the chords of E major and E minor, A major and A minor etc. The one note that changes in these chords is the third.

## Seventh chords

These chords consist of four notes, the first, third and fifth (this is a major triad again) *plus* a minor seventh interval. This interval is a major seventh interval lowered by one semitone, ie by one fret.

This chord, then, has a major third and a minor seventh in it but its name is usually shortened to seventh. It is not to be confused with the major seventh and minor seventh chords which we'll look at in the funk chapters.

This now gives you a chord vocabulary of 15 different chords; memorise their shapes and practise playing different combinations of them. You should be able to play lots of well known songs using them and there are many song books available.

You could also try picking out the notes of the chord from the relevant major scale, eg play the chord of G, then play the scale of G major starting on the 3rd fret, 6th string, now pick out the first, third and fifth notes of the scale (this is called an *arpeggio*). Now play the chord again and compare the sound. *Arpeggio* figures are useful for filling out the sound.

**C SEVENTH**
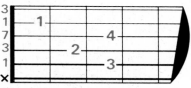

**G SEVENTH**

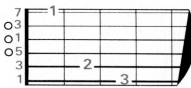

**E SEVENTH**
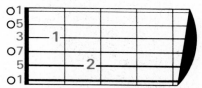

**A SEVENTH**

**D SEVENTH**

**B SEVENTH**

*Brian Setzer of The Stray Cats holding down an F♯ barre. Note the way he digs his elbow into his side*

**Barre chords**

*Barre chords* are essentially moveable chord shapes (like the major scale patterns I've already shown you) and they take their name from the fact that you use your 1st finger as a bar across the strings, taking the place of the nut, which allows you to move the open chord shapes right up the fingerboard.

Hints on playing barre chords

1  Don't worry if you can't make all six notes sound clearly at first; it takes a bit of practice. Also you'll find it's slightly easier to barre chords a little higher up the fingerboard, eg A major, A♯/B♭ major, than the lower chords of F major or F♯ major as you don't need so much pressure on the barre.

2  Remember the section on left or neck-hand positioning? Well, now make sure that your thumb is level with the first finger barre as this will help you get the required pressure on the strings.

3  Use the side of your 1st finger and bring your elbow more into your side.

**E MAJ Revised fingering**

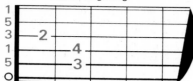

Working your way up the fingerboard you will find that you can

**F MAJ barre**

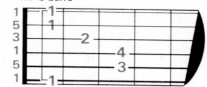

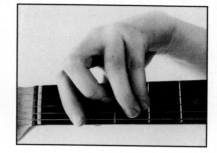

now play all 12 different major
chords. It is now definitely worth

## Major barre shapes — E shape

The first shape we're going to look
at is based on the open string chord
of E major with its root on the
6th string.

Play the chord of E major (note
the revised fingering so that your
1st finger is now free to barre).

Move the whole shape up one fret
and now bring your 1st finger down
to barre across the strings on the
1st fret. The root note of this chord
is now on the 1st fret 6th string,
which is the note of F — so this
chord is F major. If you raise the
whole barre shape one fret you
would play F# major etc.

spending some time learning the
notes on the 6th string.

Notes on the low E (6th) string

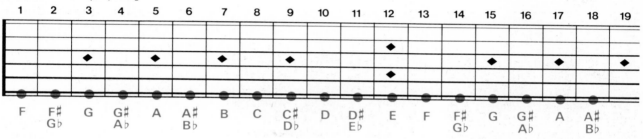

## A shape

This barre chord shape is based on
the open chord shape of A major
and we follow exactly the same
steps as for the E shape. However,
there is one important difference:
the root note is on the 5th string.

Play the chord of A major (note the
revised fingering)

Move the whole shape up one fret
and bring your 1st finger down to
barre across the strings on the
1st fret. The root note of this chord

is now on the 1st fret, 5th string —
which is the note of B♭ — so this
chord is B♭ major.

This chord is also often played by
barring the notes on the 2nd, 3rd
and 4th string with the 3rd finger.

**MAJ Revised fingering**

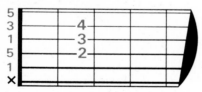

**B♭ MAJ barre**

**B♭ MAJ barre – alternative fingering**

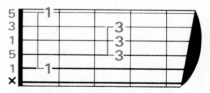

Notes on the A (5th) string

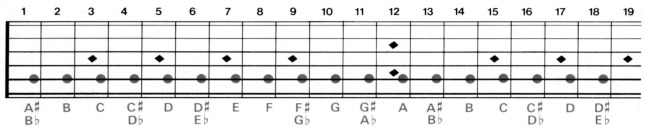

| 1 | 2 | 3 | 4 | 5 | 6 | 7 | 8 | 9 | 10 | 11 | 12 | 13 | 14 | 15 | 16 | 17 | 18 | 19 |
|---|---|---|---|---|---|---|---|---|---|---|---|---|---|---|---|---|---|---|

| A♯ B♭ | B | C | C♯ D♭ | D | D♯ E♭ | E | F | F♯ G♭ | G | G♯ A♭ | A | A♯ B♭ | B | C | C♯ D♭ | D | D♯ E♭ |

You will now be able to play 12 major chords with their root note on the 5th string, so, again, you should try to learn the notes on the 5th string. Remember, you don't have to stop at the 12th fret, the pattern of chords and notes just repeats itself from then on.

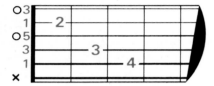

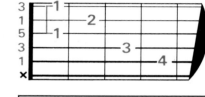

These next two major barre shapes are not so commonly used as the first two shapes we've looked at. If you're learning barre chords for the first time or you're not very familiar with them, then concentrate on the first two major shapes and the two minor and seventh shapes and come back to this section later on.

### C shape

This is based on the open chord of C major with the root note on the 5th string.

Open chord of C major with revised fingering

Moved up one fret, and with the 1st finger barring, makes the chord of G♯ major

### G shape

This is based on the open chord of G major with the root note on the 6th string but the 1st string is not used for the barre shape.

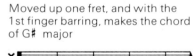

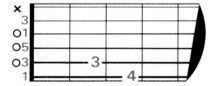

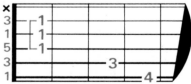

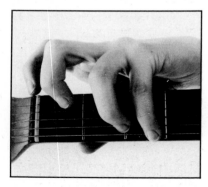

Open chord of G major with revised fingering

Moved up one fret, and with the 1st finger barring, makes the chord of G♯ major

## Minor barre shapes

The same principles apply to all

barre shapes and the two shapes we'll look at here are based on the

open E minor and open A minor chords respectively.

Minor barre shape root note on the 6th string

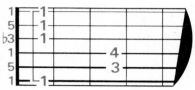

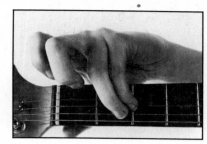

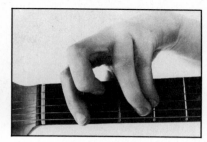

Minor barre shape root note on the 5th string

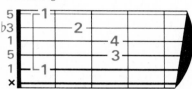

## Seventh barre shapes

These two shapes are based on the open E7 and open A7 chords.

Seventh barre shape root note on the 6th string

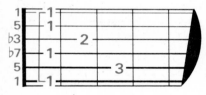

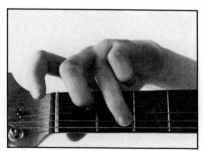

Seventh barre shape root note on the 5th string

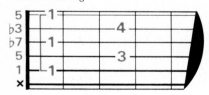

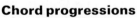

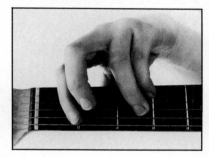

By learning the notes on the 5th and 6th string you will be able to use the 12 major chords, 12 minor chords and 12 seventh chords in two positions (root on either 5th or 6th string) making up 72 chords.

You should introduce barre chords into your playing by substituting them for open chord shapes in songs which you already know.

Remember the chord formation principles we discussed in the section on open chords:
a major chord consists of
1–3–5 notes

a minor chord consists of
1–b3–5 notes
a seventh chord consists of
1–3–5–b7 notes.

## Chord progressions

If you've been experimenting with the chord shapes I've already shown you and/or you've learnt songs from listening to records and song books, you should have noticed how some chords fit very well together and how some chord sequences are used over and over again in different songs.

Many of these chord sequences can be related back to chords you can form using just the notes from a major scale. We've already seen how you can form a major chord by building a chord on the first note of the scale and using the first, third and fifth notes. Well, you can build a chord in a similar way by using each note of the major scale as a root note so you have seven *scale chords* altogether. Three of these are called *primary* chords, three *secondary* chords and the last one is the *relative minor*.

## Primary chords

Taking the scale of C major as an example, let's identify each chord in the key by a Roman numeral:

C D E F G A B C
I II III IV V VI VII I

The three *primary* chords are built on the first, fourth and fifth notes of the scale. So in C major, you get the three primary chords of:

I  C major        IV  F major
V  G7

These chords are the basis for sequences known as the I–IV–V. In the I–IV–V sequence the V chord is always a seventh chord but you do get variations in the I and IV which can be major, minor or seventh.

We'll be looking at this chord sequence extensively in the section on the blues (p. 85), a music form which is based almost entirely on the I–IV–V sequence, but let's continue looking for the moment at the other scale chords.

## Secondary chords

The three *secondary* chords are built on the second, third and sixth notes of a major scale.

C D E F G A B C
I II III IV V VI VII I

These chords are all minor, so in C major you get the three secondary chords of:

II  D minor        III  E minor
VI  A minor

## Relative minor

The last chord, built on the sixth note of the scale, has a particular significance. It's called the *relative minor* and you can find the relative minor chord of any major chord by going down three semitones, eg C major — A minor, G major — E minor, or the related major chord of any minor chord by going up three semitones, eg D minor — F major, C♯ minor — E major etc.

## Related minor scale

The natural minor scale we mentioned earlier is sometimes called the related minor scale because it contains exactly the same notes as its related major scale.

Compare the scales of

So the natural minor scale starts on the sixth note of the major scale and uses exactly the same notes, but because its first note is different, it has a different step pattern and its own distinctive sound. This can be very useful in improvisation and we'll be mentioning this idea in the blues and funk sections.

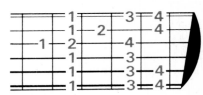

Movable shape for natural minor scale root on 6th string

## Scale chords in different major keys

|         | I | II | III | IV | V | VI | VII | I |
|---------|---|----|-----|----|---|----|-----|---|
| C major | C | D | E | F | G | A | B | C |
| G major | G | A | B | C | D | E | F♯ | G |
| D major | D | E | F♯ | G | A | B | C♯ | D |
| A major | A | B | C♯ | D | E | F♯ | G♯ | A |
| E major | E | F♯ | G♯ | A | B | C♯ | D♯ | E |
| B major | B | C♯ | D♯ | E | F♯ | G♯ | A♯ | B |
| F Major | F MAJOR | G MINOR | A MINOR | B♭ MAJOR | C SEVENTH | D MINOR | E Ø | F MAJOR |

Knowing the way chords can fit together is really helpful whether you're trying to work out a chord sequence to play or improvise over, or if you're interested in writing your own songs. The above diagram shows you what chords can be formed using only the notes in a major scale. However, as I mentioned in the section on I–IV–V sequences, you do get variations. The II, III and VI chords are played sometimes as major or seventh chords.

The best way of familiarising yourself with chord progressions is to learn and work out lots of different songs. Listen to the sound of the chords in relation to each other and also try putting the chord sequence into a different key, ie *transposing* the key of the song.

## CHAPTER 4

# Basic Bass Technique

### Playing positions

For bass, as for guitar, there is a distinct difference between *practising* and *playing*, and as Deirdre described earlier, you should find the position for each which is most comfortable for you. For practising, it's probably best to sit down because the idea is to concentrate solely on one particular aspect of your playing technique — whether it be in the left hand or the right hand — so you don't need to tire your back and legs.

In fact, you should plan your practice sessions. Make a list of what you want to work on, and then go through it methodically. But bear in mind that your brain probably can't stand more than half an hour at a time of this concentrated effort and you will need to take regular breaks. In any case, don't spend more than a couple of hours a day working in this way, although you can spend much longer on the musical aspects of your playing — working out a particular part, copying a riff off a record and so on.

# Henry Thomas

Sit on a stool or a chair without arms. Rest the body of the bass on your right thigh (or left thigh if you're left-handed), and let it lean against you. The neck should be slanted upwards and be tilted slightly back, making the fingerboard easy to cover and to see. Rest the forearm of your plucking hand on the body of the bass, so that the wrist is relaxed and flexible. With your other hand you can finger the notes in two basic ways. We'll look at both left- and right-hand positioning shortly.

For playing (and by this I mean in a band context), you'll almost certainly want to stand up and, indeed, as with the guitar, most basses are designed for this purpose.

A wide strap is essential in order to distribute the often considerable weight of the instrument more evenly. It can also help with its balance too. Usually, the neck of the bass is much longer than that of the guitar. Unless the instrument is balanced properly, you may find that your left (neck) hand has to support the neck while you're playing. Avoid this!

The height at which you sling the bass is entirely up to you. If you want to develop a slapping style, you'll have to keep it fairly high (see my chapter on funk, p.157), whereas most finger or plectrum styles can be played with the bass much lower. Just compare the likes of Mark King or Nick Beggs with Dee Dee Ramone!

*Kajagoogoo's Nick Beggs uses a Music Man bass strapped high for slapping. Dee Dee Ramone plays a Precision and isn't so fussy!*

## Tuning

Having got yourself comfortable, you need to check that you are in tune. As explained in the section on basic guitar technique, you can tune to a separate reference note provided by a keyboard, another guitar, a pitch pipe, a tuning fork, or an electronic tuner. Alternatively you can tune the instrument relatively to itself, using the '5th fret method'. If you haven't read the section on tuning (pp. 51–52), you'd better do so now.

Welcome back! When tuning to a guitar the notes of the lowest strings correspond to the four strings of the bass. The guitar sound is an octave higher but it should be easy for your ears to make the adjustment.

G string of bass = 3rd string of guitar
D string of bass = 4th string of guitar
A string of bass = 5th string of guitar
E string of bass = 6th string of guitar

### Relative tuning

As far as relative tuning is concerned, the '5th fret method' is slightly easier for bass than for guitar because the interval between the strings is the same in each case, that is a fourth.

Another form of relative tuning is the 'harmonic method'. Every note you pluck actually consists of the main note, or fundamental, plus a number of overtones which you don't normally hear. These are called harmonics. (Gary Cooper describes how you get harmonics on p. 36.) You can produce these anywhere along the length of the string. But they are strongest at the 5th, 7th and especially the 12th fret. Harmonics are particularly noticeable on the bass because of the thickness of the strings. This is how you can use them to tune the instrument.

string with your other hand and at the same time lift away your index finger. You should hear a high-pitched ring which is actually an A note. While this is still ringing, repeat the process on the 7th fret of the A string. This should produce an identical A note. Compare the two sounds. If you hear any oscillation between them, the two strings are not in tune. Adjust the A string until the oscillation disappears.

Now repeat the process, plucking the harmonics on the 5th fret of the A string and the 7th fret of the D string. Adjust the D string if there is any oscillation. Finally, pluck the

*Bruce Foxton's inventive bass lines helped make The Jam sound so powerful*

Rest the index finger of your left (neck) hand lightly on the low E string over the 5th fret. Pluck the

harmonics on the 5th fret of the D string and the 7th fret of the G string, adjusting the latter if any oscillation is detectable.

The bass should now be in tune. If it isn't, try again. If you're still not having much luck, do as Gary suggests. Compare the sound of the 12th fret harmonic with the sound of the fretted note. If they're out, you've either got a warped neck, or the bridge needs adjusting, and you may need to go to a repair shop.

It's worth remembering harmonics. You can use them in your playing, either for solos, or for brightening up a riff. Just listen to 'The Fish' by Chris Squire on the Yes LP *Fragile*, or Bruce Foxton's playing on 'Down in the Tube Station at Midnight' by The Jam.

## Left-hand technique

The function of the left (or neck) hand is to finger the notes you want to play and to deaden or dampen the ones you don't. Unwanted noises such as finger-squeak or open strings ringing, can be a problem — especially at high volume. Damping with both the left and right hands is

★ Pluck the open low E string a few times. While doing this, rest the index finger of your neck hand *lightly* on the other three strings, being careful not to press them onto the fretboard.

★ Now pluck the open A string. Using your index finger to cover the D and G strings, bring your thumb over the top of the neck to cover the low E string.

★ Now pluck the open D string, using your thumb to cover both the low E and A strings and your index finger to cover the G string.

When played continuously, the above exercise produces a circular motion in the hand. Try it slowly first, then build it up into a continuous motion, playing up and then down. You can now dampen open strings with the left hand. Keep practising this until it becomes automatic and you don't have to think about it. It'll add a lot of punch to your sound.

As for positioning your left (neck) hand, there are two main ways of doing this: the classical position and the rock position. (These have been described in Deirdre's section on basic guitar technique, pp. 48–51.) Personally, I find that I use both positions, depending on the part I'm playing and on how much damping I want to do with my left hand, but generally I prefer a kind of classical position. I rest the ball of the thumb behind the centre of the neck, using it as a pivot for the rest of the hand. Keeping the fingers straight and at 90° to the fretboard, I hold the strings down with the flat tip of each finger, well behind the fret.

I often find that in this position, the index finger acts as a barre — especially on riff-based numbers where I repeat the same finger pat-

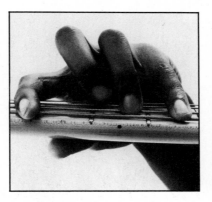

tern — and this style makes the most economical use of my left hand.

As Deirdre says, you must use one finger for each fret. On the bass, with its longer neck, wider frets, and heavier strings, this can be difficult to do at first, especially when it comes to the little pinkie!

Try this exercise to strengthen your fingers and improve your neck hand co-ordination. Place the fourth finger on the octave G of the G string, that is, just behind the 12th fret, and keep it there. Now fret the previous three notes with your other three fingers: the E, F, and f♯. Try playing this pattern:

You might find it difficult at first, but keep working at it! It might be easier to think of the pattern of movement rather than the notes you're playing. So if your fingers are numbered from 1 to 4, the pattern would be: 3–4, 2–4, 1–4, and you make each movement eight times.

Having worked out this pattern, move onto the D string and, starting again at the 12th fret, do the same thing; now move onto the A string and, finally, the low E string. Go back to the G string, but move your hand back one fret, that is, down one semitone, and repeat the same exercise over all four strings. Keep doing this, moving one fret (or one semitone) back each time, until you reach the bottom of the neck. Don't be surprised if you get pains across your knuckles and soreness at the tips of the fingers. Your hand will get used to it with practice.

When you can do this exercise fairly easily, try writing out on the stave all the notes you are playing. Use the line of music I've written out below as your starting point. This may seem boring, but it will help you to recognise where notes come on both fretboard and stave.

Once marked, a note stays sharpened or flattened until changed by a 'natural' sign.

one of the most important techniques you'll need to learn, so it's good to get it right from the start.

★ Lastly, pluck the open G string. Your thumb should be covering the low E and A strings, while your index finger covers the D string.

## Right-hand technique

Whereas with the guitar it is the left (or neck) hand that does most to bring expressiveness to your playing — through vibrato, string-bending etc — with the bass, it's probably the right (or plucking) hand that will shape your sound the most. Bass strings can be plucked, picked, slapped or pulled. *How* you do it and *where* you do it along the length of the string will make an enormous difference to the quality and attack of the note produced, as we'll see throughout this book.

Let's start by looking at the basic two-finger pluck. This is the standard technique used by rock bass players since the mid-1960s and is still widely favoured today (check out John Taylor or Mikey Craig).

Resting the thumb on the top of the pickup, pluck the low E string eight times, using the first two fingers alternately.

Now play the A string in the same way, but move the thumb down so that it's resting on the low E string.

Now play the D string and rest the thumb on the A string.

Lastly, play the G string, resting the thumb on the D string.

Remember to use alternate plucking with the 1st and 2nd finger, eight notes for each string. Try to play evenly. Start slowly and speed up as you get better.

Next, still using the 1st and 2nd fingers for the 1st and 2nd notes you play, try alternating between the strings in this order:

If you number the strings like this: G=1st, D=2nd, A=3rd, E=4th, the sequence order would be:

4–1, 3–1, 2–1
2–4, 2–3, 2–1
3–4, 3–2, 3–1
1–4, 1–2, 1–3

Watch the thumb! Make sure it moves in the right place. Listen to the sound; it should be even and smooth.

You'll find that this is not only the most economical way of using your plucking hand (it saves having to stretch the fingers too far), but it also enables you to damp the strings you are not playing with your thumb.

Try the above exercise again, but this time bring up your left (neck) hand to damp the strings in the manner described earlier. By combining these left- and right-hand damping techniques, you will produce short staccato notes even though you are plucking open strings.

Not every bass player uses this technique and you needn't either. It really depends on the style of music you're most interested in playing. But I still feel it's a good *general* technique and it's worth learning it before you develop too many bad habits!

*Geddy Lee of Rush. Note the right-hand style with the thumb resting on the E string*

The next thing to do is to try moving your hand to the bridge end of the strings and plucking the notes from there. You should get a sharp trebly tone. Compare this with the sound you get when you pluck over the pickup. This should be more rounded and middly. Now move your right (plucking) hand over to where the neck joins the body. The sound you get by playing here should be bassy and boomy. Many bassists (for example, Robbie Shakespeare), will move their plucking hands to these different positions according to the sound they want to create for a particular song.

If you want to use a plectrum, which will give your sound a cutting, twangy edge, look at the plectrum exercises discussed in Deirdre's section on guitar technique (pp. 48–51). Plectrum style can be very useful in getting certain rhythms in boogie or disco playing. Use a heavy gauge plectrum and remember that your wrist will have to move much further than if you were playing guitar.

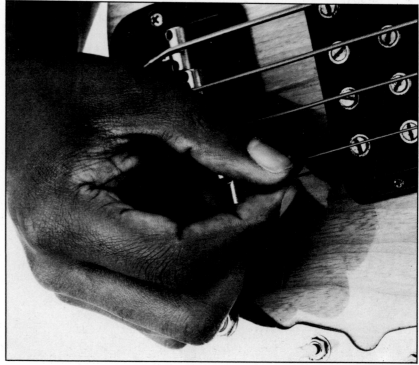

## Simple bass parts

Playing the bass in a band is extremely challenging. Your job is to
fit in with the other instruments,
enhancing both the chord work and
lead breaks of the guitar, and
the rhythm and fills coming from the
drums. What you do underpins the
rest of the band and gives the music
its drive and depth. Consequently,
you need to *listen* to the other

instruments and understand what it
is they're doing. At this basic level,
the guitar part will give you ideas for
the notes you can play, and the drum
pattern will indicate the rhythmic
emphasis. It is therefore vital that
you read Deirdre's section on scales
and chords before you go any further
(pp. 52–63). And remember to look
at Geoff's drum sections in the style
chapters when you get onto them. If

you're not sure how to read music
or tablature or standard drum notation, use the information at the
beginning of the book to help you.
The simplest kind of bass line
uses just the root notes of the
chords which are being played on
the guitar. Say you're playing a fast
r'n'b or punk-type number made up
of the chords of C, F and G7 played
in the following rhythm:

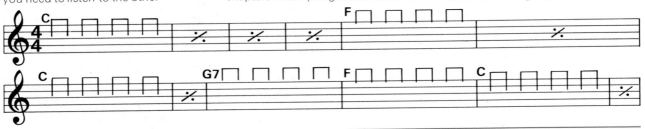

You would only need to play a C
while the guitar was playing a
C chord, F for the F chord and G

for the G7 chord.
But that becomes pretty boring
after a while. So your next move is

to find the octave of C, F and G. You
can now add some dynamics to your
bass part, like this:

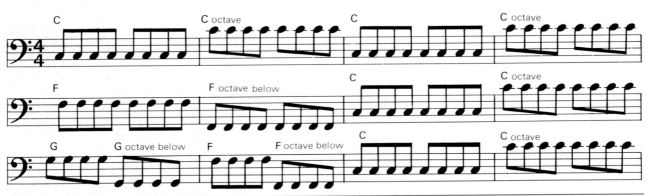

Listen to the drums. You could use
the octave notes to follow the bass
drum and snare drum pattern. This
would have the effect of breaking
up the bass line. If the drummer
does a fill, you could slide up to or
down from the octave along the
length of one string in time with it.

The next stage is to look at the notes
of the chords being played on the
guitar. As Deirdre shows, basic triad
chords are made up of the first, third
and fifth notes of the scale, whether
major or minor. In the case of a
C major chord, these are C–E–G
from the C major scale. You could

play these notes one after the other
under a C chord, moving up to the F
(and playing F–A–C) and G7 (playing G–B–D–F), as the guitarist
changes. You can choose either to
ignore the seventh in G7 or to emphasise it according to what you
think sounds best.

(This pattern does not emphasise the seventh note.)

A variation in this pattern would be
to go back to the octave idea, but fill

in the gap between the two notes
by playing the fifth. So you would

play C, G, C, F, C, F, G, D, G, in
this pattern:

etc …

Sex Pistols fans may recognise this as being similar to the beginning of 'Pretty Vacant'. But bass lines using the root, fifth and octave crop up throughout rock. Just listen to John Entwistle's playing on tracks such as 'The Real Me' and 'The Punk and the Godfather' from The Who's 1973 LP *Quadrophenia*. Of course you can also use the root and the fifth note below it to produce this simple, but widely used baseline.

## Chords and keys

The chord structure we've been using is based on three primary scale chords from the scale of C major. Because they are derived from the first, fourth and fifth notes of the scale (C, F, G) they are called I, IV, V chords. (Roman numerals are used to avoid confusion with the numbering of intervals.) Most of blues, rock'n'roll, rockabilly, r'n'b,

and indeed a lot of mainstream rock is based on the I–IV–V chord structure, or variations of it (see Deirdre's section on blues guitar, p. 85).

Because C, F and G are related in this way, the key signature is easily identifiable as being C major. So in this case you would draw your main inspiration for bass lines from the scale of C major.

## Passing notes

Let's go back to the triad of C; C–E–G, the first, third and fifth notes in the scale of C major. Now you can fit in other notes between these that lead you to or from them, the octave, or the next root note you will have to play as the chord changes.

These extra notes are called *passing notes*, and they are described as being either diatonic or chromatic. The *diatonic* passing notes in this case are the notes from the C major scale: the second (D), fourth (F), sixth (A) and natural or major seventh (B). The *chromatic* passing notes are the semitones that fall between the notes of the C major scale: C#, Eb, F#, G# and Bb.

Here are a couple of examples using passing notes. Play the triad notes of C major one after the other. Now add the sixth note (A), followed by the dominant seventh (Bb). When you play this pattern up and down, you get the so-called 'walking bass line' on which most of rock'n'roll depends:

You can use chromatic passing notes to produce quite flash bass

lines. Try this example. It's still over the same three chords of C, F and

G7, but now it's getting quite interesting!

You will have noticed that with several of the above examples, the movements your fingers make on the fretboard are similar — it's just a question of starting off from a different root note. Try building up a mental catalogue of these movable patterns, so that you can apply them to different chord progressions, or use them for improvisation.

As a general rule, try to bear in mind that with simple bass lines, you are trying to lead the ear from one chord to the next, smoothing over the chord changes and giving the music a feeling of continuity.

So construct your bass lines so they lead up or down to the root note of the next chord and time them to reach it as the guitarist changes to that chord.

| 1 | 2 | 3 | 4 | 5 | 6 | 7 | 8 | 9 | 10 | 11 | 12 |
|---|---|---|---|---|---|---|---|---|----|----|----|

Here is the finger pattern for the classic walking bass line in C major,

with the root note on the 3rd string and on the 4th string:

The electric bass has three main sections: head, neck and body. It is straddled by roundwound metal strings (see p. 26) which run through the tail-piece onto the bridge across the pickups and on to the neck. Strings are held in position by grooves cut into the nut (top of the neck) which channel them to their respective tuning pegs. This allows great adjustment of each string.

The fingerboard is divided up by frets, metal bars sunken into the neck which protrude an $\frac{1}{8}$''. This enables you to alter the pitch of a string by pressing the string on to the fingerboard just behind a fret. Dots on the fingerboard are always placed at frets 3, 5, 7, 9, 12, 15, 17 and 19 as a quick visual reference for notes and hand position.

The pickup's design and function is described on p. 24.

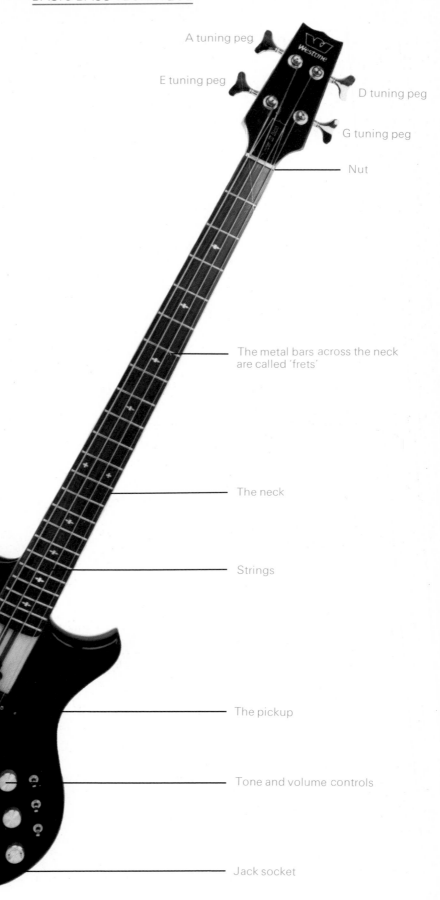

A tuning peg

E tuning peg

D tuning peg

G tuning peg

Nut

The metal bars across the neck are called 'frets'

The neck

Strings

The pickup

Tone and volume controls

Tailpiece

Jack socket

*Sometime Crusaders drummer Stix Hooper seen here at London's Capital Jazz Festival in 1982*

# CHAPTER 5

# Basic Drum Technique

## Geoff Nicholls

### The evolution and components of the drum kit

★ The drum kit, like jazz, is an American invention. Indeed, it owes its start and its evolution primarily to jazz, which itself derived from the marching bands of New Orleans around the turn of this century. In these bands the bass drums, military (snare) drums and cymbals were played by separate individuals (as they still are today). The drum kit began when these instruments were set down and played by a single, seated, individual. This was accomplished by adding a foot-pedal to the bass drum, which left both hands free to play on the stand-mounted snare drums. Additional effects were obtained from wood-blocks mounted on top of the bass drum and from a small cymbal mounted on its own stand.

A dramatic improvement in this set-up came with the invention of the hi-hat pedal, which enabled two horizontally mounted cymbals to be clashed together by depressing the left foot. More tonal colour was provided by the addition of tom-toms, one mounted on the bass drum, one standing on the floor. The small cymbal became larger and larger, and by the 1930s and 1940s (the 'swing' era) the main rhythm had largely transferred from the snare drum to the cymbal, which became known as the 'ride' cymbal.

Up until this period much jazz music — particularly the big swing bands with their vocalists — was synonymous with popular music. But in the 1940s and 1950s, with the development of small-group jazz (the 'be-bop' era), the left hand on the snare drum and the right foot on the bass drum became increasingly syncopated and 'independent', with the result that the music became rhythmically more sophisticated and less easy to dance to — and hence less 'popular'. The rhythmic gap was soon filled in the early 1950s by the arrival of rock. Simpler than be-bop and more raw than swing, rock rhythms have formed the major foundation of popular music right up to the present day. ★

---

*'If you go back to square one, the time is what the drummer gives you. Everything is controlled by time, so if there's a leader for the piece of music you're playing, a conductor, then it has to be the drummer. He controls how fast you play, where the accents go, and the feel of the thing. So, okay, you might be at the back of the stage, but really, you're leading it. It's the only way it can work properly.'*

*IAN PAICE*

### Function

By the time of rock's emergence, logical and practical functions had evolved for the various components of the basic drum kit. The high and staccato tones of the hi-hat or ride cymbal can play the faster part of the rhythm, which implies the time of the tune, and holds the band together — a function derived from the use of gourds, maraccas, shakers, etc in African and Latin musics. The bass drum provides the foundation, stabilising the rhythm (often marking the beginning of each bar) and adding punch to the notes of the bass guitar. The crack of the snare drum meanwhile adds the punctuations and syncopations which enliven the beat (taking over from hand clapping in primitive or folk music). The tom-toms add different tones either in fills and solos, or as an integral part of the rhythm. Finally, cymbal crashes, particularly in unison with the bass drum or snare lend extra weight to accents, and mark out the starts and stops in the music.

### Tuning

Before you play a drum you must get a sound from it that pleases you, and the other musicians in the band. This is not as simple as you might think. First you must eliminate all rattles and buzzes: take the drum apart if necessary and reassemble it making sure that every nut and bolt is tight and squeak-free. Next put the heads back on the drum and tension them — this is the most crucial step. Finally, dampen the drum if necessary or preferred.

*'Nobody can tell you a drum is out of tune. If you've got a two-head drum with the skins actually mis-matching so that the drum is fighting with itself, then you can say it's out of tune. But whether you tune it high or slack, is up to you. If it sounds good to your ear, don't ask for anything more.*

*'My preference is to tune my snare drum very high. I like it to be sharp and positive and I don't like a lot of duration on the note. For the toms, I like exactly the reverse. I like them deep and I like an after-note. So when you hit the drum, you get an initial tension of the impact, and then you get the roll-off as the skin relaxes and comes back to its normal tension.*

*'So that way you've got the difference between the snare drum which is really sharp and should cut through anything, and the mellower, longer notes of the toms to sweeten it all up.'*

*IAN PAICE*

There is some controversy over the term 'tuning' as most drummers do not tune a drum to a specific note, rather they *tension* it to a satisfying but indeterminate pitch. Obviously if you take the trouble to tune the heads to a particular key and the band then plays in a different key you could have an out-of-tune drum set! However some top drummers do tune their drums to particular notes. For example, in the studio, the drums might be tuned to the key of the song being recorded. Suffice it to say that it's a good idea to try specific tuning at some stage for the reason that tensioning drums is almost an art in itself and such an exercise will inevitably improve your ear and increase your awareness of the scope of your drums.

## Procedure

Place the new head on the rim after carefully cleaning around the drum edge (it's amazing how much dust collects there). Take up the slack on the tension rods all around until the wrinkles in the head have just disappeared, but it's still slack and is fairly even.

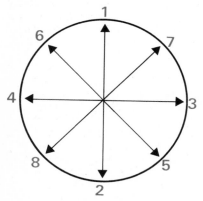

Now 'seat' the head by pressing down on the centre with the palm of the hand. Continue to tighten the head a half-turn at a time, criss-crossing the drum diagonally as in the diagram. The object is to take up the tension as evenly as possible.

When you get near to the sound you're looking for, try tapping round the head near the edge close to each tension rod. You may be surprised to hear the variations in pitch from one area to the next. Keep on tapping and criss-crossing, taking up a bit here and there until the whole head is vibrating at the same pitch. This can get frustrating as your ears give in and you hear countless overtones! However, a little time spent persevering will be greatly

*Reggae session superstar Sly Dunbar is an expert in damping techniques*

*Ringo Starr used extensive damping in the*

rewarded by the cleaner and fuller tones the drum will give you.

A variation on this procedure is to take up the tension around the drum in a clockwise direction going from one lug to the next. This is akin to the practice of tympanists.

## Single and double heads

In recent years single-headed drums have become very popular. Roto-toms and octo-bans for example, as well as single-headed tom-toms, can all be tuned to specific pitches. Indeed one manufacturer refers to its single-headed range as 'melodic' toms. With double-headed drums the vibrations go back and forth from one head to the other giving more resonance and tonal variation. When hitting single heads, the sound is emitted unimpeded with less vibration but tends to be louder.

Tuning double-headed drums obviously requires more care. The bottom head can be the same tension as the top head, or tighter or slacker. It is probably most common to tension the bottom more than the top. But one variation, for example, is to have the top head taut to make it easier to play on, and have the bottom head slacker to give depth and tone. There are no rules and you just have to experiment to find what sounds best for you. However, listen out for unpleasant overtones and

ringing or 'beats' (oscillations) when the two heads are just slightly out of tune with one another.

The snare drum presents a slightly different situation in that the bottom ('snare') head is usually a special, transparent, lightweight type which doesn't require so many turns on the rods to produce a high 'ping' when tapped. Generally the top ('batter') head should be fairly taut to give a sharp clean beat, while the snare head should be tight enough to give a good resonant snare response (too slack and the snares will 'choke' or buzz). The tension of the snare itself is also crucial to the clarity and 'attack' of the sound.

The bass drum can also be single or double headed. Because of its size and because it is struck with a beater rather than a stick, the bass drum has a greater tendency to boom than the other drums. This can be overcome by damping (see p. 77). A third common variation is to cut a hole in the front head, varying in size from a few inches in diameter to virtually the complete head.

Finally, I should mention that some drummers develop particular tuning idiosyncrasies to cope with certain situations. For example, turning the top two bass drum rods up and down to vary the sound on different numbers; or slackening the rods next to the snares to give a

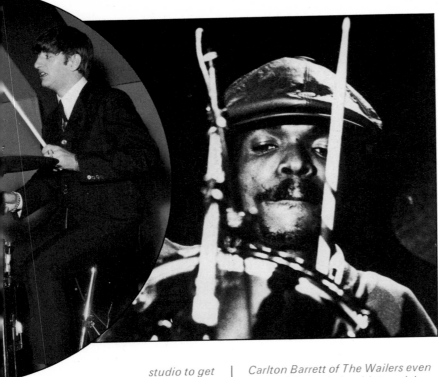

*studio to get his sound*

*Carlton Barrett of The Wailers even damps his cymbals with towels!*

particular snare response. Having taken the care to get your heads evenly tuned, you might try tightening or slackening a particular rod or two to see what special effect this gives you. Doing this can also sometimes lessen excessive ringing on an evenly tensioned head.

## Damping

Whatever heads you use and however you tension them, you are likely at some stage to need to effect some damping. Some drummers playing particular sorts of music (eg heavy rock) use little damping, preferring to allow the drums to speak out with maximum power and tone. Others (eg many reggae drummers) use a lot of damping on single-headed drums to get a very dry and flat sound.

*'I use a lot of damping on the kit. I like to go for a real dead sound. If you take the damping off, you get a pan sound. But you don't want that. A dead sound is better for recording.'*
SLY DUNBAR

Drums have traditionally been manufactured with internal 'tone controls', felt pads which can be adjusted to muffle the underside of the drum head. In rock these are virtually

useless as the power of the drum stroke soon loosens the pad from the head, and they often start to rattle or squeak. Many players take them off as soon as they acquire a new kit. Also, muffling from *beneath* the batter head impedes the natural movements of the head when it is struck. Nowadays manufacturers are producing external clip-on dampers which should prove much more successful.

However, by far the most common method of damping is the rather scruffy, though very adaptable method of putting sticky tape over

*'I used to use a wooden beater on the bass drum, but I found it gave too much of a disco "slap" effect, and I didn't actually get enough sound out of the drum. So for the last four or five years, I've been using a felt beater and very little padding inside the drum. I have one felt strip down the front head, with nothing on the batter head except a piece of moleskin where the felt beater actually hits. The felt beater seems generally to give a lower note, and I think on the bass drum that's really important, especially to get under the bass guitar.'*
CARL PALMER

the edges of the head. The amount used depends on the extent of the damping required. Pads of foam or tissue can be stuck down by tape too. The bass drum is often heavily damped by putting a blanket or pillow inside the drum, weighted against the bottom of the batter head. As the fashion for double-headed and livelier bass drums returns, felt damping strips on the inside of the heads are coming back into use. A piece of damping on the batter head at the place of contact with the beater is also common.

Another new development is the use of manufactured loops of foam which are either stuck to the underside of the batter head or held in this position by a circular plastic mould inserted beneath the batter and sitting on the rim. These have the distinct advantage of not covering any of the playing surface of the drum, but once inserted it is necessary to remove the head if you want to adjust the damping again.

Cymbals are also sometimes partially muffled, particularly ride cymbals where a clear 'sticky' tone is required with few overtones. I've seen Carlton Barrett of The Wailers (live) and Ringo Starr with The Beatles (in the studio) put a towel over the bottom hi-hat cymbal (in Ringo's case over the drums as well) to get a particular sound.

Damping and tuning are highly personal and can greatly affect your sound. There are many variables to consider. The way in which a drum is struck is crucial; drummers can sound quite different on the same kit. A drum tuned high can sound much lower when heard from a little way off or when struck hard. A large drum can be tuned quite high and still give a good deep tone.

Damping can make a high-tuned drum sound lower. You may often have to adjust your tuning and damping to different rooms and stages or to adjust to a different style of music. Studio engineers often prefer a certain tuning with a fair degree of damping to obtain a relatively clean signal to work with. Depending on the situation this is something you may or may not wish to go along with. If you're doing a commercial session it's best to go with the engineer and producer who have a picture of the overall sound; if you're recording with your own band you may well want to persevere to obtain a close rendition of your personal sound.

> *'When recording, I go for a live sound with very little damping. I find that miking the drums really close doesn't work all that well for me. The drum is an acoustic instrument, remember, and it's designed to make the sound travel. So, to get the overall spectrum of the drum kit, I like to use a combination of close and distant mikes.'*
>
> CARL PALMER

Finally, from a playing point of view, it is easier to get a bounce from a high-tuned drum, but then your sticking will have to be that much more controlled. Going from a highly tensioned snare drum to a low spongy floor tom requires an adjustment in stick control.

## Snare vibration

This is an irritating problem which occurs from time to time. Assuming the snare drum itself is properly tuned, the snares may vibrate in sympathy with another drum or instrument or as a result of vibration from an amplifier etc. A slight adjustment to the tension of the snares or to the offending tom-tom should minimise the buzzing. With loud bands and loud amps you have to go for a compromise. As a last resort in the studio you can try putting a little bit of tape over one end of the snare wires, but obviously this can severely choke the response.

## Cymbals

Cymbals in rock have two basic functions: to state the rhythm and to punctuate the rhythm. For the former you need a pair of hi-hats and a ride cymbal; for the latter you need a 'crash' cymbal. Your actual choice of these primary cymbals will depend on the sound you prefer and the style of music you play.

The ride cymbal (usually between 18'' and 24'' diameter) is the heaviest cymbal, the mass giving it little vibration, a high pitch and high volume. You can therefore play clean rhythmic figures on it without the vibrations building up and clouding the sound. The crash (usually between 16'' and 20'') has less mass and thus vibrates more, particularly when struck on the edge with the shoulder of the stick.

The ride cymbal should be played with the tip of the stick within the ride area, clarity of stroke increasing as you approach the bell. The bell area can be played with the tip or the shoulder of the stick. Because the bell is the thickest part of the cymbal the sound here is exceptionally clear and 'bell'-like.

### CRASH CYMBAL

CRASH AREA                RELATIVELY SMALL MASS

By striking the crash cymbal with the shoulder of the stick, increased vibration is set up in the relatively small mass of the cymbal with the result that there is a fast response and correspondingly fast decay for clear punctuation.

To get the best from the cymbals they should not be mounted too tight on the stands. And crash them with a glancing stroke, not flat or edge-on.

There is now a bewildering range of cymbals available. Don't be overwhelmed. They are all there to serve the basic function of rhythm and punctuation. But they enable you to colour your sound enormously.

> *'I use both an 18'' and a 22'' crash, along with 24'' China, and a 20'' ride. So I have two choices. I have the very tight 18'' sort of crash sound for very close work, perhaps accenting something with the bass player, but not in a big way; and then I have the bigger crash sound for the whole band, which I can use when everyone is playing fortissimo.'*
>
> CARL PALMER

## Sticks

Drumsticks are usually made of wood (mostly hickory or oak), but occasionally other materials such as graphite are used. In general, the more expensive the stick, the better the grain consistency and straightness. You should always check a stick for true by rolling it on a flat surface – it's amazing how many sticks are warped (particularly the cheaper ones). Most sticks are between 15'' and 17'' in length but their shape and weight varies considerably. Some models have nylon tips over the wood to give a sharper 'ping' sound on the ride cymbal.

> *'I found that the neck of the stick is one of the most important parts. I don't like to have any whip or movement here, and a lot of drumsticks you buy give a little at the neck when you use them. When they give, it makes them sound different.'*
>
> CARL PALMER

Choice of stick type is entirely personal, but individuals tend to stay with one type once they are used to it. The balance of the left and right stick can be crucial, although a lot of rock drummers use the left stick the 'wrong' way round to get a heavier snare drum sound. Indeed some drummers use both sticks the wrong way round for particularly heavy playing.

> *'I'm not very fussy about drum sticks, so long as they're the right length, and, generally, that's about 16'' for me, and the right diameter, which I think is about $\frac{9}{16}$ths'' or $\frac{5}{8}$ths'', and the weight is right, I don't actually care what shape they are. In rehearsal, I use the sticks as they should be used — bead end out. On stage, it's totally the reverse. All I really need on stage is absolute power, and using the sticks the wrong way round can give me another 20 Db!'*
>
> IAN PAICE

Using the left stick the wrong way round is also particularly effective for good rim clicks on the snare drum, and since this is a characteristic of much reggae music it has led Sly Dunbar to use a different type of stick in each hand.

### RIDE CYMBAL

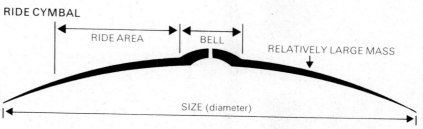

RIDE AREA        BELL

RELATIVELY LARGE MASS

SIZE (diameter)

> 'I use a heavy stick in my left hand, a lighter stick in my right — two different sticks, two different sizes.
> 'I wrap tape around the end of the lighter stick to balance them up. That helps cut out some of the notes on the hi-hat too — keeps you more in line with the music.'
>
> SLY DUNBAR

## Grip

There are two methods for holding and using the sticks: the 'matched' grip and the 'orthodox' or 'traditional' grip. The traditional grip has descended from that used by marching snare drummers who slung their drums to the left-hand side at an angle in order to make marching easier. This imbalance necessitated the development of an unnatural grip for the *left* hand (of right-handed players), whilst the right hand was free to hold the stick in basically the same way as the average non-drummer would instinctively. In the 'matched' grip, both right and left hands hold the sticks in the same manner — ie like the *right* hand in the traditional grip.

> '... the orthodox grip only came through the fact that it was a military style, for marching with a snare drum angled across the leg. On a modern drum kit you don't actually set the drum like that, so what's the point of using it? You can be just as fast, just as precise with a matched grip as you can with an orthodox grip. The orthodox grip just makes things harder, I feel.'
>
> IAN PAICE

Before we look more closely at the two methods I should say that there has been quite a controversy about the merits of each style, particularly over the last 20 years as the matched grip has gained popularity. This controversy seems to be dying down as drummers now feel free to use whichever method suits their purpose. An increasing number seem to me to use both, as the occasion demands, although I've no statistical evidence to back up this observation! The evidence *against* the traditional grip however seems very strong:

★ The two hands in the traditional grip can never be 'equal' since the method of holding each is different;

★ The traditional left-hand grip involves many fewer muscles of the arm and hand, and must therefore be weaker;

★ The traditional grip makes it more awkward to play around the drum kit — particulary today's extended layouts;

★ The tuned percussion instruments are invariably played using the matched grip.

The case *for* the traditional grip is simply this: some of the best and most *powerful* drummers alive today regularly use it — from jazz players like Buddy Rich, Louie Bellson and Elvin Jones, to rock players like Carl Palmer and Stewart Copeland. One further point: some drummers believe that sensitive finger control of the left hand is better served by the traditional grip.

> 'I personally think the matched grip is a better way to play, mainly because the whole of the percussion family uses this particular grip — timpani, vibraphone, glockenspiel, even tubular bells. I use the orthodox grip myself, because that was the happening grip when I was learning to play, and although I think there are drawbacks to it, I wouldn't change now. Not after 22 years!
> 'One thing you do have from the orthodox grip is a little bit of extra finger control, which can help you with intricate patterns played by the left hand. I can play a one-handed single-stroke roll on the snare that way!'
>
> CARL PALMER

## The matched grip

Before beginning to play it is essential to be comfortable. Pick up the sticks and sit behind the snare drum. Your body should be relaxed with the centre of balance going through the base of the spine straight down through the stool, leaving the arms and legs as free as possible to perform. Your arms should be hanging loosely at your sides, elbows neither sticking out nor digging into your middle. The sticks are like an extension of your forearms. Grasp the stick about one-third of the way from the butt end between the

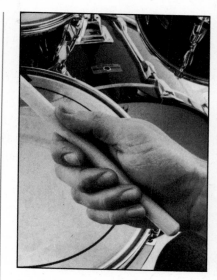

fleshy part of your thumb and the first joint of your forefinger. This is the fulcrum at which the stick turns. The other fingers wrap round the butt of the stick. The palm faces down and the tips of the two sticks

arm, depending on the amount of fine control or power that is required. Beats can be played using the snap of the fingers with no wrist movement at all. Normally beats are played using a combination of wrist and finger control. For loud playing, movement of the forearm will also be necessary. A variation on the matched grip is the 'timpani' grip which is essentially the same but with the hand turned over so that the thumb is upwards. You may find for example your right hand turns into this position as it moves across to the ride cymbal, and as you go around the drums to the right. To start with, however, use the matched grip for practising on the snare drum.

strike the drum a little way equidistant on either side of the centre. Movement of the stick is effected by the fingers, the wrist and the fore-

## The orthodox or traditional grip

With the traditional grip the fulcrum is at the base of the crotch between the thumb and the index finger. The first joint of the thumb crosses over the first joint of the index finger. The stick protrudes between the second and third fingers resting on the middle section of the third finger. Be careful not to bend the wrist forward or backward. The stroke is achieved by turning the whole forearm clockwise; the wrist in fact does not turn relative to the forearm. (In the matched grip the wrist *does* move up and down relative to the forearm.) The left-handed player would of course hold the *right* stick in this manner.

## Rudiments

Many people still have the idea that the drummer is an uncontrolled intuitive monster — thrashing out primitive rhythms as they occur to him or her, with little form or musicianship. This is not so. Drums of one sort or another are the oldest of instruments and drumming is a deeply rooted art depending on highly coordinated skills for its effect. To achieve this coordination it is useful to practise certain tried and tested exercises called 'rudiments'. There are 26 standard rudiments which you can find in many tutor books, plus infinite variations stemming from these. Also, in rudimental

snare drumming there are conventions regarding stroke height and stick positions before and after certain beats. These are interesting to study and can be a great aid in developing technique, but are beyond the scope of this book. Similarly it is not our purpose to go into all the standard 26 rudiments here but as an introduction to technique we'll look at the basic rudiments commonly used in rock.

There are two ways to practise the rudiments:

1 Start the exercise playing very slowly and evenly, concentrating on making every stroke perfect. Lift the sticks well away from the drum — try to draw the sound out of the drum rather than bear down on to it. Then oh-so-slowly increase speed until you've achieved a faster but controlled pace, at which point you slow down to your starting speed with the same control at which you began. This is a purely technical exercise aimed at developing control, power, speed and dexterity.

2 Practise the same exercise but at constant tempo. Choose differing metronome speeds (or play along to different records) and mark time with your feet. This is the way you have to play in real situations and you will quickly discover that some things are just as difficult to play very slowly as very quickly. Keeping good time is arguably the most important asset a drummer can develop, so this sort of exercise is of vital importance.

> 'The ability to change the notation of your hand makes life easier. The fact that you do it, doesn't mean to say you've got to use it, but in those cases where it's necessary to do something quite fast or quite intricate, then you should find the easiest way of doing it. There's no point in struggling and slaving over it when there is a very simple way of doing it.'
>
> IAN PAICE

## The single-stroke roll

This is the most familiar drumming technique, involving simply playing one hand after the other, left, right, left, right, and so on. Alternate strokes should be practised leading with the left as well as the right — in fact all rudiments and rhythms should be practised in this way. The range of effects which can be produced by

> 'I think that learning rudiments will let you have more freedom later, once you've achieved a certain speed. I think that your powers of creativity will be enhanced if you feel comfortable and just play something off the top of your head, knowing that your technique will let you do that. So, obviously, you've got to put a little time into your technique so that you can get the ideas out.'
>
> CARL PALMER

playing single strokes around the kit, on different drums, and with accents on different beats is unlimited.

## The double-stroke roll

This roll involves playing two strokes with each hand alternately — L L R R L L R R etc. It is also known as the 'mammy-daddy' roll. Although initially more difficult, it is excellent practice for strengthening and de-

## The flam

The flam is the drum-equivalent of the note plus grace-note, ie a strong beat of the right or left hand is preceded as closely as possible by a lighter beat of the opposite hand. In rock, flams are often played as two

## The paradiddle

This is the only one that might not seem obvious on first acquaintance. The point of it is to introduce you to mixing single- and double-strokes in either hand:

L R L L R L R R etc

This is important because in going round the drums sometimes you might find yourself on the 'wrong'

veloping control of wrist and finger muscles. It can be played 'open', ie with each beat clearly enunciated, and 'closed', ie with pressure exerted by the fingers so that the beats blur into one another and the familiar snare drum roll is obtained. This is the only sustained sound possible on the drums.

### Ruffs

Three-stroke and four-stroke ruffs are used regularly by rock drummers. The three-stroke is simply:

The four-stroke is played as a triplet:

You'll find they crop up everywhere, but don't forget the importance of practising leading with the left, and also try putting accents on the first beat, on the last *and* in the middle.

beats of almost equal power very close together; they serve as very effective punctuations.

hand going back into the rhythm. The only way out is to slip in a double stroke with one hand. Flexibility with singles and doubles allows infinitely greater scope with unlimited rhythmic patterns. It can also help you out where the alternative would mean awkward crossing over of hands (see below):

By using a paradiddle, all the snare drum beats in this funk rhythm are played by the right hand while the left hand stays on the hi-hat.

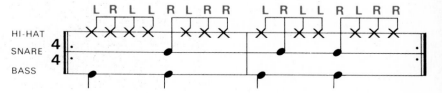

## Foot technique

Flexibility with the feet is obviously more of a problem than with the hands. It is a good idea to practise the rudiments with the feet as well as the hands, and with the feet and hands combined.

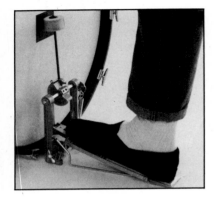

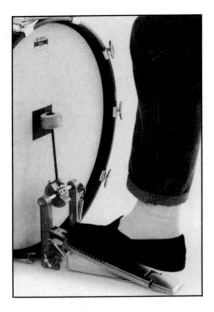

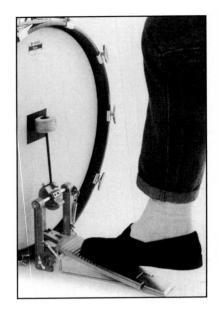

The bass pedal can be played with the foot resting on the plate so that most of the work is done by the ankle. When things get louder most drummers lift the heel off the plate and play with the ball of the foot and sometimes the toes. If the foot is brought part-way down the pedal even more leverage can be achieved.

> '*I would say to anyone wanting to improve their foot technique, to start by going through different notation, playing straight crotchets, then quavers, then triplets. Try playing these things against a regular straight pattern played by the hands. I think this will give you a bit of ground work for most rock patterns — even those bass drum triplets which seem to impress everybody so much. There's nothing magical about them, you know.*'
>
> CARL PALMER

It is possible to develop a rocking motion where the first stroke is played by the whole foot with almost an upward motion while the second stroke is played down by the ball of the foot with the heel lifted. As with stick technique the aim is to draw the sound out of the drum so the beater should be released immediately after the stroke. This can prove quite tricky at first.

The hi-hat is played in a similar way, though of course there is not the same need for heavy playing. Nonetheless a lot of players do play with the heel off the plate and achieve a better balance this way.

## Notation

In order to make examples of rhythms as clear as possible I've adopted the standard drum notation scheme which uses a flexible stave with one line per drum or cymbal. Drums are denoted in the normal way: ♩; cymbals by: ×. It is standard technique in rock, as in jazz, to depress the hi-hat pedal on beats 2 and 4 when playing on the ride cymbal. For graphic simplicity I have omitted this in the examples. You may wish to play this or some other hi-hat pattern with the left foot, but whatever you choose, don't *neglect* the left foot! Also, in rock, playing so-called rim shots on the snare drum (and sometimes the tom-toms) is common. A rim shot is achieved by striking the batter head with the tip of the stick at exactly the same time as the shaft of the stick contacts the rim.

The effect of this is to produce a louder and sharper beat. I have not attempted to notate this; it is up to the individual drummer to decide when and where (if at all) he or she wishes to use rim shots.

The blues has a long and complicated history stretching back to the days of American slavery, and before that, to Africa. But the music we think of as 'blues' only really emerged during the 1940s and 1950s with the migration of many black workers and ex-soldiers to the industrial cities of the north. Here, in the crowded, noisy bars, the electric blues was born with players like Muddy Waters, Little Walter and Otis Spann. The influence of black artists such as these is still felt in rock today. Furthermore, the social conditions which created this music still exist in the many urban ghettoes of America, producing 'street' figures like the blind Reverend Pearly Brown, seen here in Macon, Georgia, during the mid-1970s

# CHAPTER 6

## Blues guitar
### The 'triplets feel'

The blues uses four pulses or beats to the bar, which is a standard time signature in all rock music. However, as explained in the chapter on drums in this section (see p. 104), the blues, and particularly the slow blues, has a very strong 'triplet feel'. To get the feel of this before you play, count a *slow* steady 1–2–3–4 and tap your foot to each count. Now clap three even claps to each beat giving you a '3 over 1' feel.

Now play through the following chord sequence using four down-strokes to the bar — one to each beat — but make the second and fourth strokes short, like this:

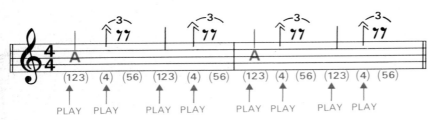

You have just played a standard 12-bar blues in A — the most important chord sequence to learn in rock. It forms the basis of most blues, rock'n'roll and r'n'b music.

### The shuffle rhythm

This is one of the most common rhythms found in blues and when played faster sounds like a r'n'b or rock'n'roll rhythm.

To play a simple shuffle rhythm on the first chord of our sequence (A), we'll be concentrating on just two strings, the A or 5th string and the D or 4th string. Play the open A string simultaneously with the note E (4th string, 2nd fret) twice and then the open A string simultaneously with the note F♯ (4th string, 4th fret) twice in the rhythm shown left (note the triplet feel again):

Another way of thinking of the shuffle rhythm is that you're playing the root of a chord simultaneously with the 5th and then the 6th note.

To play this rhythm to the D chord, simply transfer the whole pattern up to the 3rd and 4th string, and for the E7 chord play the pattern on the 5th and 6th string. The open string you play each time is the root note of the chord.

Your right (plectrum) hand should be using all downstrokes and to get a more chunky sound, dampen the strings by resting your hand on the strings just after the bridge saddles (pictured left). The nearer the neck you move your hand, the more dampened the sound will become.

When you can play the whole A blues chord sequence through smoothly using the shuffle rhythm, try this variation using the flattened seventh interval (see right):

Again transfer this pattern to the other chords.

Great, now you can play a 12-bar blues in A. But what happens if you want to play in another key? This is where you must use barre chords. Play an A major barre chord, root on the 6th string. To play the shuffle rhythm, use the bottom two notes of the chord — the root and fifth:

Then, to move up to the sixth note, play the 5th string, 9th fret with the little finger.

You can use the same pattern if you're playing a barre chord with its root note on the 5th string.

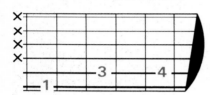

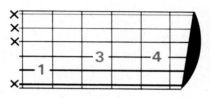

Notice that if you're playing any I–IV–V sequences with barre chords, how near the root notes are to each other no matter which key you're playing in (see below).

I *tonic* chord
C major: root note on the 5th string

IV *sub-dominant* chord
F major: root note on the 5th string, same fret as I chord but one string higher.

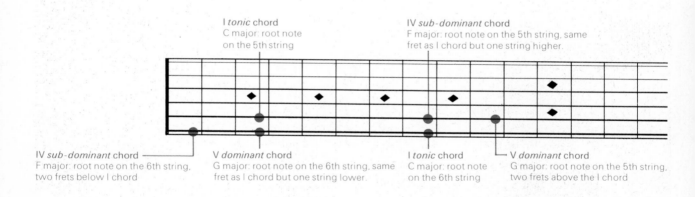

IV *sub-dominant* chord
F major: root note on the 6th string, two frets below I chord

V *dominant* chord
G major: root note on the 6th string, same fret as I chord but one string lower.

I *tonic* chord
C major: root note on the 6th string

V *dominant* chord
G major: root note on the 5th string, two frets above the I chord

*Bringing it all back home. Albert King on stage in 1976. This classic picture by Valerie Wilmer captures the pain and power of the blues*

## Blues solos

We've already examined the major scale which has 7 notes. But guitarists often base their solos on scales which contain 5 notes — pentatonic scales. The C major pentatonic contains the notes C, D, E, G, A. You hear this a lot in country music.

However, the scale which gives the blues its voice is the *related minor* pentatonic, or 'blues' scale (shown overleaf). It only consists of five different notes, yet is one of the most important ones a guitarist can learn, as it is the basis for all blues and rock guitar solos.

*'It's all pentatonic scale, I guess. But it's the feel you happen to inject into it when you play it that makes it special — all you've heard and all you've been all your life . . .'*

CHET ATKINS

## BLUES SCALE IN A

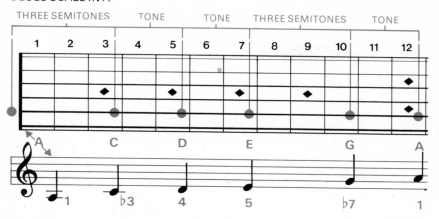

## OPTIONAL FINGERING

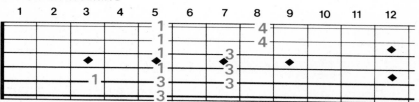

Here is an optional fingering pattern, playing the C note on the 5th string, 3rd fret. Some runs and patterns are easier using this fingering.

Again, this is a movable shape which can be started anywhere on the low E (6th) string. I've written it out in A, starting on the A note

(6th string, 5th fret). I've shown it ascending up to the C note because it's often usual to start riffs on this note.

You should try practising this scale over the A blues 12-bar sequence. Either record yourself playing the chord sequence several

## BLUES SCALE IN A
over two octaves – movable pattern

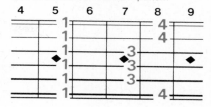

Some guitarists play this scale without using the 4th or little finger. Personally I think you should develop the use of this finger — you have more flexibility using four fingers and if you want to play other musical styles, then it's essential to be able to use all your fingers.

> 'If you're playing blues, the scale falls within two or three frets, so it's easy to get round with the first two or three fingers . . . but really you should bring your little finger in, to stop it being a passenger.'
>
> GARY MOORE

times, or practise with a friend and take turns playing the scale and the chords. When practising, try and break the scale down into smaller sections which sound good to you.

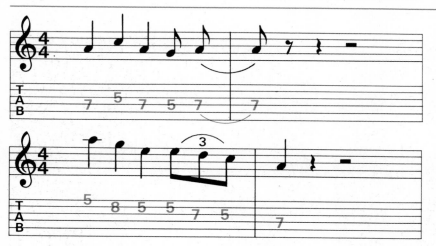

Here are a couple of riffs — simple note sequences which can be played over the whole 12-bar sequence.

You could play these riffs every two bars of the A blues 12-bar. They work over all the chords.

Try playing the 12-bar chord sequence, the blues scale and the riff examples in different keys, eg in C (root note of the scale, 6th string, 8th fret), or in G (root note, 6th string, 3rd fret) etc.

A classic key to play the blues in is E because you can use the open

strings in the E blues scale, though of course you can also play the

E blues scale starting on the 6th string, 12th fret.

Play open string first then fretted note

## Blues scale exercises

Here are a couple of ways you can practise the blues scale and you'll hear that these 'exercises' are often used in part during solos.

I've written these exercises out for the A blues scale.

'It goes back to the same thing. Any kind of modern music I think goes back to the black slave thing — the early blues . . .

LEE ROCKER

### DESCENDING RUNS

### ASCENDING RUNS

All these scales and exercises should be moved around into different keys. However, a very important part of learning to play an instrument is listening to other musicians. Try to get hold of records by people like T-Bone Walker (one of the first, if not *the* first guitarist to bring electric guitar to the blues), Muddy Waters, B B King, Freddie King and Buddy Guy. These were some of the black composers and guitarists whose styles and ideas were copied to great effect by white British guitarists like Eric Clapton, Peter Green, Jeff Beck, and many others.

Listening to these guitarists you'll hear many inventive ways of using the blues scale, but, of course, it's not just the notes used but the *way* that they're used that is important, and there are many techniques you can learn which will make your playing more expressive and soulful.

Muddy Waters

Eric Clapton

## Slides

Sliding the notes you play is important for fluidity — it is a way of moving very quickly up or down the neck and linking different blues scale positions together.

To slide a note up or down, pick the 1st note, then slide your finger to a 2nd note without picking the string again. Refer back to the original A blues scale, optional position (p. 88) and try sliding your 3rd finger up from the note D to E (A string, 5th to 7th fret). You could also try using your 1st finger to slide from the C to D note (A string, 3rd to 5th fret). Also try the same slides descending — this is a bit more tricky.

You can also slide up a note without starting on a particular note. Try

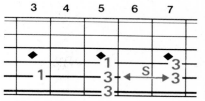

3rd finger slide

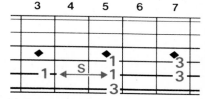

1st finger slide

this riff which starts on this sort of slide.

Now try sliding two notes at a time — one of the most famous examples

of this is used by Chuck Berry at the beginning of 'Johnny B Goode'.

## Vibrato

Putting vibrato on a note will increase the sustain and make the sound more expansive. B B King is credited with first developing the finger vibrato used by all blues and rock guitarists and this involves moving the string very slightly from side to side of where it would naturally lie, thus moving the pitch of the note up and down.

I have found the best way to get a smooth vibrato is *not* by moving your finger backwards and forwards. Keep your finger fairly still on the note, and grip the neck lightly between the side of your 1st finger and thumb. Move the string from side to side through your hand, by rotating the wrist and forearm (much like the plectrum technique).

You can try altering the speed of the vibrato from slow and leisurely

to fast, but the vibrato should always feel comfortable and sound *even*. This vibrato technique is often used when bending strings to give extra sustain.

## String-bending

On the guitar, the strings can be bent practically anywhere on the fingerboard and you usually increase the pitch of a note by a semitone, tone or tone and a half. With the blues scale, the two notes most commonly bent are the fourth and seventh. They are usually bent up one tone, ie two frets to the fifth and first note of the scale respectively — both of these notes being very strong harmonically.

The notes illustrated are usually bent with the 3rd finger. However, as with the vibrato, don't use finger pressure alone. Use the same hand position as with the vibrato and

'Maybe our forefathers couldn't keep their language together when they were taken away from Africa, but this — the Blues — was a language we invented to let people know we had something to say. And we've been saying it pretty strong ever since.'

*B B KING*

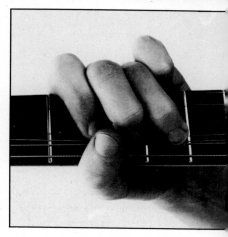

move the hand by rotating the wrist to bend the string up. With lower notes on the 4th and 5th strings, it's often easier to bend the string away from you.

Descending bends are also very effective, ie you bend the string into position before you pick it.

Most commonly bent notes (blues scale pattern)

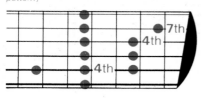

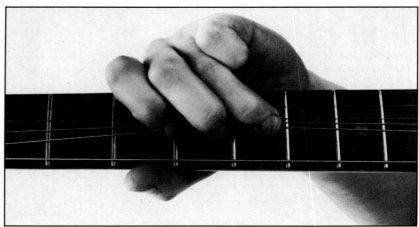

The important thing with bending notes is to reach the correct pitch. When learning to bend strings, check the pitch, eg if you were playing the A blues scale, bend the D (3rd string, 7th fret) up one tone to E, but then play the E note (2nd string, 5th fret) to check that you have bent it the correct distance.

Remember to put vibrato on the bent note if you hold it on, and practise bending on the different strings as they all have different tensions. Also try to avoid catching other strings with your fingernails when bending, because this creates unwanted noises.

Here are some ideas to use when incorporating string-bending into your playing (see right):

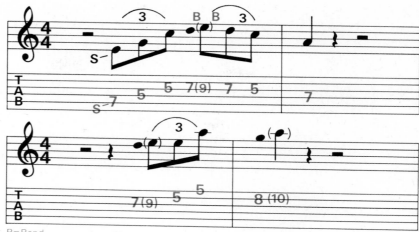

B=Bend
The note in brackets is the one you bend up to.

The note before is the one you bend from

### Minor third to major third bends

Working on the blues scale, you may have noticed that we're often using a minor pentatonic scale against major chord sequences. This

tension is part of what gives the blues its sound, but of course it also means that we can use the major third note by bending up the minor third by one semitone (one fret).

Here's a well known phrase which can be used to start a solo and which uses the minor and major third, though not bent up in this case, just fretted in the normal way.

Minor third notes in blues scale

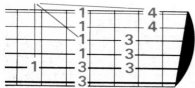

### Box positions

You should now be quite familiar with the two-octave blues scale starting on the 6th string, so next we're going to look at an extension of this first box position. (Again I'm using the A blues scale.)

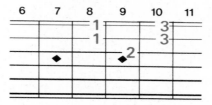

I have added in this note to finish off the scale – it's actually considered outside the box shape.

Try one of the original slide phrases we looked at, played up an octave using the new pattern.

### Third box position

Optional fingering pattern – this is the most effective one to use for sliding notes.

This is the third box position we're going to look at for the blues scale. This is a two-octave blues scale starting on the 5th string — an octave higher than our original box position.

## Using the three box positions (blues scale in A illustrated)

Work out where the fourth and seventh notes of the scale are so you know where you can bend the strings in these new positions.

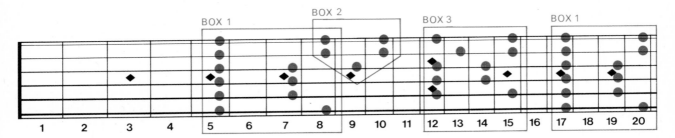

We're going to finish off this section on soloing by looking at more ways of using the techniques I've discussed, and using the blues scale in the new box positions. This first example incorporates the minor third to major third change. Use a 1st-finger barre on the top three strings at the 5th fret.

*The great Chicago blues guitarist Buddy Guy playing what looks like the min/maj 3rd lick during an appearance on 'Ready Steady Go'*

Another way of bending is to bend up a string with the 3rd finger and to use the 4th finger to play another note, while picking the bent string again. In this example (right), the 3rd finger would play the bent D to E note (3rd string, 7th to 9th fret) while the 4th finger plays the G note (2nd string, 8th fret).

Here's an example using Box position 2 (see right).

You've now got plenty of examples and patterns to work on, and as I mentioned earlier, it's a good idea to practise them over a 12-bar chord sequence so that you can hear how they all sound against the I–IV–V chords. Try playing in different keys.

You'll find more on solo playing in the heavy rock chapter and, of course, both these sections are equally relevant to both styles. Remember to use alternate strokes with the plectrum and to build up speed slowly so that you don't lose the timing or the smoothness of the phrases. Hopefully, these sections will also help you in adapting ideas from other guitarists and in developing your own solo playing style.

## Rock'n'roll

*'Well, rock'n'roll is a little bit of everything, I guess, gospel, country and boogie-woogie. I think a lot of the licks used in rock'n'roll can be traced back to the old boogie-woogie piano players. That's the first time I heard that rocking rhythm style later used by Chuck Berry...'*
CHET ATKINS

We're now going to look again at rhythm playing and at a style that derives from the blues — rock'n'roll. So far, we've looked at 12-bar sequences, triplets and shuffle rhythms. These are all contained in rock'n'roll, but it also combines influences from country and pop, and is often faster in tempo.

An important change is that the shuffle rhythm loses the 'triplets' feel and becomes 'straightened out'. Try this for yourself by keeping up a constant count of four and clapping three beats to each count. This is like the shuffle rhythm we've already done. Now clap just two regular beats to each count — you can also try increasing the speed because you are now only dividing the bar into eighths or quaver notes.

It's worth spending some time clapping rhythms like this because this will really improve your sense of timing. And if you can't feel it to clap it, you won't be able to play it well on the guitar!

Now try playing our original shuffle rhythm with the straighter, faster, rock'n'roll feel.

Use this over a 12-bar sequence to get the feel of a rock'n'roll song.

*'The only difference between blues and rockabilly is that rockabilly is a bit faster.'*
LEE ROCKER

94

Chuck Berry in full flight. This legendary rock'n'roller has been a major source of inspiration for generations of rock guitarists

## Blues bass

In its early stages the blues was performed by solo guitar or harmonica and it wasn't until blues material was recorded regularly that the double bass was introduced. Most of the ideas for bass lines came from the figures played on the low strings of the guitar and from the left-hand patterns that boogie-woogie pianists were playing 20 years earlier.

Some of the leading players were *James 'Stump' Johnson* and *Walter Davis* who both liked simple walking patterns. In Chicago around the late 1920s there was a large number of musicians experimenting with the bass figures of piano blues to create a power house sound. They seem to have been inspired by the rhythms of the locomotives which rattled past the tenement blocks! The boogie-woogie pianists and singers played in undercover bars, parties and speak-easies because alcohol had been prohibited and drinking had 'gone underground'. After the Amendment to Prohibition in 1933, the clubs and boogie-woogie re-emerged. Another well-known player of this style was *Big Maceo Merriweather* from Texas who went to

Chicago after playing in Detroit clubs for several years. One of his most famous works was 'Chicago Breakdown'. Other names were *Albert Ammons*, *Pete Johnson* and *Mead Lux Lewis*.

By the 1940s an acoustic piano was still a part of the set-up, playing fills and steady rhythms, and when drums were added they were kept very simple. A lot of emphasis was placed on the snare drum beat, which kept the audience dancing, while a triplets figure was maintained on the cymbal or hi-hat, like this:

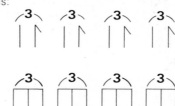

or

The electric bass was a by-product of the rising popularity of the electric guitar of the '50s. It had a shorter neck than the acoustic, and was easier to play, more portable, lighter to handle and could be amplified to the volume of the guitar and drums, making it more audible in a rock 'n' roll context. The same lines could be played on the new electric models as on the double bass and they became increasingly popular. But the instrument was still thought of as occupying a role secondary to that of the piano and guitar, providing rhythm and only the most rudimentary harmony.

## 12-bar blues

The most common chord sequence used in blues, as Deirdre has shown, is the 12-bar sequence (see p. 85). For example:

| BAR | 1 | 2 | 3 | 4 | 5 | 6 | 7 | 8 | 9 | 10 | 11 | 12 |
|---|---|---|---|---|---|---|---|---|---|---|---|---|
| CHORD | I | IV | I | I | IV | IV | I | I | V | IV | I–IV | I–IV |
| The key of a major chord | A | D | A | A | D | D | A | A | E | D | A–D | A–E |

Bass lines tended at first to be very simple, revolving round the root and fifth and changing only in tempo for different songs. In fact, you will probably realise that the examples shown in the bass technique chapter were all derived from the blues format. But because of the emphasis on the 'straight eight' 1/8th notes, the feel of those lines is completely different to that of the blues lines, which imply a triplets feel.

Here is a typical bass figure that became a classic double bass line of the late 1940s and early 1950s.

Key of E major — note the key signature!

Notice how the notes of the major triad chord are joined by a triplet rhythm:

Note also how in Bars 11 and 12 the harmony moves, forcing the song back to the beginning again. This is called a *turn around*.

| Chord | Bar 11 | | | | Bar 12 | | | |
|---|---|---|---|---|---|---|---|---|
| | HOME | then | AWAY | | HOME | and | AWAY | AGAIN |
| | I | | IV | | I | | V | |
| | A | | D | | A | | E | |

In fact, the 12-bar chord sequence represents a kind of musical journey — moving away from 'home' and then back again in time for a repeat performance. The use of the seventh in the V chord reinforces this by adding a feeling of tension which is only resolved by playing the I chord again, bringing everything back to 'normal'. Because tension and resolution are a vital part of the blues (and rock music generally), blues endings are important; and here the bass can make a valuable contribution.

The end of a blues tune always follows the same pattern using Bar 11 as the starting point. Here are some typical endings (right):

## Riffs

A *riff* is a melodic phrase played over and over again. As we'll see in later chapters, riffs have become an important element in rock composition and are often used as the basis for an entire song. In the blues, however, riffs are much more understated, merely adding to the idea of a musical journey by allowing the bass to 'walk' through the song.

Here is an example of a one-bar riff in the key of A:

The one-bar riff can be played all the way through the blues sequence simply by keeping the interval pattern the same, e.g.

| Rhythm | | | | |
|---|---|---|---|---|
| Intervals | Root 6th | 5th 3rd | 4th 5th | |

But move the phrase to the *new root* when the chords change, e.g.

| BAR: | 1 | 5 | 9 |
|---|---|---|---|
| Your root note starting point is: | A | D | E |

Now try taking the riff through a 12-bar sequence. Note the slight variation on Bars 11 and 12, which still implies a turn around, even though there actually isn't one in this piece:

A later development was the two-bar riff. Bar 1 would set up a musical 'question' which would then be answered by Bar 2. Try this next example of a blues sequence. Remember that when you have perfected this pattern, you must repeat it in *as many keys as possible*.

## Stop time

*Stop time* is a common feature of the blues. The whole band plays a phrase in unison and then stops to allow the vocalist or a solo instrument like piano, guitar or sax, to fill the space. Usually the riff is played four times, but it can be played eight times or even used as the basis for the whole song as in many Delta blues songs by Charlie Patton and Robert Johnson. *(Continued over)*

On this page are some typical blues stop time figures:
The top example is the simplest pattern. Just play the root note at the beginning of each bar and change the root as the chord changes.

Below it is a more interesting variation: Note the major feel brought about by playing the F♯ rather than a G.

*The Sensational Alex Harvey Band took perennial blues standards and gave them a 1970s rock treatment. Below are bassist Chris Glenn (left), guitarist Zal Cleminson (right), and Alex himself (centre).*

Key of A m

Key of A m

Above is a famous stop time riff that was used extensively during the blues and rock 'n' roll era and is the basis for such classics as 'Riot in Cell Block No. 9' and 'Framed'. The lower stop time phrase here was originally used by Willie Dixon on 'I Just Wanna Make Love To You', but it's probably far more widely associated with heavy rock:

In fact, bassist Willie Dixon was extremely influential in the transition from blues to rock 'n' roll. He played and recorded with Muddy Waters, Chuck Berry and Bo Diddley, as well as writing some of the most durable of the blues classics, like 'Little Red Rooster'.

*Blues maestro Willie Dixon*

## Rock'n'Roll Bass

Rock 'n' roll emerged as a speeded- up version of the blues combined with the simpler 4/4 rhythms of country music. In the late 1950s the rock 'n' roll explosion began.

Key of C

Key of A

The triplets feel was replaced by the 'straight-eight' rhythm that we looked at in the bass technique chapter. Rock 'n' roll is dance music, and the aim is to provide an uncom- plicated, solid, up-tempo beat. The role of the bass is to 'fill in' the gaps left in the beat by the guitar and drum patterns. The looseness and space of the blues has gone. But the triplets feel is not entirely lost. Via the blues 'shuffle' (described by Geoff on pp. 104–5), bass lines take on a bouncy feel, like this example in the key of F:

This, of course, is very similar to the two-bar riff shown on p. 97. But notice the difference the triplets make!

## Rockabilly

Rockabilly was originally based on a speeded-up version of the shuffle, with the guitar strumming full chords and the drummer shuffling on the snare. The bass lines are therefore simpler and slower so as to make the sound less cluttered (see example at the top of next page). The notes played tend to revolve around the root and the 5th *below*, with triplet fills leading up to or down from one root to another, as the guitar changes chords. This gives a country-type feel. You can hear this kind of line by guitarists like Carl Perkins.

*Carl Perkins — ripping it up!*

I've only summarised a few of the basic formulas used in blues and rock 'n' roll bass playing. There are as many variations to these as there are bass players! If you're interested in pursuing these styles further, check out the recorded work of people like Fats Domino, Little Richard, Bill Haley and Buddy Holly. The old blues veterans are harder to find on disc, but there are some around. And of course their work has been covered by later black American bluesmen like Buddy Guy and Freddie King, and British artists like John Mayall and Alexis Korner.

Try playing along to the records. You should be able to recognise the 12-bar chord sequence and to work out the bass lines fairly quickly.

### The artists

*Fats Domino* was born in 1928, the same year as *Little Richard*, and these two men emerged as the major instigators of the rock 'n' roll sound. The 'Fats' hits were co-written with his musical director, David Bartholomew for Imperial Records. Listen to the bass lines played on the piano — you'll get a lot of ideas from them.

*Fats Domino is best remembered for classics like 'Ain't That a Shame', 'The Girl Can't Help It', and 'Shake Rattle and Roll'*

101

*Bill Haley* and his Comets started
out as a country and western band,
but soon realised the attraction that
black music had for young white
audiences. By listening to the blues
and adding a really strong backbeat, Haley created the formula for
'Crazy Man Crazy', 'Rock That
Joint', 'Rock Around the Clock' and
'See You Later Alligator'.

*Buddy Holly* played r'n'b and blues with a strong country influence which tended to simplify the chords and straighten out the triplet rhythms into even 1/8th note rhythms. His style usually had a country guitar, as opposed to a blues guitar sound. His greatest hits were 'That'll be the Day', 'Peggy Sue' and 'Rave On' between 1956 and 1959.

## Blues/Rock'n'roll — Drums
### The 'triplets' feel
The enduring and vital ingredient of black American rhythm is 'swing'.

Although this is an elusive concept, we can go a long way to discovering what it means by identifying one common element in the rhythm of

black music. This is the triplets ride figure usually played on the cymbal or hi-hat:

JAZZ RHYTHM

SHUFFLE OR BOOGIE RHYTHM

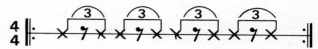

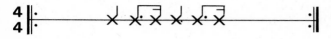

Although most often played as written, this rhythm has frequently been represented as a dotted pattern: This confusion arises partly from the impossibility of writing 'feel' into music. At different times the ride figure will be played in every variation from a deliberate staccato

dotted-note feel through to an almost straight 1/8th note feel, depending on the tempo of the mood of the song. To make it even more confusing, in some early blues and rock'n'roll recordings you can hear one musician playing triplets whilst at the same time another is playing

straight eighths!

However, the triplets feel is the most common one and it is with this that we should begin looking at drum kit patterns.

### Slow blues
When the triplets rhythm is performed at a slow tempo it opens out and is generally notated as 12/8. That is, four groups of three 1/8th notes.

So the basic kit feel is:

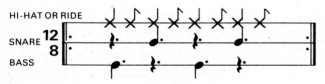

Variations in the bass drum are common:

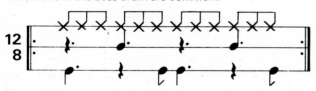

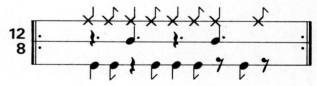

Variations in the hi-hat/ride rhythm include:

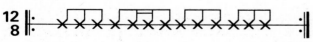

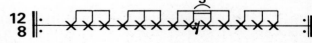

Some slow blues can be very slow indeed, and this is a great test of a drummer's taste and control. Getting a good feel and keeping the tempo steady is not easy in this situation. Generally the bass drum follows the bass guitar, but you can occasionally add to this a little so that the rhythm doesn't become too mechanical. Playing slowly and relatively softly, there is room for dynamics and shadings not practicable in a lot of

other styles. Playing different parts of the ride cymbal, for example, and occasionally catching the cymbal bell adds colour; so too, for instance, does the press-roll — a great dynamic ploy in this type of music.

When this slow blues rhythm is played a little faster we get the sort of feel pioneered by Fats Domino and others in New Orleans, exemplified in a song like Fats' 'Blueberry Hill'. Domino based many of his

songs on a slightly slowed-down boogie-woogie feel. Incidentally, this sort of rhythm was picked up from New Orleans in Jamaica and was adapted to form the basis of 'ska', which eventually led to reggae.

### The shuffle rhythm
When the triplets feel is speeded up again we arrive at what is called the *shuffle* — the basis of present-day boogie rock rhythms. The shuffle is

so-named because the feel is of the instruments shuffling along together — indeed the drummer's hands and sometimes the bass foot shuffle together also:

Within the shuffle, accents are often placed on the backbeat:

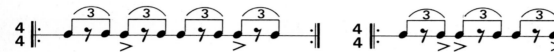

Note that at this tempo the rhythm is notated as 4/4 with 1/8th note triplets.

The style below is characteristic of Chicago blues bands and has been developed by rock boogie bands.

Again variations occur largely in the bass drum rhythm but also sometimes in the snare drum pattern:

These are just *some* of the possibilities for boogie rock rhythms. They can all also be played by using the unbroken triplets ride/hi-hat rhythm and its variations:

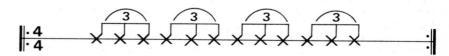

## The Latin influence

I've begun this look at blues and rock'n'roll drumming by examining the triplets feel because it is synonymous with black American music. However, a young musician starting to play today will most likely begin by playing with a straight 1/8th beat or 1/16th beat rhythm. This is because such rhythms are now far more common in rock music and in basic form are easier to play:

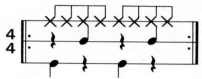

This use of 'straight' rather than swing or jazz hi-hat and cymbal playing is largely attributable to the influence of Latin American rhythms. The major Latin influences come from Brazil, Argentina, Mexico and, in particular, Cuba (Cuban music deriving from a blend of Spanish and African sources). Throughout this century of popular music there have regularly been Latin 'crazes' in North America — the 1920s tango, the 1930s rumba, the 1950s mambo.

Perhaps because of these fashionable 'crazes', the real depth of the Latin influence has been underestimated. The regular use of maraccas, cabassas, congas, bongos etc to add spice to a rhythm track may lead us to forget just how strong are the Latin roots already in the drum part. Ever since the beat groups of the 1960s, straight ride rhythms have been the mainstay of rock. The enormous success of The Beatles and the rock groups that followed ensured this. The Beatles derived their rhythmic style by listening to black blues, r'n'b and soul artists, particularly the more com-

*Bo Diddley provided rock with one of its most important rhythms. His pattern crops up in various forms throughout rock from heavy metal to reggae*

mercially successful Tamla Motown groups and Chuck Berry, who were all regularly using straight rhythms as well as triplets rhythms.

Before looking at some of these Latin-flavoured rock rhythms there

is one other black r'n'b artist whose name is synonymous with a rhythm of undisputed Latin origin. He is *Bo Diddley* and the rhythm which often bears his name is an interpretation of the *clave* — the foundation of

Cuban music. The clave is a call and response figure played over two bars:

In the absence of the triplets swing feel, the syncopation of the first half of the clave adds movement to the otherwise straight time. On closer examination it will be noticed that this first bar is in fact three beats played across the four beats of the pulse, falling on the 1st, 4th and 7th of the eight 1/8th notes:

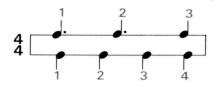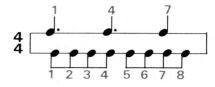

The 'push' given by this first syncopated bar is returned by the settling nature of the second. So fundamental and 'right' is this syncopation that it

crops up as the commonest accent and driving figure in the whole of contemporary music, be it rock, funk, reggae or disco. It can be

incorporated into the shuffle of blues or the swing of jazz and played on any part of the drum set — becoming very 'funky', eg

Clave beat played by bass drum

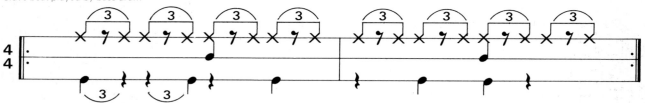

I'll be referring to the clave rhythm again in later chapters. But for now,

here are some straight ride rock beats incorporating Latin elements.

You'll notice here and there the syncopation of the first clave measure.

This snare drum figure is featured in the 'twist'

This has a samba bass figure

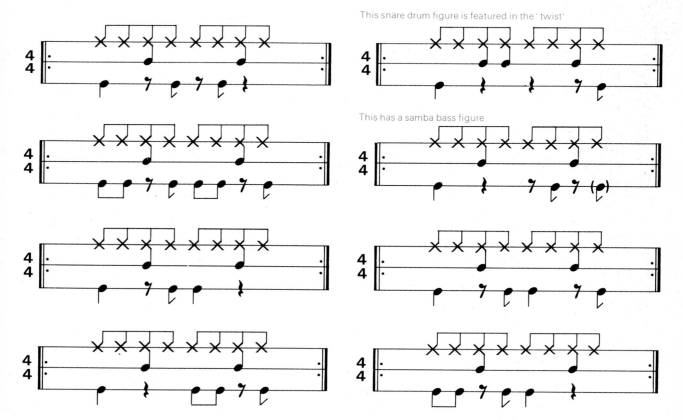

This is a reverse clave rhythm

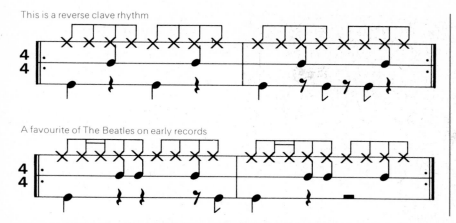

A favourite of The Beatles on early records

Some patterns repeat every two bars rather than every one, and may have a hi-hat variation (see left).

The Bo Diddley rhythm itself was made more exciting sound-wise and visually by being played on the tom-toms. On most of Bo Diddley's early records the maraccas are also strongly featured — another bow in the direction of Latin influence.

The original drummer on much of Bo Diddley's records was *Clifton James.* Drummers ever since have used variations of this idea, keeping the basic pattern but using different

*S. P. Leary trained as a ... drummer before moving over ...*

*Odie Payne worked with Willie Dixon and played on the Chess label*

combinations of tom-toms etc. During his early career, *Mick Jagger* made a feature of playing maraccas in this style — an indication of the Stones' roots.

To finish this section, there is one other rhythm common to early blues and rock which demonstrates a clear Latin connection. The snare drum and tom-tom figures are clearly modelled on a basic conga rhythm.

## Techniques and arrangements

Musicologists have managed to trace rock'n'roll-type recordings back as far as the 1930s, but to all intents and purposes rock'n'roll really came together in the 1950s. However, even on the earliest records — both rock'n'roll and blues — the bass and piano take dominance in the rhythm section. Indeed on the first Elvis and Muddy Waters records there are no drums at all. When the drums do appear they take a back seat; often brushes are used just to add colour to the solid 'walking' bass line. On faster rock tunes the bass is 'slapped' and eventually the drums start to copy the bass slap. In both rock'n'roll and electric blues, the pioneering drummers had jazz backgrounds and so employed the jazz ride figure on the cymbal or hi-hat but with a solid backbeat. In Chicago, *Fred Below* working with Muddy Waters, Otis Spann, Willie Dixon and others, was one of the first to play regular electric blues. He found he had to 'discipline' the guitarists and bassists who weren't used to playing strict time, the feel of the acoustic blues being much more open to interpretation and liberty of bar length and phrase length. It was Fred Below, along with *Odie Payne*, *S P Leary* and a few other drummers, who really established the backbeat and the shuffle, using sticks rather than brushes in the early 1950s.

*Fred Below played with Little Walter in the first electric blues band*

In rock'n'roll and rockabilly, the tempo is quite often very fast and the jazz ride rhythm is employed with a particular snare pattern derived from the slapping of the string bass.

Sometimes this pattern is played as a fast shuffle with both hands on the snare drum.

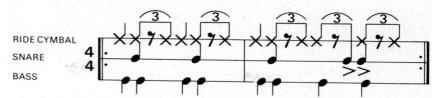

At slightly slower tempos the shuffle can be played with the right stick on the rim of the small tom-tom (to imitate the sound on early rock'n'roll records) or on the snare drum, with the left stick providing the backbeat.

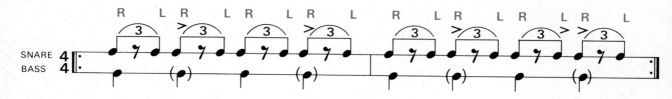

## Breaks and fills

Drum breaks and fills in r'n'b and rock'n'roll tend to be brief and to the point and occur at the beginning and the end of verses, choruses etc, or leading in and out of solos. Careful listening to some of the most innovative drummers, eg *D J Fontana* with Elvis Presley, *Earl Palmer* with Little Richard and Fats Domino, and *Jerry Allison* with Buddy Holly, reveals many ideas still relevant today. Triplet rolls on the snare drum are very effective whether the song has a straight or shuffle feel:

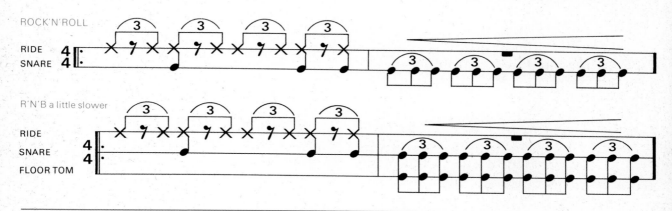

Similarly, straight 1/16th note snare drum rolls are used again in both straight and shuffle feels.

Here are a couple of more subtle 1/8th beat fills:

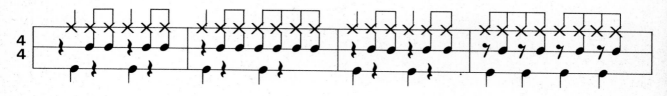

Rock Builder Evans (Slim Jim Phantom) of The Stray Cats gets an unusually big sound from a minimal drum kit: snare, bass drum, hi-hat, and ride cymbal.

## Stop time

Rock'n'roll and r'n'b arrangements frequently use a dynamic device known as *stop time*. As an intro-duction, as an ending, and/or as a recurring pattern, the whole (or part) of the band will play stop/start unison figures which act as a spring-board for the meat of the song with its complete rhythm. A classic ex-ample is the Chuck Berry-type guitar introduction:

Drums in unison with bass guitar

In the middle of a tune you might have a triplets roll leading to a section end:

The voice or guitar will then play over stop time phrases from the bass and drums:

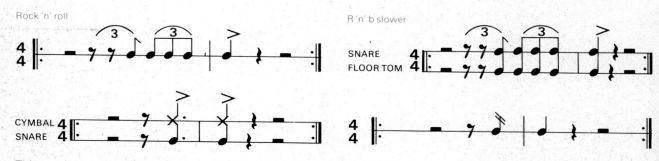

This sort of phrase is repeated over eight bars, the eighth bar being played as a lead-in to the band. Classic versions of this are Elvis' 'Jailhouse Rock' and Chuck Berry's 'No Particular Place to Go'.

Endings also have stop time phrases. Again the bass and drums will stop while the guitar plays a finishing lick.

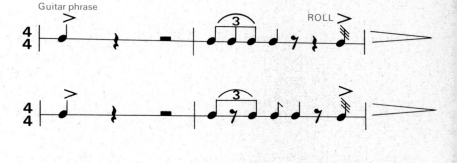

Another common variation:

It's well worth checking out old records for variations on these classic arrangements. Once the basics are mastered they make your band sound much tighter and you have a uni-versal 'language' for working with other musicians. Furthermore, having gone back to the roots you've got a much clearer idea of how today's music has come about, which must help with your own progress.

We'll be seeing in the next chapter how these arrangement devices are updated and modified for use in heavy rock and heavy metal.

# CHAPTER 7

# Heavy Rock   Heavy Metal

**HM guitar**

✳ The development of rock music in the 1960s and 1970s probably reflected more than anything else the developments that had been made in guitar sound and style.

From the early beginnings of the banjo and then through the guitar styles of Charlie Christian (late 1930s, early 1940s), B B King and Jimi Hendrix, the sound of the guitar has become increasingly elongated and abstracted from the instrument, while its range of expression has grown enormously.

We have already seen how in England in the early 1960s there was a tremendous blues and r'n'b music boom, with Eric Clapton, Jeff Beck and Jimmy Page becoming well known for their solo playing, whilst a guitarist called Pete Townshend was becoming equally well known for his songs, his style of playing rhythm power chords and smashing up his guitar!

Alongside the influence of these players, there was a growth in instrument and amplifier technology which allowed guitarists to begin experimenting with a whole new range of sounds and effects. Gary Cooper has already described these in the opening section of this book ✳

*Former Led Zeppelin lead guitarist Jimmy Page*

*Jimi Hendrix revolutionised guitar sounds and techniques in the late 1960s. No one has equalled him*

## Volume and sound

The most important part of the new sound was quite simply volume. Volume can actually facilitate certain lead techniques which we will talk about in detail later on. And, most vital of all to the heavy rock lead guitarist, volume can give you sustain and controlled feedback.

The best way to get this is to have the guitar volume and tone controls full (it helps to have a trebly sound) and turn up the amp volume. You will have to experiment a bit here with volume and positioning because feedback will only be induced in certain positions, eg facing close to the speakers. Once you have established a position and volume level where you can get feedback you should practise controlling it, eg

move away from the amp so the feedback disappears, then holding on to a high note like B (B string, 12th fret), use vibrato to make the note sustain and gradually move towards the amp so the note feeds back. You can prolong the sound indefinitely like this or you can go more over the top and have screaming feedback using a tremolo arm (if you have one) for Hendrix-like effects. This will also work well with chords. Distortion units and wah wah pedals left pressed on will help to get feedback. Many amps today are designed to be overdriven at lower volumes (master volume controls, distortion channels, etc) so hopefully you will not need to drive your friends and neighbours completely mad!

It is obvious that the *sound* of the guitar is very important in heavy rock and, as we have seen, part of this sound is sheer volume. The main part

*Leading British HM band Girlschool have carved a new role for women musicians in rock*

of this 'sound', however, comes from the actual notes you choose to play and the timing and rhythm of them, whether in solos, riffs or chords.

Heavy rock and heavy metal are epitomised by low, heavy-sounding riffs and 'power chords', and high, screaming, fast guitar solos. However, the roots of heavy rock are in the blues and rock'n' roll, and some heavy rock bands still primarily use 12-bar sequences like those we have featured. A band like Status Quo is a good example, but there is a difference here in that the bass guitar no longer emphasises the different notes in the chords but just the root notes. In most heavy rock there is a 'paring down' harmonically of the chords whilst the drive and power of them are heightened. This way of playing is even more emphasised in heavy metal.

We are going to look first at the 'rhythm' side of rock — different ways of playing the chords we have already been working with both harmonically and rhythmically, and extending our knowledge of chord sequences.

In the blues chapter we studied two rhythms:

### The 'triplets feel'

This came from swing and jazz music and has three notes to every beat though only the 1st and 3rd notes are emphasised. This shuffle rhythm is used in rock by boogie bands and we will be looking at a couple of examples with this kind of feel.

However, the more dominant rhythm in rock came to be the Latin-influenced 'straight 1/8th' feel which became popular in the 1950s.

### Straight 1/8ths

As we saw in the blues chapter, this uses two equal notes to every beat and therefore eight to the bar.

We are going to be looking at some heavy rock chords which use this rhythm. To get the right kind of 'sound', you should:

1 play only the bottom two or three strings to get a heavier sound.

2 use all downstrokes with the plectrum, for more 'attack',

3 think in terms of 1/8th notes (quavers). Count four beats to the bar and practise playing eight even downstrokes to every bar.

Try the following examples:

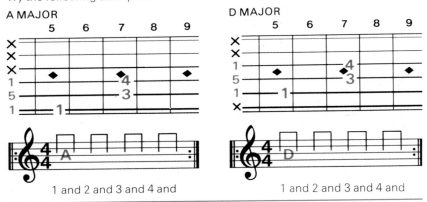

Play slowly and evenly at first, gradually building up your speed. Try this with different chords and hear how it sounds different higher up the fingerboard. Let the notes ring and then try getting a more chunky, percussive sound by damping the strings with the right (plectrum) hand. If you play this rhythm and chord shape very fast like this, you will hear the rhythm used by many punk groups — the 'chainsaw guitar' sound.

Now try playing these next examples which use only certain beats and accents (but you should still be feeling the 1/8ths).

and this variation

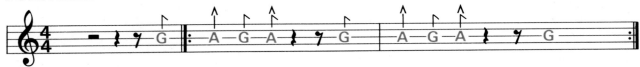

Try using different chords like C and D, F and G etc.

Accents are very important for dramatic effect, and notice also how the above sequence starts on an off-beat: 1 2 3 4 *and*. This is another classic feature of heavy rock as this 'kicks off' the chord sequence or riff — groups from Led Zeppelin and Deep Purple to Judas Priest and Girl-school use this effect. Sometimes one instrument will play even 1/8th notes, whilst both the others will play offbeat accents together.

Here is another typical chord sequence. Notice how the second chord in each bar starts on an offbeat.

You can also play this by letting the B♭ chord ring on until you play the next chord each time.

## Riffs

Another device borrowed from the blues is the riff. Heavy riffs use mainly notes from the blues scale, but it is usually the bottom strings that are used and often chords are made from the notes to give a heavier sound — a classic example of this is the riff from Deep Purple's 'Smoke on the Water'.

Below is an example of a chord-type riff which uses the triplet boogie rhythm, compared with a popular blues riff so that you can see the similarity between the two styles.

In the second example, by playing the low A note on the open 5th string you can sustain the note more and it makes playing the two chord shapes easier, though this only works in the keys of E or A.

**CLASSIC BLUES RIFF**

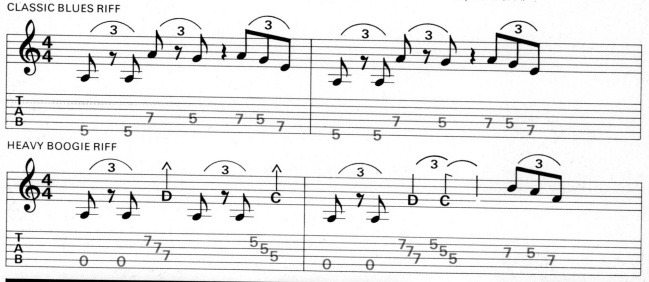

**HEAVY BOOGIE RIFF**

*Ritchie Blackmore who, as guitarist for Deep Purple, devised one of the greatest heavy riffs of all time — 'Smoke on the Water'*

116

On the right are two further examples of single-note riffs.

## Chord sequences

Though heavy rock and heavy metal are influenced by the blues, there is a move away from keeping to the I-IV-V chord sequences. You will find that often the chords are made up using the notes of the blues scale as the root notes, so if, for example, you were playing in the key of A, you could try chord sequences using the major chords of A, C, D, E and G, and in the key of E, the major chords of E, G, A, B and D. Try this for yourself in different keys, first working out the notes of the blues scale and then the chords.

I have already mentioned how you can use the bottom three notes of the E and A shape barre chords to get a heavier sound. By doing this, you are not playing a third in the chord — just the root, fifth and octave. This gives the chords an ambiguous sound, neither major nor minor — and this is also what I meant earlier by 'passing down harmonically'.

When you substitute the fourth note of the scale for the third in a chord, this is called a 'suspended fourth'. When you play the chord, you will hear that the fourth is trying to resolve back to the third. Here are some examples of suspended open chords which of course can be used to form barre chords as we did earlier on.

The rock guitarist probably most associated with these type of chords is Pete Townshend, who actually uses open shapes a lot because you can get tremendous sustain by leaving the notes ringing on.

### SUS D CHORD
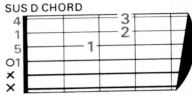

### SUS A CHORD
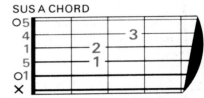

### D7 SUS FOURTH
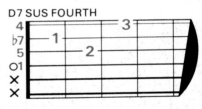

### A7 SUS FOURTH
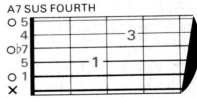

### SUS E CHORD
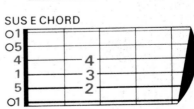

### E7 SUS FOURTH
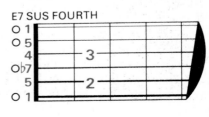

A famous chord sequence using the suspended fourth resolving to the major chord is 'Pinball Wizard' which you can play using the following shape.

Note that these notes are the top four notes of an E shape barre.

**SUS FOURTH**

**MAJOR CHORD**

Other chords which contain no thirds and use open strings are these (Jimi Hendrix is associated with this type of sound):

An alternative is not to play the 6th string with the thumb but to play instead the 1st string on the same fret using a 1st finger barre.

You can also try playing the top four notes of an A major barre chord (E shape) and use an open A string as the root. Bring your thumb over the fingerboard slightly to dampen the 6th string. This gives the chord more depth and sustain at volume.

G chord (no third)

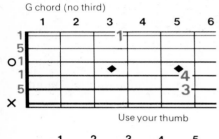

Use your thumb

F chord with added ninth (G note)

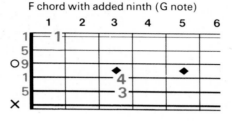

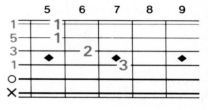

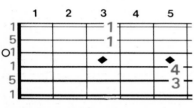

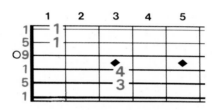

A lot of HM guitarists use this shape in their rhythm playing.

There are many ways of using and changing the sounds of chords. I have mentioned some guitarists who were associated with these sounds and techniques when rock guitar began to develop and of course they have influenced many guitarists who have become known more recently. So, you should listen to groups, past and present, and take note of the musical context in which these different sounds and rhythm techniques can be used.

We are now going to look at more soloing techniques which will increase your speed and your range of expression on the guitar.

Here is an example of an open string 'pedal' using the low E string this time. If you hit this hard at a loud volume, it will really ring and sustain. If you

play it more gently, perhaps picking the individual strings, you will get a more 'folky' sound — used sometimes by guitarists like Jimmy Page.

E chord (no third)

E7 SUS FOURTH

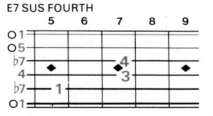

## Rock soloing

This section really continues the techniques we started exploring in

the blues chapter, but whereas the blues is concerned primarily with expression, and this is often achieved

by a sparing use of notes, heavy metal guitar solos are much faster, using more 'showy' techniques.

*Most HM guitar solos are based around the three box positions of the blues scale*

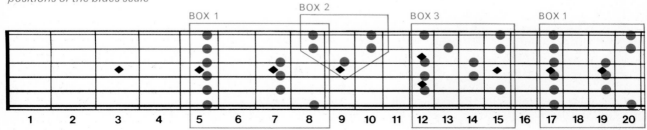

You'll see that nearly all the techniques we're going to study involve building up the speed and strength of the left (neck) hand, but we're going to look first at a different plectrum technique which is often used in soloing.

If you pick a string using the plectrum and the side of your thumb you can produce strong harmonics as well as the sound of the note and at volume this is very effective if you want to heighten the intensity of the sound. The plectrum and thumb are both picking the string at once (see right), though they're about ¾'' apart. You should also experiment with the thumb and plectrum in different positions between the ends of the neck and the bridge because you'll find you can produce different harmonic sounds depending on where you pick.

## Hammer-ons

Pick a C note (G string, 5th fret) using your 1st finger and, without picking the string again, bring your 3rd finger firmly down on the D note two frets up. This is a *hammer-on* and it allows you to play two or more notes whilst only plucking the string once. Now, as an exercise, play the A blues scale ascending using hammer-ons, ie you will only pick each string once but play two notes on every string. In tablature a hammer-on is written like this: H
Try it slowly at first and make sure

all the notes are even before you increase the speed of the exercise. Using alternate down and up strokes with the plectrum you should with practice be able to get a fast but smooth sounding pattern.

Also try coming down the strings (though you won't be playing the notes in the scale order) using hammer-ons.

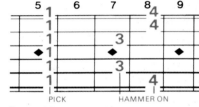

Repeat this on every string

## Pull-offs

In some ways, the pull-off seems the reverse of the hammer-on, but really it is a left- or neck-hand pluck. Pick a D note (G string, 7th fret) using your 3rd finger to fret it. Now pull this finger away from you so that it plucks the string and plays the C note (G string, 5th fret) that you should have already fretted. This technique is a little harder than the hammer-on and if you find it difficult at first, practise pulling off to an open string, eg G (1st string, 3rd fret) to open E (1st string).

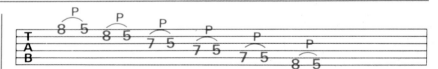

Try this on all open strings. Pull-off from the 3rd fret on the 1st, 2nd and 6th strings, and from the 2nd fret on the other strings.

Again, when it feels comfortable and both notes are of equal volume, try this exercise using the A blues scale (descending). Remember to use alternate plectrum strokes. The pull-offs are marked thus: P

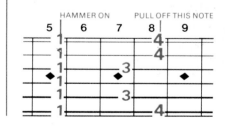

## Trills

Now if we combine the hammer-on and the pull-off using the C and D notes on the G string again we can play three notes to just one pick. Practise until you can keep the two notes alternating — only picking the string once at the very beginning. This is called a trill, and if you've

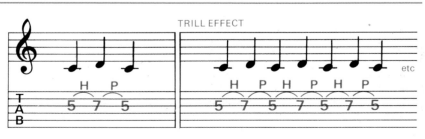

ever seen guitarists playing with just their left hand this could be what they're doing . . .

It's worth spending time on hammer-ons and pull-offs because they really do make your playing faster and, along with string-bending, are the commonest tech-

niques used in rock guitar. You can hear the following phrases — running up and down the blues scale — in many solos.

Also, you should translate all these exercises to the two-octave blues scale starting on the 5th string, and stop at the seventh note of the scale.

**Exercises**
Now here are some ideas for exercises using hammer-ons and pull-offs. Remember the exercise we did in the blues chapter coming down the blues scale? Well, try it again using hammer-ons and pull-offs this time.

There are other ways in which you can play several notes with just one pick — combining a hammer-on and slide, for example (see right).

Play the same pattern one octave apart. Pick only the first and fourth note. Notice also that the higher phrase connects with the extended blues scale (box position 2).

A variation on the blues scale is to add the flattened fifth note to the scale, like this.

**BOX POSITION 1**

Blues scale – root note on 5th string. Variation on using box position 3 for ease of playing.

**BOX POSITION 2**

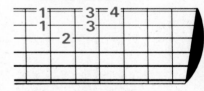

The following ideas use both the hammer-on and pull-off to play three notes to one pick, using a flattened fifth note:

ASCENDING

DESCENDING

We can also use passing notes in blues scale patterns. If we were using the A blues scale, we could use the

B (1st string, 7th fret) and F# (2nd string, 7th fret) as passing notes and you can achieve the following

effects using first pull-offs, and then hammer-ons.

You can get a really fast, rippling effect using these kinds of ideas, and if you transpose this pattern to the E blues scale using the open strings you'll find it's slightly easier to play.

If you follow all these ideas and exercises through methodically, you will become extremely fluent with hammer-ons and pull-offs. We're now going to look briefly at the string-bending technique which is mainly associated with Jimi Hendrix. I call them unison note bends because you play two notes in unison, ie of the same pitch, but one is fretted

normally and the other is bent up to the same note.

They're most effective using either the 1st and 2nd strings or 2nd and 3rd strings. Use your 1st and 3rd fingers. With practice you can get a

real screaming sound!

Guitarists like Carlos Santana relied heavily on this technique in the early 1970s and you can hear it now in the music of bands like Gang of Four.

## Soloing style

A last word about solos — don't just string together phrases for a set period of time. It's actually quite boring to listen to a guitarist playing as fast as he or she can for two minutes, using just stock phrases. Of course every rock solo uses certain ideas which are now almost cliches, but you should adapt these and try to build your own ideas on them. Keep in mind that a solo should have a beginning, a middle and an end. If soloing is quite new to you, then to get you going, work out a couple of ideas that you can use to start and end the solo and this will allow you to experiment in the middle. Finally, an exciting solo isn't necessarily just a fast one.

Try to introduce dynamics into your playing. Slower parts can be really effective too!

'I think too much is made of the guitar. Too many guitarists make records which are purely vehicles for their own ability, so they can say "Look what I can do". I really try to avoid that because I feel that the composition of the song is the mainstay of the music . . . which is why I prefer to play lyrical guitar solos, although I suppose I'm associated with very fast playing. 'If the chord sequence is right, it will inspire me to play a lot better than if I'm playing over a riff that's just chugging along. . . . What I try to do is build up the phrases in an emotional way, sort of thinking of scales as I approach each chord. I think it's important to my style of playing to do that, and it comes out as more of a feel thing than a technical thing.'

GARY MOORE

*Brian May of Queen is noted for his carefully constructed melodic solos*

You should still be thinking of *expressing* yourself and not just *impressing* your friends/audience with flash playing. You'll find in the end that individual expression will make you a much more exciting guitarist to listen to anyway.

## HM bass

There's a lot more to heavy metal music than screaming guitars and gut-rending riffs. The term HM covers a wide variety of different styles, from boogie and punk at one end of the spectrum to the semi-classical at the other. And at the very heart of the sound you'll find the bass and drums. Without the weight and power of the rhythm section, those ear-bending guitar solos and brain-crunching block chords would sound thin and weedy. If the guitar provides the 'metal' in HM, then the bass and drums provide the 'heavy'!

Originally known as Heavy Rock, HM grew up in the late 1960s when musicians began looking for ways to expand their sound, pushing both themselves and their gear to the limit. The sound got louder and heavier. The songs got longer, showcasing the talents of players in a way not seen in rock before. The backing for this large scale improvisation was still solidly blues-based, using riffs and chords derived from the blues scale, and rhythm patterns taken from the 'straight 8' and boogie shuffles of rock'n'roll. But the standard 12 bar format was abandoned in favour of open-ended riffs.

Among the most influential bassists of this period were:

★ Jack Bruce of Cream and Noel Redding of The Jimi Hendrix Experience. They both brought a touch of jazz to their lines, adding a subsidiary melody to the frantic solos of Clapton and Hendrix, emphasising the passing notes, playing in the relative minor or major, and so on.

★ John Entwistle of The Who played the bass like a lead guitar, relying heavily on the blues scale

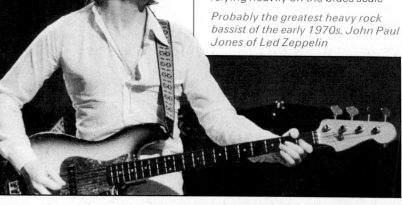

*Probably the greatest heavy rock bassist of the early 1970s, John Paul Jones of Led Zeppelin*

*Black Sabbath's Geezer Butler*

and providing a melodic interest to Pete Townshend's powerhouse chord work.

★ John Paul Jones of Led Zeppelin and Andy Fraser of Free remained conventionally blues-based in their playing while managing to inject a fresh melodic feeling. Just listen to the middle section of 'Lemon Song' and the bass riff on 'Ramble On' — both on *Led Zeppelin II* — and 'The Stealer' from the Free *Live* LP.

These musicians might describe themselves more as heavy rock bass players rather than heavy metal. During the early 1970s they were part of a movement which was making music more complex and sophisticated. It was the age of 20-minute guitar solos, 'concept' albums, spectacular stage shows. But there were heavy metal bass players too in the shape of people like Geezer Butler of Black Sabbath, Roger Glover of Deep Purple and, to a lesser extent, Gary Thain of Uriah Heep. Their lines were simpler and more driving. Just listen to classic LPs like *Paranoid* (Sabbath), *Made In Japan* (Purple), and *Look At Yourself* (Heep).

With the advent of punk in the late 1970s, there came a new brand of heavy music which relied on the basics of high volume and grinding riffs, but was this time shorter and punchier, often trimmed down to three or four minutes a song. The new wave of HM is currently at this stage and is one of the most popular rock styles in Britain.

**Sound and technique**

HM bass sound varies according to personal taste and the style of your band. The common factor is, of course, volume. Getting the bass to cut through the other instruments at high volume can be a problem and will usually require considerable experimentation on your part. Earlier heavy bassists, like those I've just mentioned, tended to go for a full, rich, clean bassy sound (with the possible exception of Bruce and Entwistle who on occasion opted for a drier, trebly feel). This bassiness underpinned the music, but left things at best indistinct, and at worst muddy and muffled.

More recently, bassists have gone for a middly, punchy sound, which allows the bass lines to cut through, while still providing the thud you need to kick the music along.

'An audible bass sound, that's the most important thing. When you go and see a band and can't hear the bass, that's not necessarily because it's not there, it's just because the sound they've chosen doesn't cut through . . . If you're too boomy, the boom will be covered by the bass drum, and if you're too trebly, you'll be wiped out by the guitars and cymbals . . .

'It took me two years to find a sound with Whitesnake that fitted in with the drums, and with two guitars, the organ and the vocal.'

*NEIL MURRAY*

To get a middly HM bass sound, try turning your amp up as high as it will go without distorting. Set all the tone controls on about half, but be prepared to make fine adjustments depending on the acoustics of the room and the sound of the other instruments. You may need to ease the Middle or Presence control forward a bit.

Open out all the tone and volume controls on the bass itself. If you've got active circuitry, switch it on, but then increase the bass setting on the amp to compensate for the extra treble of the boosted signal.

How you play the bass will also affect the sound dramatically. Most heavy bassists, I think, use the standard two-finger pluck style described in my chapter on basic technique (p. 69). If you play this way, pluck the string right over the middle pickup. One thing you must do is play *hard*.

If you use a plectrum (like Phil Lynott, late of Thin Lizzy, Alan Lancaster of Status Quo, or Chris Aylmer of Samson), you will automatically get a sharper, more trebly sound, and you will have to cut

## Rhythm patterns
Having got the sound and volume right, the next ingredient is the rhythm. Just listen to the drums, and play along with them, sticking to the root notes of the chords the guitarist is bashing out. Common rhythm patterns would be these:

'Straight 8':

Try these simple bass lines (all in the key of A minor) using each of these rhythm patterns. Remember to use the left- and right-hand damp-

back on the Middle and Treble controls on your amp.

You can also use effects and different amp combinations to get a middly sound. But the simple suggestions above will get you well on your way.

Boogie:

'American Indian':

'Classical':

ing techniques discussed earlier (pp. 68–9). Try to get your two fingers to pluck the strings alternately. Keep the sound as smooth as you can.

## 'Straight 8':

Bands like Motorhead tend to use straight 8 rhythms a lot.

## Boogie:

Status Quo, ZZ Top (pictured below), Wishbone Ash and Lynyrd Skynyrd have all used this kind of rhythm.

*Phil Lynott, late of Thin Lizzy. Perhaps best known for their twin lead guitars, Lizzy were powered by Lynott's plectrum bass lines*

'American Indian'

You can hear this used on songs like 'Eye of the Tiger' by Survivor, 'Death Walks Behind You' by Atomic Rooster and 'Immigrant Song' by Led Zeppelin.

'Classical':

Bands like Rush and Genesis might play this kind of rhythm in unison with all the instruments — even drums. This particular pattern was immortalised on Deep Purple's 'Child in Time'.

There are many variations to these basic rhythms. You should listen to different bands and try to work out how they incorporate them into their sound. Try to make up a few lines of your own, using the notes from the blues scale. In A, these notes would be: A, C, D, E, G.

## Accents

The basic rhythms I've just shown you would get pretty boring if everybody played them straight all the time. To create more interesting music you need to use *accents* in your playing. These will emphasise certain notes and beats. They should be played in conjunction with the other instruments, especially with the drums. You could try working out a few with your drummer. If you get them right, they'll add a feeling of tension and excitement to your sound. They will also make your band sound extremely tight.

Try playing the basic rhythms again, but this time put in a few accents:

### 'Straight 8':

With this one, the drums would not play a steady beat, but would accent in unison with the bass at the places marked, creating a classic HM 'stab':

This next one is a little more tricky, as it demands a high degree of concentration from the bass player. It would be played over a fast, steady 1/8th note beat:

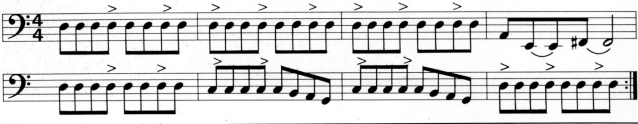

Try it slowly at first, remembering to alternate the fingers of the right (plucking) hand. You may find it easier to count the beats instead of thinking of the pitch of the notes (right):

If you still can't get the hang of it, clap out the rhythm until you've got it firmly in your mind, and then try again.

1 – 2 – 3 – **4** – 1 – 2 – **3** – 4 – **1** – 2 – 3 – **4** – 1 – 2 – **3** – 4 etc.

**Boogie**
Note how the accents here break up the beat and give a shape to what

you are playing. It's no longer just a rhythm, but a bass line with a beginning and an ending.

The 4th and 8th bars would be played in unison with the drums.

**'American Indian'**
With this example, the bass lays down the rhythm with the drums and guitar. On the 4th bar, all three

instruments hit offbeat quaver accents, ie 1/8th notes, but played against the beat. This has the effect of disrupting the whole rhythm,

before everything settles down to the basic beat again:

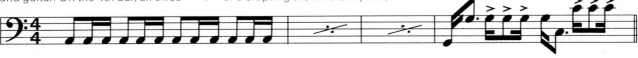

**Stop time**
Stop time can be even more effective than simple accenting in creating a feeling of power. Musical phrases are 'broken up' to give space for one instrument to stand out. Try some of these examples with your band:

This kind of phrase was used by bands like Yes during the early 1970s. Listen to the opening of 'Perpetual Change' on *The Yes Album*.

A variation of this is to emphasise certain beats with drums and bass, while the guitar or keyboard plays a rippling arpeggio figure. Genesis used to do this a lot (listen for it during the mammoth 'Supper's Ready' from the *Foxtrot* LP).

Of course, you can make the phrases more complicated than this. But the idea is for the drums and bass to punctuate the flow of the music at this point.

Mike Rutherford of Genesis

The next example features the 'American Indian' rhythm. The drums, bass and guitar lay down the

basic beat. On the 4th bar, the guitar and bass play two 1/8th note phrases with quarter note rests

in between. This punctuates the rhythm and allows the drums to fill in a little.

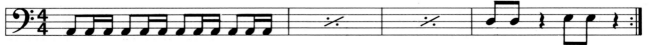

Here is a more complicated stop-time phrase. The drums would be playing a basic 'American Indian' rhythm, while the guitar and bass play the notes as marked. The drums would accent with cymbal snatches where the accents come. Note also that in order to get the low D note at bars 1, 2 and 4, you will have to tune the E string *down* by a tone before you start playing. This will mean a slight revision of your fingering for the notes played on the bottom string.

Lastly, here's a couple of easier stop-time phrases which show a distinctly bluesy influence:

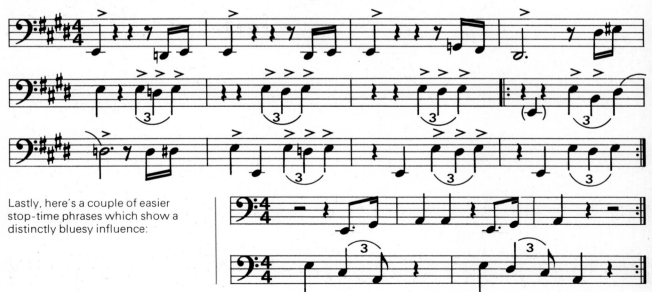

*Jean-Jacques Burnel of*
*The Stranglers (left) was the first*
*punk bassist with an identifiable*
*sound: thick, fat, and busy!*

## Riffs and lines

The riff is one of the cornerstones of heavy metal music. Deirdre provides plenty of examples and ideas relevant to the bass in her section on HM guitar. If you haven't looked at this yet, do so now (pp. 116–17).

Suitably enlightened, I hope you're now ready to proceed!

Riffs are most commonly derived from the blues scale and can either constitute the basis for an entire song (eg 'Peaches' by The Stranglers, 'Whole Lotta Love' by Led Zep), or can be used as intros, hook lines or bridge sections between verses and choruses (eg 'Wishing Well' by Free, 'Iron Fist' by Motorhead).

You can make riffs as simple or as complicated as you like, ranging from the two-note simplicity of Cream's version of 'Spoonful', to the complexity of Zeppelin's 'Black Dog'. But if you go in for flashy riffs, you should arrange the other instruments very carefully. On 'Black Dog', for example, the drums are playing a *simple* pattern in half time, and the vocals come *between* the riff sections. A heavy riff should obviously be very powerful, and you must think of ways to let it stand out as a feature of the song.

The bass will often play riffs in unison with the guitar, thickening up the sound and creating a feeling of harmonic depth (although in fact there isn't any, because the bass is simply playing the same phrase one or two octaves below the guitar, not a harmony line complimentary to it). All the examples I've mentioned so far feature unison riffs.

But you can do other things as well. If you listen to songs like 'Smoke on The Water' and 'Burn', both by Deep Purple, you'll hear the guitar playing chord riffs, while the bass simply plays a single root-note line. The Who also use this approach in songs like 'Won't Get Fooled Again' and 'Bell Boy' (the latter from *Quadrophenia* — an album that every hard rock bassist should listen to). It's a great way of building up a feeling of tension, because the chords on the guitar seem to be 'breaking away' from the bass line, and you long to have them come together again.

Let's look at some riff examples. Below is an early standard heavy rock riff. This would be played at a medium tempo in unison with the guitar. It is based squarely on the blues scale and still uses the 12-bar structure. Note that the first two 1/8th notes (quavers), followed by a quaver rest, will mesh in with the drums, matching the bass drum pattern and allowing the snare drum to stand out on the second beat of the bar. Note also the offbeat 1/8th notes played in the 9th bar, which give a pumping, heavy feel when played over the drums:

Here's an alternative version, which gets away from the 12-bar format, but still has a strong bluesy feel to it. Note the use of the octave, and again the emphasis on the first beat of the bar.

Riffs can also incorporate passing notes to create a greater melodic interest. The next example is similar to the one above, but I've put in some chromatic passing notes to give a slightly more unusual feel. The chromatic notes are marked thus ★

Don't be afraid of using passing notes. Even if a riff sounds weird at first, it may give the other members of the band some fresh ideas.

> *'I like to be as excited by the bass as I would be by the guitar, and if the bass is doing something melodically interesting or flashy, or exciting rhythmically, then to me that's better than if he (or she) is just plodding away — holding everything up, but also holding everything back.'*
>
> NEIL MURRAY

Here's a faster riff that uses passing notes. It has a distinctly rock'n'roll feel to it and should be played at fast tempo for full effect. Note the crotchet rests in bars 1, 3, 5, 11 and 12. This allows the snare drum to stand out.

FAST TEMPO

Triplets are often used by bands in their riffing. The instrumental section in Iron Maiden's 'Number of The Beast' is a good example of this. Here's a similar example. Note the way the riff builds up by contrasting the ascending triplets phrases with the low A 1/8th note played at the beginning of each bar. If you play this on the open A string and let it ring on while playing the other notes, you'll get a fat, chord-like sound (assuming, of course, that your bass sound is good to start with).

As I said earlier, you don't just have to play riffs in unison with the guitar. The bass can repeat a riff under a guitar chord sequence, or the guitar can play a riff over a simple root note phrase played on the bass.

With the examples above and below, the bass repeats a blues-scale riff under the power chords of the guitar. The low pedal note, here an A, stays the same despite the chord changes (shown above the stave):

This idea works because both the bass riff and the chord sequence are in the same key and because the chord sequence is derived from the blues scale. Individually, the chords are major, but the *progression* has a

minor feel to it, and indeed, if you played just the root note of each chord singly, you would be playing a blues scale-type phrase.
Here's another example, this time in the key of G major:

Because so many HM chord sequences get their inspiration from the blues scale, you can also play descending or ascending chromatic bass lines. You don't need to stick to the root notes of the chords all the time. The next example is played at a slow and stately tempo, and fits with the chord sequence: A, G, D, F. (It would also fit with the slightly

fancier sequence: Am, G major, F# m, F major.)

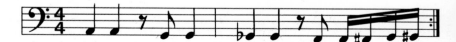

Try playing this single root note line under a driving Who-like power chord sequence of G, F and C. Tell the guitarist in your band to play the chords in the way described on p. 118. That is, with the open G string sounding on all three chords. If your drummer bashes out a simple, heavy 4-to-the-bar pattern, and you play

this bass line, you're going to sound pretty heavy!

Listen to the fills the drummer plays and try to follow them, while

still maintaining the solidity of the beat. You don't have to use any notes other than the ones marked: G, low E, F and F♯.

## Playing chords on bass

Because a lot of HM bands use a guitar, bass, drums line-up, some bassists have taken to playing chords — especially during guitar solos — to keep the sound rich and heavy. The leading exponent of this style of playing is probably Lemmy of Motorhead, and you can hear his distinctive, fuzzy chord sound on any of their LPs.

Holding down chords on the bass requires considerable strength in your left (or neck) hand. The chord shapes are usually very simple. The most common are the root and fifth, or root, fifth and octave shapes that guitarists often use in HM (see p. 115). These give you a harmonically am-biguous sound that can be used in either a major or a minor context. Of course you can play other types of chords (or more correctly, part-chords) too. The root and third, or root and minor third is often used. For a slightly jazzier sound, try playing the root and sixth, or the root and dominant seventh.

If you decide to play chords, you should really try to get a slightly more trebly sound, especially if you're strumming with the fingers of your right (plucking) hand. Using a plectrum will of course give you a sharper edge anyway.

Have a go at the following example. To hold down the first chord (which is a G), fret the D (or 2nd) string at the 5th fret with your 1st finger. Then fret the G (or 1st) string at the 7th fret with your 3rd finger. Now play the two strings at once. To hold down the F chord, take the same finger shape, but this time start from

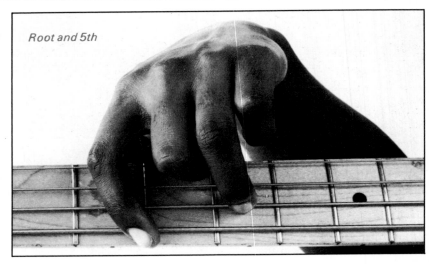

Root and 5th

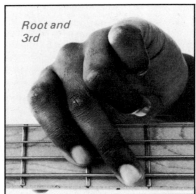

Root and 3rd

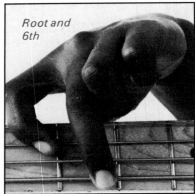

Root and 6th

the 2nd string, 3rd fret. To hold down the C chord, take the same finger shape again, but start from the 3rd string, 3rd fret. For the D chord, simply move the shape up two frets, so that you are starting from the 3rd string, 5th fret.

You can use chords in other styles too, such as funk, which we're

going to look at in the next chapter (pp. 143–66). You should read this even if you think you're not interested in anything else beside HM. You may find that there's a strong musical connection between the two styles and that you might be able to learn something from it.

Keith Moon's manic energy inspired a generation of rock drummers

Ginger Baker brought the technical finesse of jazz to rock drumming

John Bonham was unique for his combination of power and inventiveness

## HM Drums

The inspiration for drummers to let loose and play 'heavy' has to be credited to *Keith Moon*. Before Moon hit the scene in the mid-1960s there had been a revolution in British pop — the emergence of the 'beat' group. The Shadows heralded the change, but of course it was The Beatles and then The Rolling Stones who were to devastate all previous ideas of rock in Britain. The beat groups introduced down-to-earth do-it-yourself rock to the previously tame British pop scene; but The Who, and particularly Moon, was a real eye-opener for drummers. He has not been equalled since, at least in terms of visual entertainment.

Following closely on Moon was *Ginger Baker*. Using two bass drums and a large (for that time) array of gutsily tuned toms-toms, Baker was the ultimate yardstick by which aspiring heavy drummers measured themselves. With Cream, the concept of long improvisations, involving solos from all the instrumentalists was pioneered in rock. Meanwhile *Mitch Mitchell*, with his more obviously jazz-influenced technique, was the perfect foil for Jimi Hendrix, their almost free-jazz improvisations opening up another area for rock musicians to tackle. Across the Atlantic, *Carmine Appice* was getting a huge drum sound with Vanilla Fudge, while back in Britain Free took the more sensual laid-back heavy-riff approach, and Deep Purple initiated 'progressive' heavy rock.

Finally, Led Zeppelin took 1970s heavy rock as far as it could go. *John Bonham* became the model for heavy rock drummers the world over. His huge open snare and tom-tom sound, coupled with a fearsome bass drum sums up the heavy rock approach to drumming.

Since those days rock has taken off in many directions. Heavy bands went out of fashion for a while but their popularity with their own followers remained great. In the past few years heavy rock and heavy metal bands have once again become so popular, that the music press cannot ignore them. A new generation of 'HM' musicians has swelled the ranks of the original players. Their music seems generally to be much more down to earth — songs are relatively short and tightly arranged. The self-indulgence of the earlier bands has gone, at least for the time being.

*// If we go back to Deep Purple, what we were doing then was different, it never happened before. There had never been that much freedom in rock — although jazz players had been doing it for years. In rock'n'roll, nobody had more than 8 or 16 bars to solo in . . . What was happening in the late 1960s and early 1970s was that people were saying, "no, I want to extend this and see what I can get with it". Sometimes it was good and sometimes it was bad, but you had to go for it. But I don't think that's the case any more and I get bored if a second generation HM band goes on and on for hours. I don't actually think it's valid now. People won't stand for a 15 or 16 minute two-chord solo. And I don't think they should, either. //* **IAN PAICE**

## Technique

To play the drums loud you have got to increase the height and power of your stroke. You therefore need more room, which usually means setting crash cymbals a bit higher. This way you don't catch the underside or edge of a cymbal when going for the tom-toms. The hi-hat too might need to be a little higher so that the left hand has room for a solid snare beat. This has to be balanced against the extra fatigue that is caused by lifting the right arm higher. In the case of the ride cymbal it's good to keep it as low as possible — it's much less tiring that way.

Large drums and large cymbals generally give a bigger sound, but you'll also need smaller items for various effects and fills. Stands should obviously be strong with good bases to prevent them from toppling over. You'll want a deep penetrating sound particularly in the bass drum and tom-toms. This does not necessarily mean slack tuning; a large tom-tom will give a deeper sound anyway and remember, a slack head will give very little bounce, making playing that much more tiring. For the snare you again want depth, but the crispness of attack is equally important, otherwise what should be 'heavy' can become merely a dirge. Heavier sticks give a thicker

sound but once more this has to be balanced against the extra fatigue.

Everything then is a matter of weighing one extreme against another. Getting the right gear and experimenting with different heads and sticks to find the most comfortable combination is time well spent. Warming up before a gig, and learning to pace yourself are both vital: there's nothing worse than finding yourself with nothing left for the climax of the set. Sweat bands on the wrists (and head) will come in useful. Some players wrap sticking plaster around their fingers and stick butts to improve grip and prevent

blisters. And *always* have a towel handy!

## Rhythms

Since heavy rock grew largely out of the blues, r'n'b and rock'n'roll, all the rhythms and techniques encountered in the last chapter are applicable here — but heavier. In making the rhythms heavier, certain subtleties are sometimes left out, while other tricks may be added. For instance, instead of playing the hi-hat eight to the bar, a similar passage played heavy might have four to the bar, with the sound increased by slightly opening the hi-hat cymbals. Correspondingly, when playing the ride cymbal, in order to build the sound up to a crescendo, the cymbal may be played in semi-crash manner. This, however, can lead to things getting out of hand, so instead a crash cymbal might be struck with each snare beat whilst continuing on the ride cymbal. Large heavy ride cymbals are now available with loud 'ping' and bell sounds. This gives the advantages of clarity of beat plus volume. On the hi-hat, the same can be achieved by playing the closed cymbals with shoulder of the stick instead of the tip. Or you can use the sticks the 'wrong' way round . . .

## Hi-hat/ride cymbal patterns and bass drum patterns

I've started by writing out the commonest ride patterns with the snare on beats 2 and 4. This is because the bass drum usually fits in with the bass guitar pattern and all these hi-hat patterns can be tried with the following bass drum patterns. Note that some work better than others. (Experiment also with the rhythms cited in the section on blues and rock'n'roll drumming.)

*// I think when you're playing a concert for 2 1/2 hours and it's full tilt all the time, the most important thing is that the hi-hat cymbal is low and comfortable to play . . . I think the ride cymbal should also be low, so there's no stress, because a high angle is not that good for you . . . A low ride keeps the fatigue factor back and keeps you fresh. You don't lose time, you don't drag behind or speed up. You're just right and you've got plenty left for the encore! //* **CARL PALMER**

Clave over one bar

Occasionally the snare drum is played on all four beats of the bar, eg

Try four beats to the bar on the snare drum with all the above hi-hat/ride and bass drum patterns. Obviously, some will work better than others.

Boogies/shuffles
As in the previous section, the shuffle rhythms encountered in the blues and rock'n'roll chapter can be played in heavy rock. Often again the ride pattern is simplified to make it heavier (see left). (Continued over)

As the beat gets heavier and the ride is only four beats to the bar, so the boogie rhythm may be implied by the bass drum:

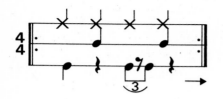 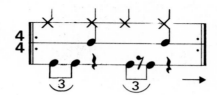 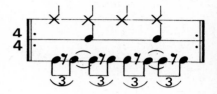

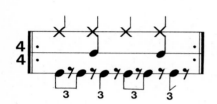 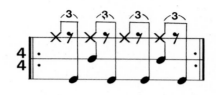

---

The triplets feel can also be implied by snare drum beats incidental to the main back beat (usually played more softly).

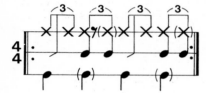 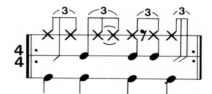

There are endless variations of this, but I've only noted down a couple as a taster. Without wishing to erect boundaries, this is nevertheless more the area of jazz-rock, although with the many brilliant drummers now working in the heavy rock field, this sort of compound rhythm is becoming increasingly familiar.

---

## Dynamics, syncopation, arrangement

One of the main reasons heavy rock and heavy metal are so popular is because they emphasise the dramatic and the spectacular. The feel is larger-than-life. Of course if you closely analyse the workings of any riff that 'moves' people you will find a subtle element, but usually in heavy rock accents and dynamics aren't toyed with — you really hit them. So while the bass player and the drummer are normally locked into a solid riff, when it comes to the pre-arranged accents everyone plays them in hard unison.

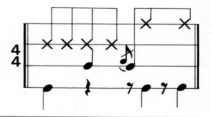

CRASH CYMBAL
RIDE CYMBAL
SNARE
BASS

Note that these accents fall on up-beats and thereby give 'drive' to the rhythm. Accents can of course be placed wherever the band wishes. The stop-time arrangements introduced in the previous chapter are also developed in heavy rock and HM. As an introduction to a song, or as a device to add drama to a middle section, or maybe to preface a doubling of the tempo, a stop-time passage will have the bass and drums (and maybe other instruments) playing stabbing accents in unison. The first three accents in the example below should be very sharp: the crash cymbal should be struck and then immediately cut short by grasp-

BASS DR

ing with the free hand. For the final two accents the crash cymbal can be left to ring. This effect can be heightened by the guitar playing

staccato 1/8th notes over the first three bars of the pattern (echoing the normal hi-hat rhythm) and then hitting heavy power chords for the

last two accents. This creates a feeling of tension and release, a development of the call-and-response idea introduced in the last chapter.

## Drum breaks and fills

As with the laying down of the basic rhythm, the playing of fills in heavy music requires a solid no-nonsense approach. Although you may want to look flash, squeezing in fast jazzy licks often won't work when playing loud. To illustrate what I mean, look at the one-bar fills on the right:

Now the first is a relatively simple 1/16ths around the kit. The second is 1/16th *triplets* and is harder and faster to perform. But because of the sheer volume of heavy music it's often more impressive to play the former at medium to fast tempos. Unless you are extremely powerful, the latter will often be an almost inaudible blur. The one drummer at the back of the hall will be impressed

by what he *sees*, but the rest of the audience will wonder where the drums went. At slower tempos however, the triplets played well can be very effective.

I'm not suggesting you shouldn't

be adventurous; I'm just suggesting that the fill must be appropriate to the music. When playing loud your ability to play fiddly patterns will obviously be curtailed and interestingly this often suits the music.

The other problem with loud playing is timing. The irony is that although the drummer seems to have it easy — no notes or chords to negotiate — it's probably harder to keep good time on the drum set than on the other instruments. There are several reasons for this. Not only is a drummer using 16" extensions to his or her hands (playing with sticks is a bit like walking on stilts), but the surfaces played on vary from hard and bouncy (snare drum) to spongy and absorbent (large toms) to mobile (cymbal crashes where the stick goes 'through' the cymbal). Moreover they have to strike with great force — no fudging; they have to go for every beat, and all beats are staccato; they must be spot-on. Finally, all four limbs are carrying a different part of the beat. This explains why drummers will often speed up a little as the song hots up and gets louder; or slow down with fatigue on fast tempos; and, most commonly, speed up a little on drum breaks.

The real point of this sob story is that by recognising the hurdles, they can be overcome. First of all most heavy-rock fills are based on single stroke patterns. Double strokes or paradiddle variations require some bounce which is difficult to get from large tom-toms, particularly when playing loud. Here are some variations on single strokes going around the toms (see right):

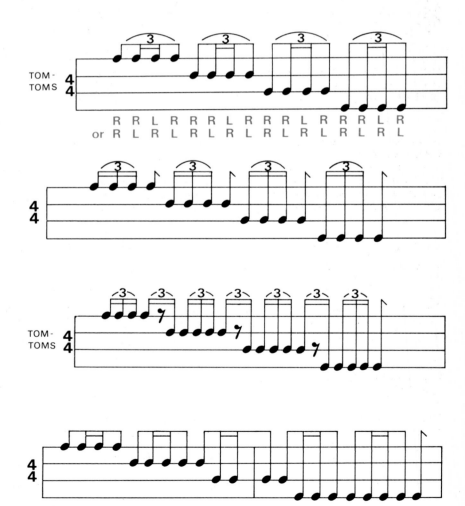

Because fills like these are often executed going around the tom-toms and ending up on the lowest floor tom, they can easily fall off and get sloppy at the end. This is exactly what you don't want. It's well worth making an extra effort to finish the

fill cleanly and really concentrate so as not to rush the last few beats.

Although all these patterns go around the kit from high to low there is of course no necessity to stick to this. Certainly, coming the other way, from low to high, and leading with

the left (for right-handed drummers) is good practice.

**Double bass drums**
Double bass drums, along with extended kits, are very popular in heavy rock and heavy metal. Not only do

they look good, they have certain real advantages for the heavy player. Firstly the player can get more power and volume out of them, for example by using both feet in unison, or by playing the left foot on beats two and four to add depth to the snare drum. Secondly, they help you to play bass drum figures which you might find difficult with one foot (especially playing loud). Thirdly, they can add a lot of excitement to a solo or to the building up of the climax of a song.

*'Philthy Phil' Taylor, formerly with Motorhead, takes the classic heavy metal approach – powerful, solid and very loud!*

To build up ability with both feet the same exercises and rudiments should be played with the feet as with the hands. Also, rudiments and beats can be practised between the hands and feet — whether for double bass drums or single bass drum and hi-hat.

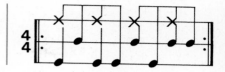

Paradiddle between left hand and bass drum

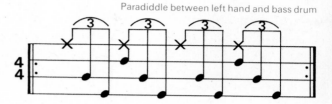

## Solos

Since heavy rock grew out of a tradition of long improvisations previously unheard of in rock, extended solos for all the instruments, including the drums, became commonplace. In recent years though, long rambling solos aren't so readily accepted and this can only be a good thing. For the drummer a solo is an opportunity to branch out and use more light and shade then it's generally possible to do while accompanying the whole band. The important thing is to approach the solo as you would a piece of music. Stop thinking solely in terms of drum licks and how to string them together, and instead try to think in terms of melody and rhythmic form. After all, this is what the other instrumentalists in the band have to do. Starting with the call-and-response idea, again it's good to keep the rhythm of the introductory tune going for a while and alternate this with one- or two-bar phrases. This gives you and the audience the chance to settle into the solo. Gradually increase the length of your phrases until you're launched into the solo proper. Here's a short skeleton passage to illustrate what I mean (see below):

'You can only play flat out for so long before physically you go off, and you'll also turn the audience off, because once you've blown your cookies, there's no more left to give . . . Light and shade in volume is really effective if I'm thundering around the kit and then go down to do some fiddly things on the snare drum, the difference can make a drum solo. Without that build up and without that diminuendo, you have nowhere to go.'
*IAN PAICE*

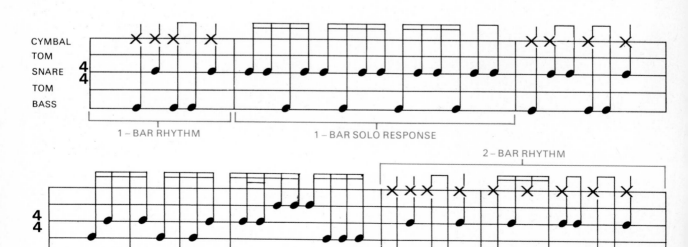

2 – BAR RESPONSE

As in the build-up above, vary this by playing on different drums LR and RL etc

TOM 1
TOM 2
BASS

3 – STROKE RUFF

TOM 1
TOM 2
BASS

TOM 1
TOM 2
BASS

4 – STROKE RUFF

TOM 1
TOM 2
BASS

TOM 1
TOM 2
BASS

TOM 1
TOM 2
BASS 1
BASS 2

Having got into the body of the solo it's a good idea to use rhythmic contrasts to keep up the interest. Alternate between straight beats and triplets, for example, and at some stage bring the volume right down. Perhaps play on the cymbals to get a different timbre before building up to a climax. It would seem that a powerful climax is generally expected unless you can conceive of a solo so devastatingly musical this becomes unnecessary!

The usual way to do this is to bring in the bass drum more forcibly. Get steady 1/4ths, 1/8ths or 1/16ths going (with one or two bass drums) and play rolls over this to reach a climax with plenty of cymbal crashes. Alternatively, get some power by actually incorporating the bass drum(s) into your stick patterns (see left).

These are some of the basic combinations, but it's surprising how much you can get out of them. For further inspiration listen to the way the top rock drummers (with single or double bass drums) do it. Then all any of us can do is get practising.

Finally there is the lead back in for the band. This is crucial, as if it is messed up it can completely ruin the hard work you've put into your solo. Make sure your cue is clear and is a figure you're happy playing. Also, choose something you can *feel* well enough so as not to lead the band back in at three times the rehearsed tempo!

George Johnson of The Brothers
Johnson, playing a guitar not often
used in funk — the Gibson Les Paul

# CHAPTER 8

# Funk and Disco

## Funk guitar

★ As with rock, we can trace funk guitar back to rhythm and blues. But whereas rock guitar developed a powerful heavy sound and was very much a solo 'voice' in the manner of the blues, funk has always been dance music and funk guitar has therefore developed a much more rhythmic role.

As always, the sound of the guitar is very important but whereas in rock the guitar plays very powerful chords and riffs, often using the bottom strings, funk guitar features fast choppy rhythms and you'll find we'll be concentrating on the top strings. This not only gives a lighter sound but your rhythm playing will be crisper, as the actual plectrum stroke covers a shorter distance. You don't need to overdrive your amp, because you'll need to keep the sound fairly clean — but you could experiment with a phase pedal or, if you own a Fender Strat or similar, try putting the pick-ups out of phase using the selector switch.

We'll start off by looking at the actual rhythms and strokes that are used, then move on to extending the chords we already know into more 'jazzy' sounds, and finally look at funky guitar riffs and rhythms using these chords. ★

## Rhythms

Funk rhythms are very percussive-sounding and you'll often find yourself doubling up with and/or playing very closely with the drums. I've explained the principles of playing a chop rhythm in the reggae chapter on page 183. Look at this first if you're not familiar with this.

Now we're going to play a chop rhythm using the top three notes of a D chord (E shape) and G chord (A shape).

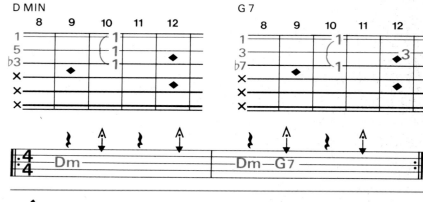

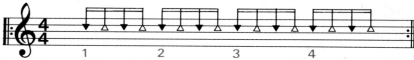

Play a sharp downstroke on beat 2 and 4 of each bar. Remember to cut the sound of the chord short by bringing up the fingers of your left (neck) hand quickly so they dampen the sound by resting on the strings. This accent coincides with the snare drum beat and crops up a lot in soul.

This is a classic soul guitar rhythm (eg 'Midnight Hour'). However, using a chop stroke by itself doesn't necessarily make the sound 'funky'. This effect is more usually achieved by playing much faster rhythms and accenting very short notes. So, in funk, the guitar often uses 1/16th notes, ie a bar of 4 divided into 16 semi-quavers (see above).

### Sixteenth notes

If you keep your right (plectrum) hand going in a steady continuous motion, the left (neck) hand selects which 1/16th beats to accent by pressing down the fingers to sound the notes at that moment. Try the two examples below.

● = stroke not sounded
▼ = downstroke sounded
△ = upstroke sounded

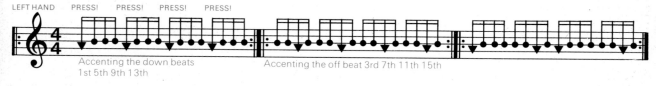

Accenting the down beats 1st 5th 9th 13th

Accenting the off beat 3rd 7th 11th 15th

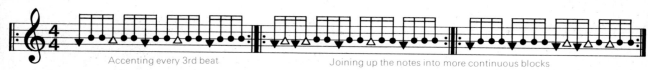

Accenting every 3rd beat

Joining up the notes into more continuous blocks

You'll find these exercises really build up the co-ordination between your left and right hand and these are the kind of patterns used in building up fast syncopated guitar rhythms.

You should try making up some of your own — just try shifting the accents about.

You may find that you're catching the open D string with the plectrum, so you should use the left (neck) hand to dampen out unwanted noise. For example, if you bring the 1st finger of this hand toward you a bit while it's barring the D minor, the tip can rest against the D string and muffle any accidental strokes.

You'll find that Funk rhythm is often a mixture of chops and continuous 1/16th note sections.

> 'It's a feeling thing and you just practise over and over again which is what I did. I used to lock myself in the bathroom for hours on end and mock banjo rhythms until it becomes second nature, and you don't have to think about it.'
>
> NILE RODGERS

This is the kind of rhythm you'll often hear in disco-funk:

These are the same chords as we used originally in our soul example but notice the difference the rhythm makes to the sound of the pattern. You should hit the single stroke beats with a hard downstroke and notice that the 1/16th only comes in for one beat but you can feel them implicitly all the time.

### Inversions

If you played a major triad and the notes were in the order 1–3–5, then this is called its root position, the root note being the lowest note. If the chord is played with the third as the lowest note, this is called the 1st inversion, if the fifth is the lowest note, this is called the 2nd inversion. So with triads, you can get three different positions or 'sounds'.

Chord inversions are an important feature of funk rhythm guitar — particularly if the chord sequence stays on one chord or is moving quite slowly. The next three examples show inversions of Em, A7 and C major. Play them using the top three strings like this:

Different inversions of E MINOR

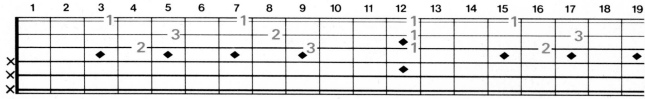

Different inversions of A7

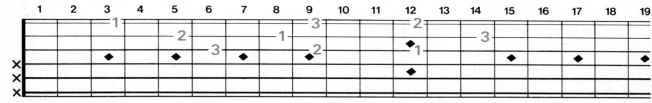

Different inversion of C MAJOR

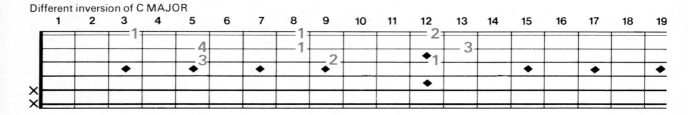

Try working this idea into your rhythm playing by moving from one inversion to another so that you're playing a rhythm but moving the sound of it as well. Another way of changing the sound of the chord is to extend it by adding extra notes. This can bring a range of new voices to your chord work. We're now going to look at ways of

'The thing that impressed me about [Nile Rodgers'] guitar playing was the inversions he used. I really thought it was fantastic, because most guitarists I knew just played one chord, and they would stay on it all night long and it drove you crazy! So when I heard somebody who could take one chord and make it sound like 10 chords, I thought it was fascinating.'
*BERNARD EDWARDS*

extending the major, minor and seventh chords that we looked at

earlier on and incorporate this with some funky rhythms and riffs.

## Chords

Chords fall into the following categories — *major, minor, seventh, diminished* and *augmented*. Let's look first at the sevenths, major and minor chords in detail.

We saw earlier on how the basic major and minor triads are made up of intervals — the major triad consists of the first, third and fifth, the minor triads of the first, flattened third and fifth. These are the intervals from the root to each note, but there is also an interval between each of the notes and this consists of a major or minor *third* (see right).

We're now going to form more complex chords by continuing the

'I think a lot of times when musicians say they want jazzier sounding chords, they want different voicings, other tonalities that normally you don't find in basic rock stuff. . . . But say to a jazz player, "play an A chord", he wouldn't play an A. I mean I know, because I used to suffer from the same disease. If I was told to play an A, I'd go "oh come on, that's corny!", so I would play all the variations of an A chord — sevenths, ninths, sixths, major sevenths — anything that would make the chord jazzy!'
*NILE RODGERS*

process of stacking major or minor thirds on top of each other.

## Seventh chords

We've already looked at one chord which consists of more than the basic triad and that is the (dominant) seventh chord. This consists of a first, third, fifth and seventh (or 1–3–5–♭7).

When we stack another third on top of a seventh chord, we create chords that go more than one octave, so the notes are called by extended names, and the chords are called *extended chords*.

The next chord in this family is called the *ninth* and consists of the following notes: 1–3–5–♭7–9.

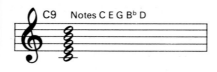

This is the most popular shape for the ninth on guitar. The root is on the 5th string.

The next chord is called the *eleventh* and this consists of notes 1–3–5–<sup>b</sup>7–9–11.

C11    Notes C E G B<sup>b</sup> D F

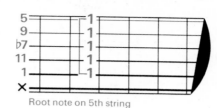

Root note on 5th string

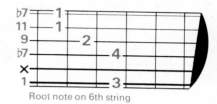

Root note on 6th string

The final chord in this series is called the *thirteenth* and this consists of notes 1–3–5–<sup>b</sup>7–9–11–13.

C13    Notes C E G B<sup>b</sup> D F A

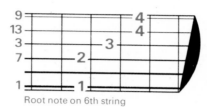

Root note on 6th string

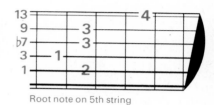

Root note on 5th string

C MAJ 7
or sometimes written CΔ 7    Notes C E G B

## Major chords
We can do the same with major chords. If we add the major seventh interval to the major triad we get a *major seventh* chord (below left).

So this consists of notes 1–3–5–7. It can be played in several different ways. Here are three examples.

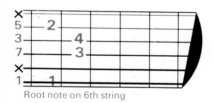

Root note on 6th string

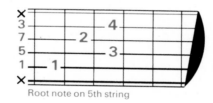

Root note on 5th string

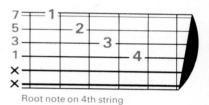

Root note on 4th string

If we add the ninth we get the *major ninth* consisting of notes 1–3–5–7–9.

CΔ 9    Notes C E G B D

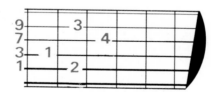

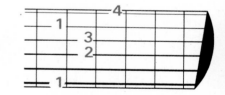

## Minor chords
We can also do the same with minor chords. If we add the minor seventh to the basic minor triad we get a *minor seventh* chord. This consists

of notes 1–<sup>b</sup>3–5–<sup>b</sup>7.
With this shape, if you hold down the 1st finger barre and hammer-on the other notes, you can get a percussive-sounding rhythm, prob-

ably best known as played by the Doobie Brothers (eg 'Long Train Running' or 'Listen to the Music'), but this rhythmic technique is used quite extensively in funk.

C MIN 7    Notes C E<sup>b</sup> G B<sup>b</sup>

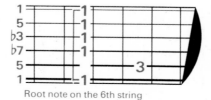

Root note on the 6th string

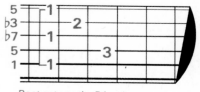

Root note on the 5th string

We can also add the major seventh to the minor triad and get a min/maj seventh chord.

C MIN/MAJ 7    Notes C E♭ G B

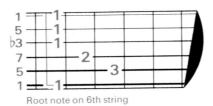

Root note on 6th string

You will probably be most familiar with the sound of this chord used as

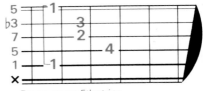

Root note on 5th string

a passing chord between the major and minor seventh chords.

We can also add the ninth and get a minor ninth chord. This consists of notes 1–♭3–5–♭7–9.

C MIN 9    Notes C E♭ G B♭ D

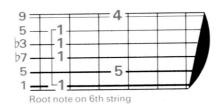

Root note on 6th string

Root note on 5th string

Obviously I'm not showing you every chord possible but I hope you will now have a good idea of chord construction and shapes.

We've used the 1–3–5–7 and the extended notes 9–11–13 of the scale to show how chords are built up, but what if we just add notes 2, 4 and 6 to the basic triad?

## More major chords

If we add the sixth to a major triad we get a sixth chord. This consists of notes 1–3–5–6.

C MAJ 6 or C 6    Notes C E G A

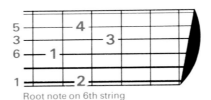

Root note on 6th string

Root note on 5th string

If we add the second to a major triad, the chord is actually given the name *added ninth* (probably to avoid confusion with the 2nd inversion). It consists of notes 1–3–5–9.

C MAJOR with added ninth
Notes C E G D

Root note on 4th string

## More minor chords

If we add the sixth note to a minor triad, we get a *minor sixth* chord. This consists of notes 1–♭3–5–6.

C MIN 6    Notes C E♭ G A

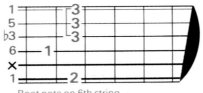

Root note on 6th string

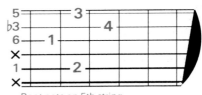

Root note on 5th string

If we add the second to a minor triad, we form a *minor added ninth* chord. This contains notes 1–$^b$3–5–9.

We've already looked at what happens when you add a fourth to the triad in the chapter on heavy rock. This is called a *suspended fourth* (see pages 117–118).

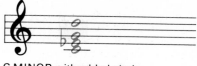

C MINOR with added ninth
Notes C E$^b$ G D

Root note on 4th string

## Diminished chords

These consist of three minor thirds stacked on top of each other (1–$^b$3–$^b$5–$^{bb}$7). Because this divides the octave equally into four, each diminished chord shape can be named by *any* of the notes contained in it (see right).
If you move this shape up one fret you cover four new diminished chords, and up another fret, four more diminished chords, so you

C diminished, C°, C°7
or E$^{bo}$ 3rd inversion or G$^{bo}$ 2nd inversion
or A° 1st inversion    Notes C E$^b$ G$^b$ B$^{bb}$ (A)

have now played all 12 diminished chords. Experiment with this shape for yourself. Notice also how you

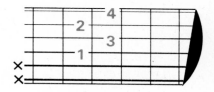

form a different inversion of the same chord by repeating the shape every three frets.

## Augmented chords

These consist of two major thirds stacked on top of each other. This divides the octave equally into three, so it has some similarities to the diminished chord.

C augmented, C+   Notes C E G♯

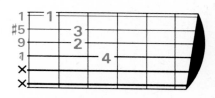

### Chord summary

In this chord summary, flattened or minor sevenths are simply indicated by the number '7'. Major sevenths have been specifically named. A major seventh chord simply has a seventh note from the major scale added to the basic triad, while a seventh chord (whether major or minor) invariably takes the flattened seventh. This is probably one of the most confusing things about chords and I have deliberately written it this way so you can see how the chord takes its name. Also, in the minor chord section, the minor name always refers to the minor *third*, not to the seventh.

You should practise fingering and listening to the sound of these different chords. Some of them you'll find easier to play than others but persevere so that you can play them with each note sounding clearly.

Learning chords is obviously an essential part of playing the guitar but of course you need to know different ways of using them and be able to recognise their sound.

### Major chords

| | |
|---|---|
| MAJOR | 1 3 5 (triad) |
| MAJOR SIXTH | 1 3 5 6 |
| MAJOR SEVENTH | 1 3 5 maj 7 |
| MAJOR NINTH | 1 3 5 maj 7 9 |
| ADDED NINTH | 1 3 5 9 |

### Minor chords

| | |
|---|---|
| MINOR | 1 $^b$3 5 (triad) |
| MINOR SIXTH | 1 $^b$3 5 6 |
| MINOR/MAJ SEVENTH | 1 $^b$3 5 7 |
| MINOR SEVENTH | 1 $^b$3 5 7 |
| MINOR NINTH | 1 $^b$3 5 7 9 |
| MINOR ADDED NINTH | 1 $^b$3 5 9 |

### Seventh chords

| | |
|---|---|
| SEVENTH | 1 3 5 7 |
| NINTH | 1 3 5 7 9 |
| ELEVENTH | 1 3 5 7 9 11 |
| THIRTEENTH | 1 3 5 7 9 11 13 |

**Suspended fourth** 1 4 5

**Diminished seventh** 1–3$^{bb}$3–$^b$5–$^{bb}$7

**Augmented** 1–3 ♯5

### Sliding

Let's look at seventh chords for a moment. This is a very widely used chord in funk though often it's played with a 9th added to it — in other words the ninth chord. Play an E9 chord with the root note on the 5th string. This shape is particularly good for sliding the chords, which is another characteristic of funk guitar. Practise sliding up from the E$^b$9 to the E9 in this rhythm. Strike one downstroke for the first chord and slide into the second one without striking the strings again (see top left of next page.

This type of chord and rhythm can really sound like a brass section. To add more to it you can make this ninth shape into a thirteenth simply by fretting the top string two frets up with the 4th finger (see thirteenth chord shape, root on 5th string, page 142).

Now try this rhythm (page 149, right) which incorporates the thirteenth.

Use all down-strokes except for the second to last stroke. I've shown

the bar divided into 1/16ths because it will make it easier to count at first, but this rhythm actually uses short chop strokes.

This type of guitar sound is very typical of early funk. Try listening to James Brown records from the

1960s, and you will hear that once again the chord sequences followed are usually very similar to the I–IV–V formula. Try playing this pattern as a 12-bar and you can hear the r'n'b/funk crossover. Use the same chord shapes for the whole sequence.

You can see how ninths, elevenths (though we haven't used this with this particular pattern) and thirteenths can be played instead of just sitting on the sevenths for the whole 12 bars or whatever. This is an important part of chord embellishment.

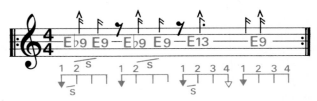

## Altered chords

You can also alter notes in the chord. We're not going to study this in detail but we will look at one sound which is very popular in funk, the raised ninth.

As the name implies, this consists of a ninth chord with the ninth note raised or sharpened like this: 1–3–5–♭7–♯9.

Again, this is a good shape for sliding the chord.

C 7♯9    Notes C E G B♭ D

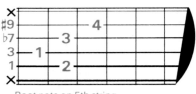

Root note on 5th string
Most popular shape used

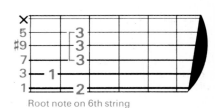

Root note on 6th string

If you're rather unsure how these more complex chords fit into the I–IV–V theory or whatever, let's go back to how we harmonised a major scale (as in the introduction), but this time we'll add another interval of a third to the triads we formed originally. Let's take C major again as an example.

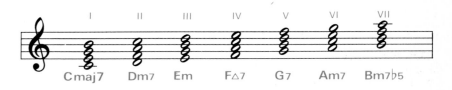

| I | II | III | IV | V | VI | VII |
|---|---|---|---|---|---|---|
| Cmaj7 | Dm7 | Em | F△7 | G7 | Am7 | Bm7♭5 |

| So if someone said to you play a you could play | I | VI | II | VI in C |
|---|---|---|---|---|
| | C | Am | Dm | G7 |
| or | C△7 | Am9 | Dm7 | G9 |
| or | C△9 | Am7 | Dm9 | G13 |
| or | C add 9 | Am9 | Dm9 | G9 etc |

This should help you in trying out your own ideas, using different sequences, eg I–II–III–I etc. Also, listening to records and groups and analysing what they do will really help you understand how chords can relate to each other.

## Soloing

The sound of the soloing guitar in funk varies enormously from the melodic jazzy feel of someone like George Benson to a slightly harder sound, for example Kelvin Bell of Defunkt, to the screaming rock solos of Eddie Van Halen on the

Michael Jackson single 'Beat It'. It all depends on the melody, chords and feel.

Funk songs often utilise only one or two chords for quite long periods or repeat a fairly simple sequence and you'll find that the blues scale will work. However, with songs that

use more jazzy chords or emphasise a 'major' sound you might come unstuck. This sequence is in G, but try playing the G blues scale over it.

If you're playing the scale correctly it should sound horrible!

‖: G△7 / / / | Am7 / / / | Bm7 / / / | G△7 / / / :‖

However, you can see that this sequence utilises the scale chords I, II and III so you could use the G major scale. Sometimes a song might use these chords for 16 bars then modulate into a different key. If you become familiar with chord sequence and know the scale chords you'll become adept at changing scales to suit the chords.

Alternatively, with this sequence you could use a related minor scale — the natural minor (see page 63).

Notice how the notes of the blues scale are the same as five notes of the natural minor, so you can use the blues scale as a related minor scale. So, for the above chord sequence you could use G major, E natural minor or E blues scale, but *not* the G blues scale!

## Funk bass

### Introduction

For the origins of funk we have to look to the negro spirituals sung by black slaves in America, which used two highly dissimilar elements, the rhythm and melodies of Africa with European harmonic traditions. The Afro-Americans embraced Christianity and transformed it into their own unique expression of faith, 'gospel music'.

Church gatherings in the Deep South were held in the open and led by travelling preachers, but in some remote rural areas they were held in make-shift chapels. Many thousands of slaves found their way to these chapels formed by an enclosure of tents and covered waggons, and listened eagerly to the preacher's message of redemption and his promises of relief from their burdens in the next life. The congregation would come forward in response to his call of repentance, enthusiastically joining in the singing of gospel songs which allowed more intense and personal expression than the old European hymns. Singers of gospel music were recorded from the 1920s onwards and formed the source of inspiration for soul music after the Second World War, when the lyrical content became more secular.

### The artists

Singers and musicians of the soul r'n'b era all seemed to relate identical stories, 'I used to get up to sing and play in church'. One of the most eminent artists of that era was *Ray Charles*, born in Albany, Georgia in 1930. His musical style came from New Orleans and the south and he managed to fuse and popu-

larise r'n'b, blues and gospel, and became one of the few black artists to cross over to a middle-class white audience. He even recorded country and western tunes such as Don Gibson's 'I Can't Stop Loving You'. His other important hits were 'What'd I Say', 'Georgia on my Mind' and 'Hit the Road Jack'. But the most important artist for the black American was undoubtedly *James Brown* who was born in 1928 at Pulashi, Tennessee, and made his first record at the age of 20. Within 10 years he had become a giant box-office success, his biggest hit being 'It's a Man's Man's World', recorded in 1966. His music was the street funk of America, pure dance music which was to pave the way for the new funk bands of the 1970s. Two of his best numbers were 'Papa's got a Brand New Bag' and 'Sex Machine' recorded in the late 1960s and early 1970s.

*Kool and the Gang are best known for smash hits like 'Celebration'*

*Funk-rock pioneer Sly Stone seen here in a rare British appearance at White City Stadium, London, 1973*

Sly and the Family Stone stand alone as the fusion of r'n'b rhythms and soul with rock guitar, drums and the west coast influence of theatrical psychedelia. Sly Stone created a sound which was accessible to white audiences, and playing in his band was the pioneer of 1980s funk, the man who invented the slap bass technique, *Larry Graham*. He went on to form his own band Graham Central Station and with his bass rhythms inspired a new musical style: jazz-funk.

Some of Graham's best-known hits were 'Feel the Need in Me' 'Turn it out' and 'My Kind of Music'.

Other bands which led the field in 1970s funk were Earth, Wind and Fire, Tower of Power, the Ohio Players, Rufus, Kool and the Gang and the Commodores.

## Funk rhythm

To get to grips with funk, one must first try to understand what is happening rhythmically. There is nearly always an implied 1/16th note feel to the bass line even if the 1/16th notes are not played. Notes like this:

in funk are played more like this:

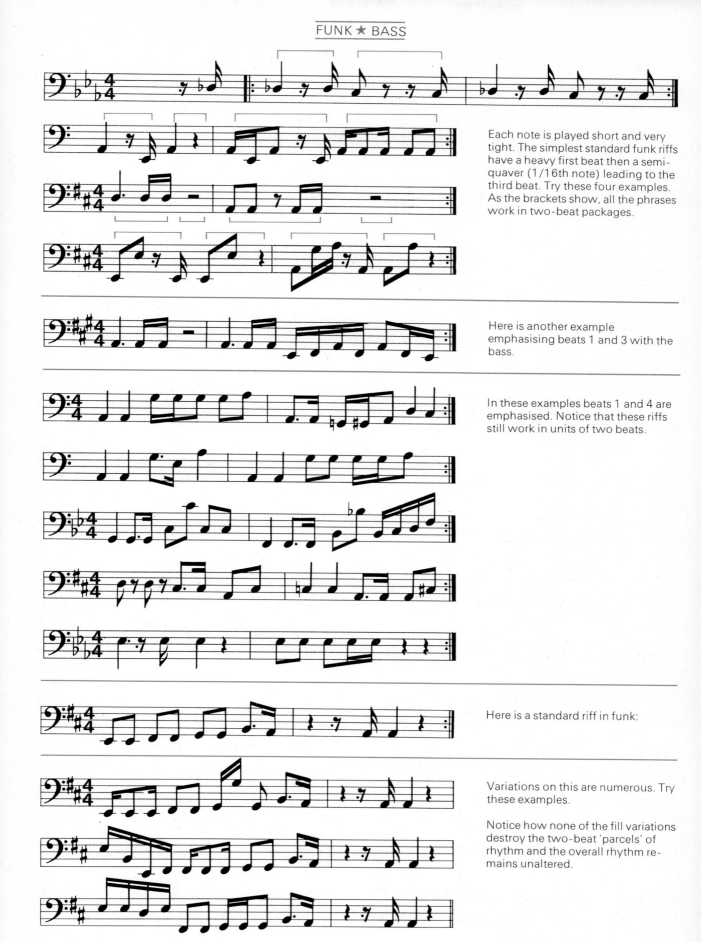

Each note is played short and very tight. The simplest standard funk riffs have a heavy first beat then a semi-quaver (1/16th note) leading to the third beat. Try these four examples. As the brackets show, all the phrases work in two-beat packages.

Here is another example emphasising beats 1 and 3 with the bass.

In these examples beats 1 and 4 are emphasised. Notice that these riffs still work in units of two beats.

Here is a standard riff in funk:

Variations on this are numerous. Try these examples.

Notice how none of the fill variations destroy the two-beat 'parcels' of rhythm and the overall rhythm remains unaltered.

Often in funk you find accents played across groups of semiquavers, e.g.

This is accenting 1, 4, 7, 9, 12 and 15 of even 1/16th notes. For example:

Another common accent is to miss out the first and second 1/16th notes, accenting instead the 3rd, 6th and 9th, for example:

The third most common accent in funk puts the accent on 1, 4, 6, 8, 9 and 11 of even 1/16th notes.

The three most common one-beat rhythms are as follows:

Those of you that have read the HM bass section may recognise these next two rhythms (see page 126):

## Technique

Apart from the different rhythms in funk, you also have a new technique which involves hitting the strings with the thumb whilst plucking with the fingers. As we have seen, the man who applied this to electric bass and turned it into the style we know today is *Larry Graham*.

A funky bass note is created by the *thumb-bone* striking the string against the finger-board and then bouncing off. In order to do this, it is important to try to keep the thumb as flexible as possible from the hand, wrist and forearm. Here are some exercises designed to help this:

With the fingers together in a vertical plane and the thumb extended, move the thumb 360° without moving the hand or forearm.

Place the palm of the hand on a flat surface with the fingers together. Now raise the thumb 1″ from the surface (absolutely *no* movement of the hand, wrist and forearm allowed!) and tap out a clear audible beat, increasing the tempo as you get better.

## Achieving the right sound

Rest the fingers over the strings. Now play the open E string with the thumb-bone anywhere between the last four frets of the bass neck. The wrist and forearm should be totally relaxed. Listen carefully to the sound. The note should be clear with a definite click at the start of each sound. If it isn't, you may be making one or more of the following common mistakes:

★ tensing the hand and wrist so that they push into the string together:

★ letting the fleshy part of the hand get in the way when striking with the thumb;

★ holding the thumb in position *after* hitting the string, thus dampening the string vibrations.

Once you can obtain a clear sound on the E string, move on to A, D and G respectively and repeat the same process.

Always listen carefully. Record yourself and listen back for mistakes.

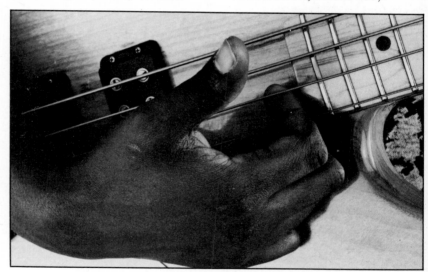

*Slapping with the thumb (above), and plucking with the first and second fingers (below). The best place to get the funkiest sounds is immediately over the top end of the neck, where it joins the body*

Start at a very slow tempo and increase as you get better.

As you advance with this technique try fretting a note with the left (neck) hand, and thumbing with the right 4 times on each string. Make sure you have a clear sound. The next stage is to take the notes in a scale and play them with the correct sound and technique starting at a slow tempo, then speeding up as you improve.

## Pulling and plucking

For this you use the 1st and 2nd fingers, with the palm of the hand placed flat across the bass strings. Curl the 1st and 2nd finger underneath the top G string with the tips of the fingers pointing towards the bridge. Pluck underneath the strings, with the 1st finger and then 2nd finger, exerting just enough energy to create a 'twang' sound. Each finger moves towards the palm of the hand after releasing the string, with the wrist and forehand staying perfectly relaxed. Try to keep the movement of each finger as small as possible. After each 'twang', move the fingers back to their original positions.

Practise even plucks on each string:

G 1–2, 1–2, 1–2, 1–2
D 1–2, 1–2, 1–2, 1–2
A 1–2, 1–2, 1–2, 1–2
E 1–2, 1–2, 1–2, 1–2

★ Always listen carefully to the sound. Control is what you are aiming for
★ Now try barring with the left-hand 1st finger while plucking.
★ Now play a major scale across the strings and make sure that the notes are even

★ Always start with slow tempos, then speed up gradually.

Besides using the thumb to slap and the 1st and 2nd fingers to pluck, you can also use the flat of the hand to hit the strings or even just your nails. These techniques are explained below.

## Flat of the hand

Using this area of the hand simply slap the flat of the hand against the bass strings. Keep the fingers out-stretched. The movement should be

from the wrist with the forearm hanging down vertically, acting as a pivot. Remember the bones in the fingers create that percussive sound.

## The nails

Try striking the strings with the fingernails as a flamenco guitarist would. Fold the hand into a loose fist shape and then flex the fingers outwards and downwards to strike the string. This technique is very effective on the D and G string. Now try this musical exercise.

Play these phrases in different keys and tempos

## Hammer-ons and pull-offs/slurring

When a note is sounded, whether by thumb, nail, slap or pluck, the left hand may change notes either by fretting down with extra fingers (hammering on), or slurring up or down a fret with the fretted finger.

Here's an example of a hammer-on and pull-off for sustaining a note with the left (neck) hand.

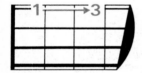

After the 1st note sounds, hammer on with the 3rd finger (left hand)

After the 1st note sounds, flick off the 3rd finger onto the 1st

Sustains can be created by trilling with the left hand. Phrases can employ more than two notes so the later examples will indicate this.

These are the main techniques used in funk and there are many variations, but the main point is that you are using the hand as a percussive instrument. So, as long as clear,

coherent rhythm patterns and notes are created, the technique is valid. I prefer thumb, pluck and nail techniques as these afford me the greatest amount of control.

## Thumb and pluck control

It is important to practise co-ordination between the thumb and pluck of the 1st and 2nd fingers.

Practise scales in octaves using this exercise. Perfect the sound at slow

tempo and then increase speed as you gain confidence.

Once you can coordinate the thumb and pluck, you can go on to play some standard octave lines which are to be found in the music of the late 1970s and early 1980s. Try the examples shown here and over the page.

(All the notes are played with the thumb or fingers except where indicated by P (pluck).)

## Choking notes

Often in funk, notes are 'choked'. The fingers of the left (neck) hand hold down a note without letting the string touch the fret-board. Then the note is plucked with the fingers of the other hand or with the thumb. This produces a thudding sound which has a similar pitch to the tom-tom on a drum-kit. Often a bassline will have 'choked' and 'sounded' notes, for example:

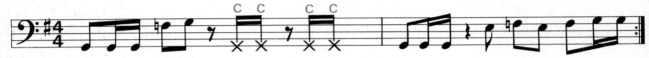

So try and practise 'played' and 'choked' notes in the same phrase.

Now try this exercise with the thumb, from a slow to a fast tempo.

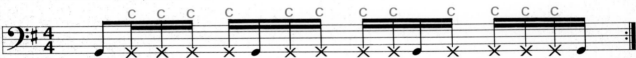

## Developing ideas

It is often hard when one has composed a riff, to then think up variations. Here is a very simple system which can be applied to all the patterns you play naturally.

Take this simple rhythm. Now pull on any note, but only once in the pattern.

Examples:

Louis Johnson of The Brothers Johnson, getting down to some hard core funk. Slapping is probably the most visually exciting way of playing the bass

## Funk drums
### Introduction

Funk is a broad term which has been attached to music from diverse roots: rock-funk, jazz-funk, disco-funk and even reggae-funk (the album title 'Funky Kingston', by Toots and the Maytals comes to mind). Without therefore attempting to analyse the term funk in any great depth, I shall in this section concentrate on the type of drumming which can loosely be described as dance-oriented, or disco-oriented. This area in itself might include anything from Chic to David Bowie, from Spandau Ballet to Earth, Wind and Fire, or from Level 42 to Herbie Hancock!

Funk grew out of the r'n'b, soul and gospel music of the 1960s. As this music got more sophisticated, the drum rhythms got slicker. The top American session players like *Al Jackson* and *Bernard Purdie* set the scene for the more and more intricate drum licks which culminated in the virtuoso displays of the jazz-rock-funk players like *Gerry Brown*, *Lenny White* and *Alphonse Mouson*. Meanwhile the bass guitar had also been liberated so that rather than playing the melodic lines of the Tamla or Stax songs, the emphasis was more on the rhythmic slapping style formulated by *Larry Graham*. Sometime in the 1970s dancing came back into

fashion with the emergence of discos and the result was disco music. While the bass came up-front with overtly rhythmic slapping, the drums became metronomic—solid four-to-the-bar bass drum with the snare relentlessly on 2 and 4. With the electronic advances of the 1970s it soon became possible for such rigid drum parts to be programmed electronically so that there was no chance of the beat wavering. This phase is now passing and the drum parts are starting to get more varied again whether played on the conventional kit, or on some form of electronic device, or by a combination of both.

## The funk kit

As in heavy metal, the drum sound in disco and funk is big and powerful. However, it is also tighter and 'cleaner', with fewer overtones. The basic beat comes from the relentless bass drum and snare drum, both of which have an attacking edge — almost a 'slap' — but also depth. In the recorded sound this is sometimes achieved by getting a solid meaty snare drum sound and then triggering a 'clap-trap' or similar device to add the sharp crack in sync with the snare beat. Drum fills tend to

*Spandau Ballet successfully blend funk with New Romantic pop*

be used sparingly, just involving maybe snare, bass, hi-hat and crash. When tom-toms are used, though, the fills are often very musical; the tom-tom sound is again clean and punchy and a wide range of sizes may be used. The important thing is not to stray too long or too far from the beat.

Since this is dance music, metronomic 'click-tracks' became very widely used as a guide in recording. Then, as drum synthesisers became more advanced and as a simple drum part was often all that was required, synthesised drum tracks inevitably became more common. This practice is infiltrating other areas of modern music also,

and quite often a synthesiser will be used for recording while a real drummer will play the live gig. The next step is for the programmed drum parts to become more unusual — and I've recently heard quite a few tracks which would be technically impossible for a drummer to reproduce live! Where this will lead to is anybody's guess, but more creative drum ideas *do* seem to be coming through. Whether synthesised or real, the unswerving monotony of a lot of 1970s disco beats seems to have had its day.

*Al Jackson played on the 1960s soul hits of the Memphis* Stax *label*

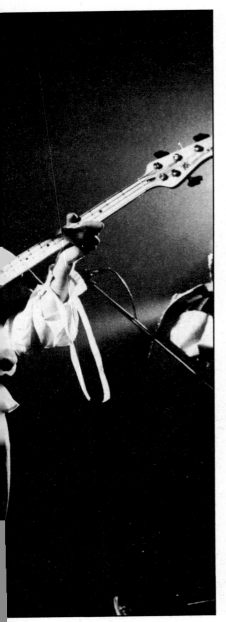

## Funk and disco drum rhythms
Funk and disco drumming starts with the basic 4/4 beat, the bass drum solidly kicking out all four beats of the bar:

These are the fundamental closed hi-hat variations, the choice of hi-hat pattern depending on the tempo of the song and the arrangement, ie what the other rhythm instruments are playing. The last of these

four patterns often involves playing with both hands on the hi-hat RLRL and so on. In this case the hi-hat beats in brackets (see below) will be missed as the right hand strikes the snare drum.

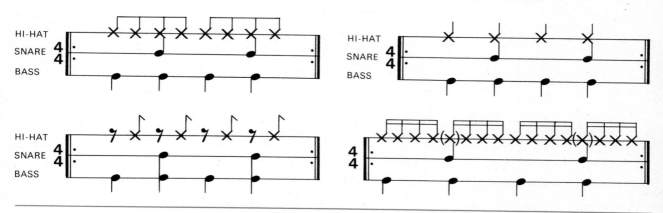

In a lot of recent recordings these basic rhythms, being easily programmable, are executed by drum synthesisers. The important thing is the solidness and regularity of the snare and bass beat, and often the hi-hat is very low in the mix. This should be remembered when you play; hi-hats have the sort of frequency which cuts through very easily, so you may find you have to hit the snare drum very hard while playing much softer on the hi-hat. In fact the hi-hat can sometimes be quite obtrusive and because of the particular arrangement on some songs, the rhythm works better with no hi-hat at all. You will hear some records today where the drum beat is simply this:

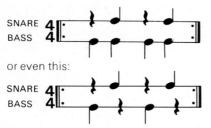

or even this:

Though this seems the ultimate in stark simplicity if it is all that is required to move the song, don't be afraid to play it. Very often the simplest idea played well is the best.

## The 'disco' hi-hat
Having stripped the beat to its simplest form, we can now start to build on it. Since the bass drum and snare are laying down a solid 4/4 beat, something may be needed to

*'A heavy downbeat is really important, especially when you are playing music to dance by . . . for example, if the bass is giving that heavy downbeat with the bass drum, and the snare is carrying the backbeat, then the horns, the guitar, the keyboards could do practically anything else, and it'll never get the dancer or the listener confused.'*

*LARRY GRAHAM*

'lift' the rhythm. A new way of doing this was discovered in the mid 1970s and became known as the 'disco' hi-hat. To play this style, your *left* foot plays four-to-the-bar on the hi-hat in unison with your right foot on the bass drum. This means that the hi-hats are open on the 'an'' of each beat, and if you strike the open hi-hat with the right stick on each of these beats you get the distinctive disco 'bark'.

**C** = closed   **O** = open

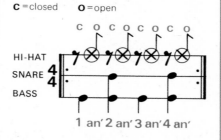

Since the old convention in jazz and rock is to close the hi-hat on beats 2 and 4, playing on all four beats may feel a little strange at first; but it is soon mastered.

The next step is to free your right foot, so that while continuing to play the disco hi-hat, you can vary the bass-drum patterns. Again this independence may require some practice at first (perhaps start by playing rhythms with the feet alone, and bring in the hands one at a time). Here are some examples:

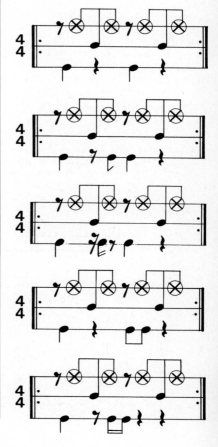

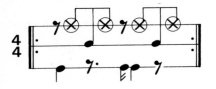
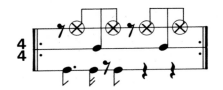

Clave over one bar

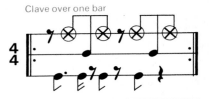

Sometimes a syncopation on the snare drum is added:

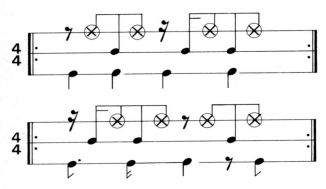

There are occasions when, to vary the sound, all of the above rhythms can be played with right-hand on the *closed* hi-hat, or the bell of the ride-cymbal or even on a China-type cymbal. In these instances the left foot can continue to play four-to-the bar on the hi-hat, or, if you prefer, just on beats 2 and 4.

As you can see, this direction leads on to ever more complex rhythms. Listen to some of the jazz-rock drummers and you'll hear just how far things have developed. In funk and dance music the application of the more complicated beats is usually unnecessary;

> '*I guess that's why they call it a rhythm section. It's basically three people playing together to make a rhythm pattern that sounds like one overall rhythm pattern, instead of three distinctly different patterns.*'
> NILE RODGERS

but the flexibility acquired by practising these patterns is invaluable, and sometimes one or two bars can be dropped in as a rhythmic fill which enhances the flow of the steady beat.

The important thing is to listen; listen to your bass player, to the guitar, the keyboards and, not least, to the vocals. Getting into rhythmically advanced music like this can be very perplexing for rock drummers. The secret is to listen to the *whole* band: is it really happening or not? The separate parts played by each musician must interlock to produce something which moves as an entity. This requires empathy and communication between the individuals. If the bass player has a particularly funky riff, the drummer doesn't have to compete to find something equally flash; instead you lay down something solid and simple which *enhances* the bass line. Conversely if the bass is playing something heavy, with spaces (ie not too many

> *You've got to complement each other. I mean, you can create things where you're fighting each other or you go against a groove for a moment. But for the basic dance thing, it sounds better if everything is kind of flowing along together.*'
> BERNARD EDWARDS

notes) you can probably weave around this to lift it.

Then again, this does not mean you go out to fill *all* the gaps. If there's a lot going on over the top — a busy instrumental or vocal — then both the drums and the bass may be better employed keeping it simple. It's best to think of the whole band as a drum-orchestra: ie forget the notes for a minute and see that everyone is playing a rhythm pattern that enhances the whole rather than clashing with it. Each musician is a member of a team and carries a specific and essential part of the rhythm.

## Hi-hat variations

The disco hi-hat can be varied to incorporate 1/8th and 1/16th beat patterns, eg:

These hi-hat patterns can be tried with the bass drum and snare drum beats above: some combinations work better than others

as you'll soon find out. Remember to listen to the overall band sound: don't crowd the rhythm.

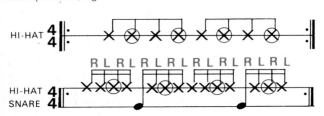
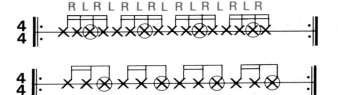

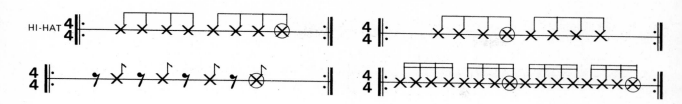

## Hi-hat 'snatches' and accents

The hi-hat in the disco beat is usually opened and closed regularly four times each bar. Of course there is no rule which says this has to be so and hi-hat lifts or accents can be placed as frequently or infrequently as you feel is right for the music. A few examples will show you what I mean:

In each of these examples the hi-hat is opened a little, struck as indicated, and closed on the immediately proceeding beat. Thus, according to whether the struck beat is a 1/4th, 1/8th or 1/16th beat, the left foot has to close down with corresponding speed. When the beat is 1/16th or less (depending on the tempo), striking the hi-hat in this way pro-

duces a sharp accent or 'snatch'. Such snatches can be a very effective way of punctuating the beat. Sometimes when playing 1/8th or even 1/4th beats on the hi-hat, you may wish to put in hi-hat snatches. In this case, however fast or slow the regular hi-hat beat might be when you come to the accented beat, open the hi-hat a little, strike with the shoulder of the stick, and close it down as quickly as possible. This has to be done without upsetting the steady rhythm, and requires a bit of nifty footwork, but it's a most effective technique when used in the right place.

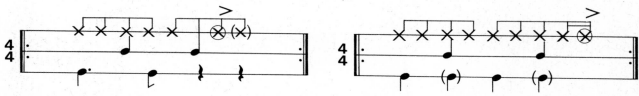

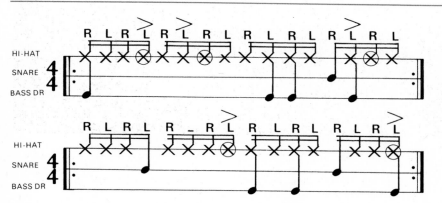

The effect of these accents when played tightly is to put very funky syncopations into the rhythm. This technique has again been fully developed by the jazz-funk players, and snatches can be placed on any 1/8th or 1/16th beat of the bar. To give you an idea of the sort of thing you can try, here are two rhythms with the snatches played by the left stick, while carrying on the 1/16th beat rhythms on the hi-hat (see left).

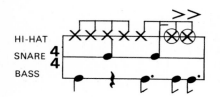

To make accents even more pronounced, hi-hat snatches are played simultaneously with the bass drum. This is a technique favoured by r'n'b and soul-funk players like *Bernard Purdie* (one of the top

American session players) and *David Garibaldi* (of Tower of Power). Such accents are usually on upbeats and often in unison with the bass guitar:

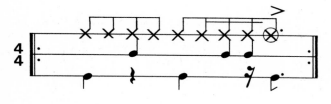

Here are a couple of bars of typical Bernard Purdie soul-funk | solo drums with some intricate bass drum and hi-hat work:

## Triplets rhythms

The influence of jazz and the blues is again shown in funk by the use of triplets rhythms. While perhaps not so familiar as the boogies of heavy rock, when a triplets feel *does* crop up in funk it can be quite unusual. For example, in this first rhythm the only indication of the triplets feel is in the bass drum:

*Billy Cobham came to prominence in the '70s with his technically brilliant and innovative jazz-funk drumming*

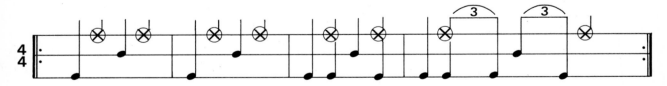

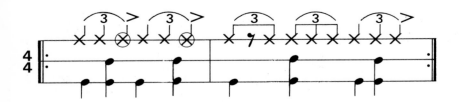

And in this second rhythm the triplets feel is seen in the hi-hat 1/4th beat triplets, occasionally interspersed with 1/8th beat triplets (see left).

End of section

Break played on snare or around the Tom-Toms

Half-time feel. Second bar has snare drum syncopation as a fill

Break played on snare or around Tom-Toms

Tom-Tom fill

TOM-TOM
TOM-TOM
TOM-TOM

HI-HAT
SNARE
BASS

HI-HAT
SNARE
BASS

HI-HAT
TOM-TOM
SNARE
BASS

## Funk rhythms, fills and breaks

Here are a selection of typical drum rhythms with appropriate fills. The fills tend to come between changing sections, ie not too frequently. These examples are typical of bands like Chic, Imagination, and many others. These are all rhythms and fills I've heard in recent months, some played conventionally, some synthesised. As you can see, the fills tend to be short, briefly syncopating the rhythm, and leading into the strong first beat of the next bar. By coming back in on the first beat of the bar the rhythm is re-established and the flow maintained – essential for dance music.

# CHAPTER 9

★ Reggae is like a heart-beat. It is hypnotic and trance-like, simple and repetitive. It uses simple folk harmonies and call and response vocals. The word 'reggae' first appeared in 1967 on a record made by the Maytals called 'Do the Reggae'. Toots of the Maytals, when asked to define reggae, is supposed to have said 'Reggae means coming from the people, like an everyday thing, from the ghetto, from the majority, an everyday thing that people use, like food. We just put music to it and make a dance out of it. Reggae means regular people who are suffering' ★

## Reggae Drums
### The reggae kit

Because of the specialised nature of reggae music, the drum kit is often modified. One of the most characteristic aspects of early reggae is the snare drum sound. The drum would be very highly tensioned and often played with the snare off to get a high pitched shallow tom-tom sound. With the snare on, rim shots produce a metallic almost timbale-like sound (listen to Carlton Barrett with The Wailers). Latin-flavoured snare drum rim clicks are also a reggae trademark. If the left stick is used the 'wrong' way round a much more solid rim click is obtained. More recently a timbale (or a snare drum with the bottom taken off) is mounted in the position normally occupied by the floor tom-tom, or one or two timbales are mounted above the hi-hat next to the small tom-tom. The timbale can then be used as an integral part of the kit as opposed to a separate part of the percussion section. Likewise syn-drums, and other electronic drums, are popular with some drummers (including Sly Dunbar and Aswad's Drummy Zeb) to give rhythms and fills a different sound. The tom-toms are often single-headed and damped to give a low pitch and penetrating fills with few overtones.

The ride cymbal is absent or infrequently used, the rhythm being invariably carried by the disciplined, clipped hi-hat patterns.

### Reggae drum patterns

As in all styles of dance music, the bass and drums in reggae work very closely together developing a formal relationship. A tried and tested bass and drum riff is called a 'riddim'. The relatively small circle of Jamaican musicians who produced the vast majority of seminal reggae recordings have names for many of the riddims (often derived from the original recording of the bass line), so they can be referred to and used again — preferably in the original key. From the point of view of the drums, however, we can distinguish three main areas of style:

1 'one-drops'
2 'steppers'
3 contemporary rock/funk reggae

In each of these styles reggae is performed with straight 1/8th, 1/16th and shuffle feels as in the other categories of music we've looked at.

### One-drops

This is the technique which stems from the late 1960s/early 1970s classic reggae period; it is a technique which is totally unique and at variance with other drum kit styles. Experienced drummers hearing reggae for the first time feel that something is the wrong way round — or upside down. Why is this? To begin with we notice that the distinguishing feature of almost all of reggae drumming is its half-time pulse. This means, rather than the snare drum backbeat falling on beats 2 and 4 as in rock:

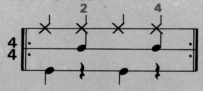

the snare drum beat falls on *3* with the accents on beats 2 and 4 being transferred to the hi-hat and beefed-up by the rhythm guitar and keyboard right hand. Further, the bass drum is played simultaneously with the snare drum, both 'dropping' on the third beat of the bar:

The unsettling feature of this pattern is that there is no strong downbeat (from the bass drum) on the first beat of the bar, as there is in most funk and rock. Sometimes the bass guitar provides the stabilising role on count one, but not always. This is what caused so much perplexity among non-reggae drummers. The snare drum is also usually played on the rim, ie the butt end of the left stick strikes the rim while the tip end rests on the batter head (see below).

167

Brinsley Forde (right) and Drummy Zeb of premier UK reggae band Aswad. Based in the Notting Hill area of London, Aswad are now getting international recognition for such classics as 'Not Satisfied', 'African Children', and 'Drum and Bass Line'

Played synchronously with the bass drum this gives the percussive edge to the drop. The snare mechanism is sometimes turned off so that the sound is very clean and dry. Finally the hi-hat (almost never the ride cymbal) is used to state the rhythmic feel. It is also played in a very tight and staccato fashion — 'sticky'. The hi-hat cymbals are mostly shut tight, but for variety they may be opened and shut either in the normal disco 'barking' fashion, lasting a whole 1/4th, 1/8th or 1/16th beat (according to tempo), or for a much shorter stabbing accent. This is achieved by opening the hi-hat slightly, crashing the top cymbal with the shoulder of the stick and closing the hi-hat as swiftly as possible.

hi-hat bark:

hi-hat stab:

## One-drops: 1/4th and 1/8th note feels

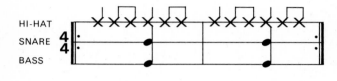

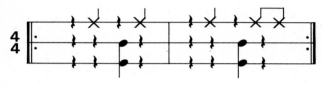
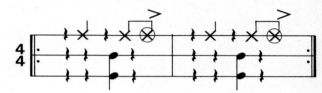
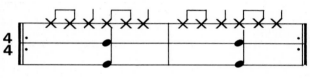
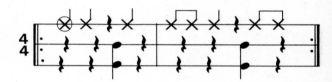
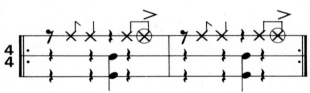

## 1/8th and 1/16th note feels

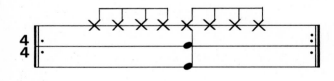
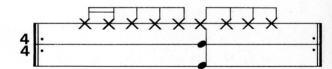
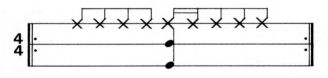

## Triplets feel

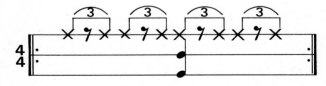
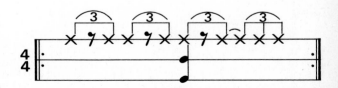

### Steppers

The tempo of reggae gradually slowed as the music became more political, so that by the mid-1970s a new style emerged where a heavier feel was obtained by playing four to the bar on the bass drum — steppers, or 4-drop. This is the basis of the 'militant' and 'rockers' styles and was pioneered by Sly Dunbar and Leroy Horsemouth Wallace. The drop on the snare is still on the third beat, although, because the tempo is often slower, there is room for doubling up, as some of the following examples show. But there is nearly always a return to the half-time feel.

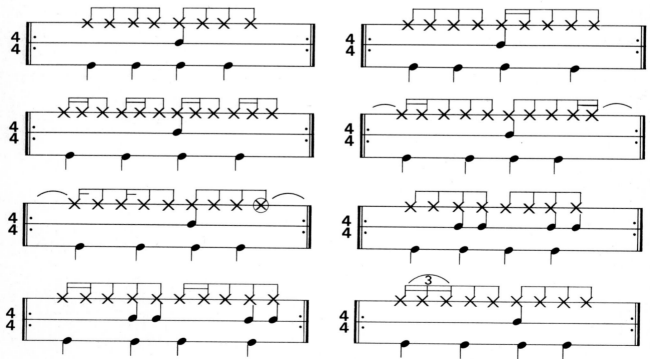

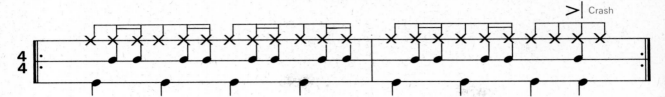

## Triplets feel

All of the triplets-feel hi-hat patterns cited in the one-drop section can be used with steppers.

## Contemporary reggae

In recent years, as reggae has become international, reggae drummers have absorbed techniques from other music styles such and rock as funk. The result is a blend of rock and funk bass drum and snare beats but with the characteristic half-time spacey feel unique to reggae. The quality of the recorded sound has become much more sophisticated,

and the snare drum is played much more often on the batter head (rather than the rim). A typical two-bar rhythm might be:

REGGAE

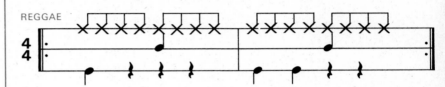

ROCK

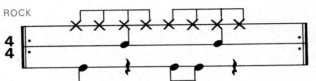

which is a standard rock beat played over two bars instead of one (left).

Here are two more examples of rhythms in regular use:

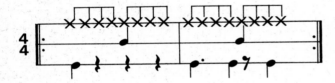

Once, again different hi-hat patterns and shuffle rhythms can be played in this style. However, because there

is more variation in the bass drum, there is a tendency to keep the hi-hat pattern simple and regular.

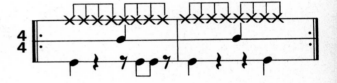

## Fills and compound rhythms

Having got the hang of the principal styles, we can now look at how the incorporation of little fills and accents put life into a rhythm. The best reggae drummers have built up

their own fills. Let's look at some. Starting with a one-drop rhythm you can syncopate the bass drum and the snare-drum rim click, and add short fills on the snare with rim shots on the batter head, like this:

But don't overdo it; don't lose the basic feel. Carlton Barrett with The Wailers is a master of this, and there's lots of musical one-drops on (for instance) Toots and the Maytals, and Burning Spear tracks.

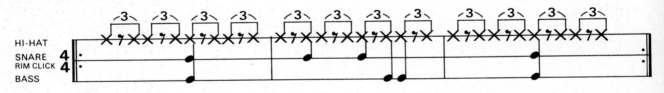

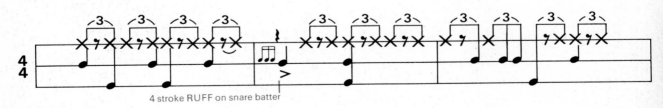

4 stroke RUFF on snare batter

When playing steppers or in the modern rock style, it's possible to incorporate the tom-toms and the

timbale into the rhythm whilst playing either on the snare rim or the snare batter — or even both.

*JA reggae superstar, Winston Rodney, of the vocal trio* Burning Spear

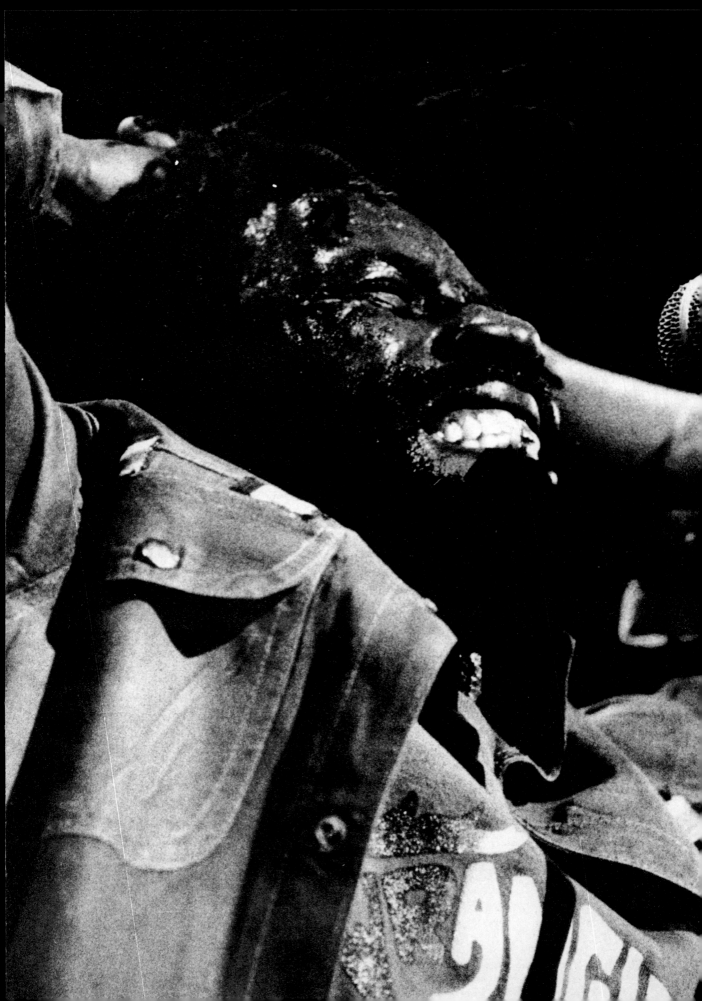

Try these examples:

### Reggae technique
Here are some other techniques regularly employed by reggae drummers:
1  Sometimes instead of striking the snare batter head cleanly, the stick will be 'buzzed', as in a one-handed press-roll.
2  The hi-hat ride rhythm can be accented on beats 2 and 4 along with the guitar 'clip'.

3  The stick can be played on the bell of the hi-hat cymbal to give a bright (but light) effect.
4  Cymbal crashes on the first beat of the bar at beginnings of verses/choruses etc — common in other types of music — are not often used in reggae. Rather the crash comes simultaneously with a rim shot on the third beat of the bar or on the 'and' between the third and fourth beat.

### Drum breaks and fills
Reggae songs usually lead off with the drums. A drum break may be just a couple of beats or may extend over two or more bars. The rhythm is then stated for four or eight bars. During the third and fourth or (more usually) the seventh and eighth bars, there may be another fill which introduces the vocal or the horn riff. The rhythm then settles in.

Here are a couple of typical Sly Dunbar-type breaks:

One of the great things about reggae being a new and ever-developing style is that reggae drummers are constantly searching for new variations on fills and breaks. This sometimes leads to really eccentric drum intros and breaks; there's an element of competition amongst reggae drummers to come up with the most original idea. Try these three examples:

'Rumour has it that King Tubby was once fixing this two-track machine, and one track dropped out of sync with the other and there was a certain amount of feedback... And someone just said 'Hey, that's great!'. So people started doing it more and more, introducing harmonisers, phasers, flangers, chorus echo and all kinds of gadgets just to cover up the sound...'

DENNIS BOVELL

**Dub**
Dub is essentially a recording technique whereby a song can be mixed in an infinite variety of ways. In effect the studio mixing desk becomes a musical instrument which is played by the engineer/producer. Varying degrees and types of echo and reverb are added to each track of the multitrack recording, and then in playback

*Dubmaster Dennis Bovell. Formerly lead guitarist with Matumbi and now recognised as a top record producer*

the tracks are faded in and out. The resulting dub mix has a spacey and unreal quality totally different from the conventional song mix. A great deal of care and expertise is used, eg single drum beats may be isolated and 'spun' off by 'space echo' in exact time with the track or, commonly, in triplets across the four-beat pulse of the track. As the echo diminishes another part of the track will come into focus. Meanwhile the various instruments in the band are dropped in and out. The guitar and keyboards for instance may suddenly disappear leaving just the bass and drums laying down the basic rhythm. In fact the emphasis is very much on the bass and drums. But any instrument or combination of instruments may be taken in or out in this manner.

The effect can be dramatic and cliff-hanging and yet you always feel the pulse is in there somewhere. Remarkably, reggae bands have developed ways of performing dub live. Whereas a rock group might go into a lengthy guitar or keyboard solo, a reggae group will go into a dub passage. Any one of the instrumentalists may simply drop out for a few bars and then come back in; combinations of instruments may dub in and out. The effect live is of a shifting of emphasis in the composite rhythm which serves to highlight aspects of the rhythm and paradoxically strengthens it. The live mixer can use echo through the PA system to 'spin off' various instruments just as in the studio. Also the musicians can mimic echo effects in their play-

> 'The art of dub is to deviate from the beat to play something quite outside the beat, but within the tempo. Just play something alien to what's going on — but not too long, just long enough to make it sweet.'
>
> DENNIS BOVELL

ing. For instance, on the drums, instead of simply dropping out, it is possible to play a triplets figure and gradually decrease in volume (and maybe speed up, then slow down) to nothing. Then after a short gap the drums simply come back in rhythm — almost as if nothing had happened. The following are rough guides — you'll have to listen to the real thing to get the full idea.

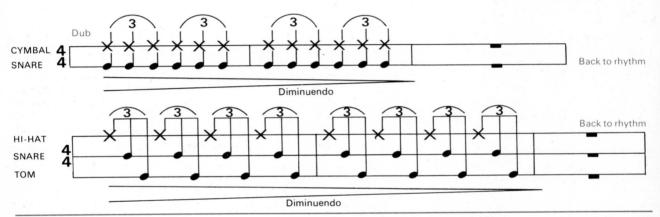

Another technique is to play a continuous pattern on the drums (often mainly the snare) which is reminiscent of echo being applied to a short drum figure. For example

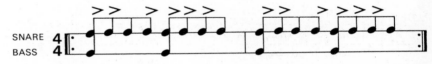

If echo or reverb is then added to this figure a whole drum-orchestra of polyrhythms emerges.

One more dramatic technique is the use of accents and syncopations to produce classic tension and release passages — again, almost as if

the instrument has been cut by an outside operator and just as arbitrarily dropped back in. I can best describe the effect by likening it to a clockwork toy train being picked off the rails: the wheels continue to turn and when it is replaced the motion con-

tinues unaware of the interruption. Of course in reggae the effect is finely calculated and requires a deep understanding of the rhythm. The tension and resolution may fall on various beats of the bar as the following examples show:

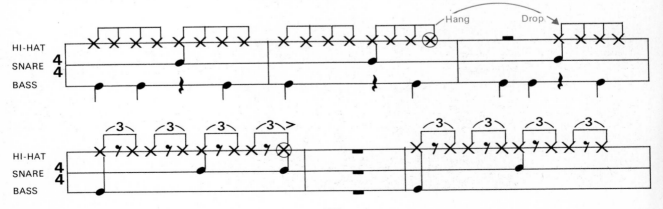

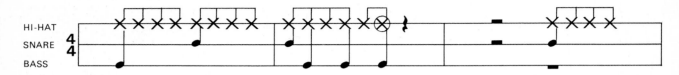

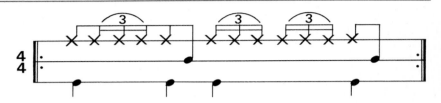

One final note about dub. Because dub albums are primarily instrumental the drum rhythm is often more experimental and sometimes busier than usual. For instance:

## Reggae bass

Reggae bass lines are simple and yet melodic. They provide an anchor and a focal point by weaving in and out of the drum patterns. The notes are deceptively simple, yet the rhythm phrasing and feeling of space is unique. The original bass players in reggae were *Leroy Sibles*, and *Aston Family Man Barrett* who played with the Aggravators and the Wailers. They were followed by *Robbie Shakespeare* who was heavily influenced by Barrett. Robbie is now the principal bass player in reggae today.

## Bass rhythms

Bass lines tend to be very laid back, almost dragging behind the beat rather than stating the downbeat as in rock. The feel of a line is closer to a triplets feel in that the first note of

each two notes is emphasised more heavily than the second.

So this rhythm might be played:

If line two is played with a heavy third beat, you are approaching the

This rhythm pattern (above) appears a great deal in reggae. Just listen to bands like Chalice.

feel of reggae. In reggae you are usually dealing with two-bar phrases where the third beat is stressed heavily, especially on the second bar of a phrase.

BAR 1

To add to this unusual feature the drum plays a half time feel, dropping on beat 3 of each bar with snare and brass drum together.

Practise the following variations of this rhythm but phrase to end on the third beat of the second bar:

Sly Dunbar is the acknowledged master of modern reggae drumming, and has played on countless hits, from 'Double Barrel' (Dave and Ansel Collins), 'Welding' (I-Roy), and 'Police and Thieves' (Junior Murvin), to more recent work by Black Uhuru, Mighty Diamonds, Dennis Brown etc. For ten years he's partnered Robbie Shakespeare in one of the hottest studio and live rhythm sections in the world.

Robbie Shakespeare was taught how to play bass by Aston 'Family Man' Barrett of The Wailers, and played on two Bob Marley tracks 'Concrete Jungle' and 'Stir It Up'. He's toured with many reggae stars, including Peter Tosh, Bunny Wailer, and Jimmy Cliff. His bass sound is unusually light and often low in the mix in comparison to the roots sound adopted by others. His style provides a perfect melodic counterpart to Sly's rhythmic precision, as many international rock artists, from Ian Dury to Bob Dylan, are beginning to find.

Now you've got an idea about phrasing you can leave notes out.

1/8th note or 1/4th note rests on the first beat of the bar are very effective.

Here are some examples. Notice that beat 3 is still heavily emphasised.

Eventually, by missing out all sorts of beats, you get a pattern like this,

which works well with a one-drop drum pattern.

## Bass lines

It's not just the rhythm you play that counts, of course, it's the notes you choose as well. The reggae bassist tends to play lines that create tension against the chord which nicely matches the up-in-the-air feeling of the rhythm. One way of doing this is by phrasing to the *fifth* note of a chord instead of to the root. Compare the bass lines on the right.

The subtle change of phrasing in reggae creates a melody across the chords as well as providing an anchor. Below and on the next page are some bass lines that incorporate the minor third:

The idea of using arpeggios in bass lines is not new. It appears in mento and calypso music. Calypso was originally from Trinidad and became the main music of the islands in the early 1950s. The characteristics of the music are very simple — two or three chords, fast tempos and rude lyrics! The guitar and piano emphasise the off-beats, while the bass plays simple syncopated arpeggio figures:

These lines easily change into reggae bass lines when played at slow tempo.

New Orleans r'n'b was also an influence on Jamaican musicians in the 1950s. Look at this r'n'b bass line:

This became simplified, the guitar chopped on beats 2 and 4, and the result was ska:

Ska was replaced by rock steady which was at a much slower tempo and much heavier. The bass players in bands like The Maytals, and The Wailers were influenced by soul and funk and to a lesser extent rock from Europe and America.

In the examples here and over the page, soul and funk patterns are transformed into reggae riffs.

**Key of A**

At half tempo this becomes

The reggae version simplified would be

This line

Becomes heavier and laid back

By the late 1970s and early 1980s an increasing use of funk and rock | patterns in reggae bass lines and bass drum figures was being made:

This Reggae riff could be a rock riff

**Key of F**

**Key of Am**

Possible funk pattern

**Key of C**

**Key of A m**

*Toots and The Maytals have been together since 1961, producing classic songs like 'Pressure Drop'*

## Reggae guitar

Reggae is a Jamaican music which has developed over the past 15 years into one of the most influential styles of music today. The guitar provides a key rhythmic role emphasising beats 2 and 4 of the bar (a role usually occupied by the snare drum in other music styles we've looked at) and this is one of the most distinctive and easily recognised characteristics of this music.

## Background

It is useful to look at the beginnings of reggae because the sharp rhythmic sound of the guitar was established in the era of ska in the early 1960s and this sound has remained constant through rock steady and into modern reggae, though the actual rhythm of the music has slowed considerably and become heavier.

In the 1930s and 1940s, calypso, mento (a Jamaican folk music) and jazz were popular in Jamaica; however, in the 1950s, Jamaicans began tuning into radio stations like WINZ, broadcasting from the southern states of America, to pick up the latest rhythm and blues — a new, black, danceable sound featur-ing musicians like Fats Domino and Louis Jordan. Some of the well known American musicians did come over and tour but as the demand for the music grew, so the sound systems run by record shop owners began to develop and assume great importance. They played the latest imports and sound system men like Sir Coxsone Dodd and Duke Reid began recording aspiring Jamaican musicians.

Gradually a new Jamaican sound began to emerge which sounded a bit like the r'n'b shuffle rhythm (we looked at this in the blues chapter,

*A rare shot of ska session pioneer Ernest Ranglin (on guitar), jamming with trumpeter Roy Burrowes at Ronnie Scott's Club, London, 1964*

p. 85) but with a heavy accent on the off-beat usually played by the guitar — this was the sound of ska. Clue J and the Blues Blasters with guitarist *Ernest Ranglin* were the first group to record ska and shortly afterwards the most influential ska group — the Skatalites — was formed. Led by trombonist *Don Drummond* and with guitarist *Jah Jerry*, they produced classic ska music from 1963–1965.

## Reggae rhythm

We're going to look first at the transition from r'n'b shuffle to guitar shank.

This is the shuffle rhythm

This is an offbeat ska rhythm

and it was often 'straightened out' so that it lost the triplet feel (again | like the 'straight 1/8th' feel we talked about in the rock'n'roll section).

In ska the guitar rhythm is usually played as an upstroke and this is a fast jerky rhythm. However, as I mentioned earlier, with the advent of rock steady in the mid to late 1960s the beat became literally 'steadier' and in turn this was gradually replaced in popularity by reggae | which was slower still. With this slower beat, the way the music is usually counted is different. It's counted twice as fast as the above example with the result that the guitar changes from playing on the offbeat to playing on the beats 2 and 4 of each bar.

This is usually played as a down-stroke and you can hit the strings quite hard, but what is more important is that you don't let the chord | ring on and to achieve that characteristic, sharp, attacking, chop stroke sound you need to use left (neck) hand damping.

## Chop strokes

As with funk, reggae rhythm playing tends to concentrate on the top three or four strings of the guitar — this will help you get a sharper sound.

Try playing an Am chord using just the top four strings.

Fret the chord and play a single downstroke. Note how the chord rings on. Now play the chord again but bring the fingers of the left (neck) hand up quickly so that they rest on the strings — you should notice that | the chord sound is cut off by this damping technique.

Try the following example (below) remembering the previous points.

If you listen to reggae guitarists like Earl 'Chinna' Smith or Binghy Bunny you'll hear that there are many subtle variations in sound and rhythm.

One variation in sound is to play the chord using heavy left hand damping all the time. If you rest your fingers on the strings in the chord shape and just press down lightly

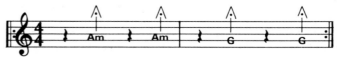

on the strings without actually fretting the chord you'll get a very 'clicky' sound with just a hint of the chord. If you set the guitar and amp on a trebly setting this will give you a great percussive rhythm sound. Try the previous example using this technique.

The type of rhythm that you use will depend on the feel of the song but don't be afraid to experiment and, again, listen to other musicians.

> *'In reggae, you're generally looking for a percussive, scratching sound. When you're playing the chord you don't actually press the strings firmly onto the fretboard, you just hold your hand in the position of that chord and hit the strings, so it sounds like there's a chord there, but it's being muffled.'*
>
> DENNIS BOVELL

> *'Quite often reggae tunes are based on just two chords. So, instead of showing what a brilliant musician you are, how many chords you know, it shows how well you can play a limited amount of chords in that timescale and how tight you can get it, so it's all wrapped up in the sound.'*
>
> DENNIS BOVELL

## Chord sequences

Now let's move on to look briefly at chord sequences. We've seen that ska contained a strong r'n'b influence, and ska songs often followed the I-IV-V sequence. Likewise, reggae tends to stick to the simpler chords — the major and minor triads and sevenths. With the slower feel and heavier bass lines, however, there has also come a tendency to emphasise minor sounding chord sequences, and often a song will remain on just one or two chords.

Even great songwriters like Bob Marley mainly used chord sequences based on simple scale chords (see p. 63) because a strong, repetitive melody (similar to blues singing and playing) and swaying, compelling rhythm are the most important components of a reggae song, not a complex chord sequence.

## Reggae riffs

Apart from playing chords, the guitar can also play riffs throughout a song. As in funk you often want a very percussive note sound and this calls for right (plectrum) hand damping

(refer to p. 85 in the blues chapter for this technique).

This percussive note style was very popular in the rock steady era of the late 1960s (listen, for example, to 'Rock Steady' by Alton Ellis), but it is still widely used. Often the rhythm guitar will play chop strokes whilst the lead guitar will play melodic lines and riffs. Other good examples of this are 'Bettah Must Come' by Delroy Wilson, 'Slaughter' by Black Uhuru or 'Could You Be Loved' by Bob Marley and The Wailers.

Most of the percussive guitar lines are slightly embellished versions of the bass line, bringing out the bass notes but adding a percussive attack to the rhythm. In a classic rock steady number like 'Return of Django' the guitar and bass play the melody almost identically so it's easy to hear, but you often need to listen carefully to pick out the subtleties of this style.

Here are some examples of these reggae guitar lines.

This could be played over the chord of F major (see below).

This example would be played over the chord of Gm and repeating the same note using a fast rhythm is a common device.

One idea to help you to start making up these kind of melodic lines yourself is to begin by picking out just the notes contained in the chord in a rhythmic pattern.

So if you were playing a chord sequence that went:

and used the following shapes:

C MIN

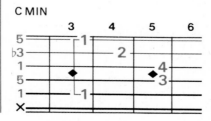

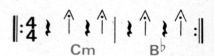

you could try playing the riff shown on the next page:

Bᵇ MAJ

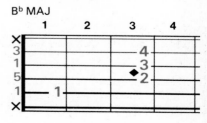

*Geoffrey 'Mao' Chung has played guitar on many Sly'n'Robbie recordings, including Black Uhuru albums like 'Red', and all the Grace Jones LPs*

Notice how these notes and the resulting fingerboard pattern relate to the two chords in the sequence.

## Rhythmic soloing — dub sounds

Finally, another feature of playing reggae is not so much melodic improvisation as rhythmic improvisation.

In reggae the instruments in a group fit together in a subtle pattern of interlocking rhythms and feels. As each instrument has its own area, this in turn creates a feeling of space in the sound as a whole.

There are always subtle shifts of rhythm and pace happening in a reggae song but another stronger influence has been dub. Studio-created dub records have always

been very popular since the early 1970s. This effect is done at the mixing stage when tracks are brought in and out of a song and often have effects like echo added to them to create 'spinning off' effects and repeated sounds. Groups have been influenced by these studio sounds to create their own 'live' dub. The two most common techniques used are first, simply to stop playing for a few bars, let the bass and drums continue by themselves for a while then start playing again. You might find yourself playing with just the drums over a few bars. Or you could try dropping some beats — try playing

one stroke to a bar instead of two. If you do this in a group it can sound very strange at first and the whole song could collapse, but if you keep the pulse or beat going strongly in your head or keep tapping your foot it should work. Remember, no matter what you do or don't play, that central rhythm must keep going constantly.

The other technique is to play triplets; this is to simulate the effect of an echo machine. Try these exercises just resting your left (neck) hand on the strings to create a damped sound — don't worry about playing chords.

These are called quaver triplets — three quavers in the space of two quavers (two quavers 1/8th notes being equivalent to one crotchet 1/4th note).

These are called crotchet triplets — three crotchets in the space of two crotchets. They are more difficult to play and can make you sound like you're playing slightly out of time.

These are the triplets usually played though in guitar dub effects. When you're able to play them easily you can try incorporating them into your playing and even actually speeding or slowing them so that actually you

are playing out of time but then make sure you come back firmly in time at the end of your rhythmic improvisation!

This last section on dub sounds is not easy, so you should expect to

spend quite a bit of time practising this, particularly in a group context. However, it's really exciting playing around with the beat of a song and it will really improve your rhythmic feel and playing.

*Handsworth revolutionaries* Steel Pulse

It's at this stage that we could say 'OK, you've covered the basics, now go out and take the world by storm!'. Of course, it doesn't work like that. Music isn't just a matter of following the rules; it's also about pure inspiration. And you can't analyse that!

However, as we've seen in this book, rock is based on a shared vocabulary of common rhythms, chord sequences and scales. So let's conclude by reminding you of some of the most frequently used devices in rock. If you have got nothing else from this book, we hope that you've grasped these.

## Rhythm

Rock rhythm, as we have seen, come from two broadly distinct sources: African and Latin. Through jazz and blues, a crucial African influence on rock has been the *triplet* pattern. This crops up regularly in every style. You have only to flick through some of our musical examples to see how common the triplet feel is.

Triplets can either be played on all the instruments at once to give you shuffle and boogie feels, or on each instrument in turn, as in reggae, opening up a whole range of syncopations in the beat. Alternatively they can be played by each instrument individually, while the others play something else.

The Latin influence has given rock the 'straight eight' and 'clave' rhythms. A lot of rock is based on the straight-ahead, driving feel of playing eight 1/8th notes (quavers) to the bar. The 'clave' or 'Bo Diddley beat' is used both for continuous rhythm patterns, and for accents and stabs. It can be played in unison by different instruments, or on different parts of the drum kit, giving a very loose, funky feel to the beat.

By getting different instruments to cover different parts of the rhythm pattern, you can build space into your sound, which will mark you out from other bands that pound monotonously away on the same beat. Just listen to the way the top funk and reggae bands achieve this.

## I-IV-V

These form the basis of the 12-bar chord structure on which most of blues, rock'n'roll, r'n'b and a lot of 1960s rock and pop are based. As a starting point and a source of inspiration these chords are still relevent today. Try playing them in a different order, using different rhythms, over different numbers of bars.

Start with    V-IV-I
Then try     IV-V-I
Next        V-I-IV      and so on.

## The blues scale

Lastly, the blues scale is one of the most important things for rock guitarists and bassists to learn. It provides the most flexible and expressive melody line in rock, especially when played using the vibrato and string-bending techniques described on p. 90. The blues scale not only provides inspiration for guitar solos in blues, rock'n'roll, r'n'b, heavy rock and heavy metal, it is also the mainstay of funk bass lines too. In addition, most guitar and bass unison riffs are derived from it, and a lot of rock chord sequences come from it. The blues scale is important.

The strength of rock lies in the number of overlaps that exist between each style. By understanding this you can begin to explore the differences *between* the styles too. The more flexible you are and the broader your influences, the better a musician you will be.

Rock music is continually growing and developing. Every musician is capable of bringing something new to it. We hope that this book will help you on your way. Get out there and do it!

**Picture credits**
ATLANTIC RECORDS 133; COURTESY BLUES UNLIMITED 109 *top*; ADRIAN BOOT 77 *right*, 167, 168–169, 173, 187; CBS FENDER 18 *top left*; DECCA INTERNATIONAL 14 *bottom*; EFR GUITARS 17 *right* (Max Kay); EMI 175; FCN MUSIC 73; ISLAND RECORDS 178–179 (Kris Puszkiewics); BOB KOMAR, BBC © 40 *below*, 41, 48, 51, 56–57, 58, 60–62, 64, 67–69, 70 *bottom*, 80–81, 83, 85, 86, 90 *bottom*, 91 *bottom*, 93 *left*, 119, 131, 156, 167; CHRIS LENT, BBC © 8, 53 *top*, 144; LFI 100, 101, 102, 115, 117, 153, 160, 165; MELODY MAKER 11, 12 (Ian Dickson), 21 (Andre Csillag), 44 (Robert Ellis), 50 (Ross Halfin), 76–77 *centre*, 103, 106 (Robert Ellis), 132, 142, 157 (Chris Horler); CAROLE MONTAGUE, BBC © 53 *bottom*, 94; NICK OAKES 74; BARRY PLUMMER 10–11, 13 *top*, 15, 17 *left*, 18 *top right*, 19, 20–21, 22–23, 24, 26, 27, 30, 32–33, 37, 38, 42–43, 46–47, 49, 59, 64–65, 66–67, 70 *top*, 89 *right*, 98–99, 111, 113, 116, 121–124, 127, 128, 150–151, 152, 182, 190–191; PREMIER PERCUSSION 40 *top left*, 40 *top right* (Neville Chadwick); NORMAN REID 76 *left*; REX FEATURES 31; ROLAND UK LTD 28–29; ROSSETTI LTD 9, 13 *bottom*, 14 *left*, 14 *right*; RICK SAUNDERS 138–139; SIMMONS ELECTRONICS 45; VAL WILMER/FORMAT 18 *bottom*, 79, 84, 87, 89 *left*, 90–91, 93 *right*, 95, 99, 108, 109 *bottom*, 114, 132, 161, 184–185; YAMAHA 16.

Front cover illustration by Brian Robins

Notation and diagrams by Tony Spaul